DANGEROUS CROSSROADS

DANGEROUS CROSSROADS

Popular Music, Postmodernism
and the Poetics of Place

GEORGE LIPSITZ

VERSO

London · New York

First published by Verso 1994
© George Lipsitz 1994
Paperback edition published 1997
All rights reserved

Verso
UK: 6 Meard Street, London W1V 3HR
USA: 29 West 35th Street, New York, NY 10001–2291

Verso is the imprint of New Left Books

ISBN 1–85984–054–X

British Library Cataloguing in Publication Data
A catalogue record for this book is available from the British Library

Library of Congress Cataloging-in-Publication Data
Lipsitz, George.
Dangerous crossroads : popular music, postmodernism, and the
poetics of place / George Lipsitz.
p.   cm.
Includes bibliographical references and index.
ISBN 1–85984–054–X
1. Music and society.   2. Popular music—Social aspects.
3. Popular music—Political aspects.   4. Postmodernism.   I. Title.
ML3470.L57   1994
306.4′84—dc20   94–20455

Typeset by York House Typographic, London
Printed and bound in Great Britain by The Bath Press, Bath

CONTENTS

ACKNOWLEDGMENTS

We live in an age where dangerous crossroads are not difficult to find. Inequality and injustice all around the globe promote the disintegration of social ties and provoke violent outbursts and insurrections. Concentrated political, economic, and military power leave most people unable to determine their own destinies or to advance their own interests. Yet, as one of the characters in Jack Conroy's novel about Depression Era America argues, "Things that seem solid as a rock may be fragile enough to collapse at a pinch. But you've got to pinch first."[1] Knowing what to pinch and when, is no small matter. Only by networking – by listening to anyone who will talk and by talking to anyone who will listen – can we go beyond the limits of our own experiences and situations. This book is a contribution to that conversation, but it grows out of it as well. I am grateful to anyone in that conversation for the things they have taught me, but at this point, I want to express particular gratitude to all of the people who have helped bring this book into existence.

Mike Davis and Colin Robinson of Verso offered important encouragement and support. Margaret Finnegan, Violaine Thompson and Bonnie Wright provided expert research assistance, while Brian Cross, Greg Landau, Yvonne Reineke, and Sarah Simmons came through with needed materials at crucial times. Raul Fernandez, Juan Flores, Rosa Linda Fregoso, Robin D.G. Kelley, Charlie Kronengold, Lisa Lowe, George Mariscal, Susan McClary, Michael Omi, Tricia Rose, Jose David Saldivar, Marta

Sanchez, Barbara Tomlinson, and Rob Walser contributed much-needed advice and criticism.

Finally, I want to acknowledge the important example set by the members of United Auto Workers Local 879 at the Ford Plant in St. Paul, Minnesota in January 1994. They voted to "adopt an organizer" at the Ford Assembly Plant in Cuatitlan, Mexico to promote worker exchanges and to provide information about bargaining, injuries, and disciplinary firings to workers in both countries. Through what they call the "Cleto Nigmo Memorial Agreement" (named in honor of a Ford worker shot and killed during a protest against pay cuts and classification changes in the Cuatitlan plant in 1990), the St. Paul workers agreed to pledge $300 a month from shop floor contributions to support the work of the Mexican Ford Workers Democratic Movement. "Cleto Nigmo has become a symbol all across North America for autoworker solidarity and courage. This is the best way we can remember him," proclaimed a member of Local 879's Community Action Program.[2]

The "Cleto Nigmo" agreement is just one of many examples of networking between workers in different countries in today's age of transnational capital. Augmented by personal visits, computer "mail," and shared cultural commodities, this kind of networking provides a possibility that popular movements for justice and equality may yet become as mobile as capital. Because the members of Local 879 obviously know what to pinch and when, it is to them that this book is dedicated.

GEORGE LIPSITZ,
San Diego, California,
1994

NOTES

1. Jack Conroy, *The Disinherited* (Westport, CT: Lawrence Hill and Company, 1982), 288.

2. Tom Laney, "UAW Local 879 Adopts Organizer," *Impact: The Rank and File Newsletter* vol.1 no.11–12 (February/March), 1994, 1, 12.

1

Kalfou Danjere

BOUKMAN EKSPERYANS

According to a story often told among jazz musicians, Clark Terry experienced some exasperating moments when he first joined the Duke Ellington orchestra in 1951. The great trumpet and flugelhorn player had rehearsed every complicated technical maneuver in his repertoire in anticipation of the opportunity to impress his new boss and band mates. But when he got to his audition, all Ellington wanted him to do was "to listen." Terry complained that he was a musician who needed a chance to play, that anyone could just sit and listen. But the ever enigmatic Ellington informed him, "There's listening and there's listening, but what I want you to do is to *listen*."

Eventually, Clark Terry came to see what Ellington wanted. He had been so preoccupied with his own skills, and what they could offer to the orchestra, that he had not taken time to hear what the other musicians needed from him. He had not yet learned to listen to the voices around him, or to understand the spaces and silences surrounding them. Ellington already knew that his young trumpeter had talent as a virtuoso, but he felt that Terry had to bring his virtuosity in harmony – both literally and figuratively – with the rest of the orchestra.

Ellington's admonition serves as a useful way of beginning to think about the problems, politics, and poetics of place within popular music in the contemporary world. At this moment of unprecedented danger and unprecedented opportunity, virtuosity entails *listening* as well as speaking. It requires patient explorations into spaces and silences as much as it demands bold and forthright articulation of ideas and interests. Most important, it calls for an understanding of how people make meaning for themselves, how they have already begun to engage in grass-roots theorizing about complicated realities, and why and when that theorizing might lead to substantive change for the better.

In our time, social and cultural crises often come to us in the form of struggles over place and displacement, over transformations in our relationships to both physical places and discursive spaces. The relationship between popular music and place offers a way of starting to understand the social world that we are losing – and a key to the one that is being built. Anxieties aired through popular music illumine important aspects of the cultural and political conflicts that lie ahead for us all.

Popular music has a peculiar relationship to the poetics and the politics of place. Recorded music travels from place to place, transcending physical and temporal barriers. It alters our understanding of the local and the immediate, making it possible for us to experience close contact with cultures from far away. Yet precisely because music travels, it also augments our appreciation of place. Commercial popular music demonstrates and dramatizes contrasts between places by calling attention to how people from different places create culture in different ways.

A poetics of place permeates popular music, shaping significantly its contexts of production, distribution, and reception. New Orleans jazz and sambas from São Paulo circulate freely throughout the world, but they never completely lose the concerns and cultural qualities that give them determinate shape in their places of origin. Through music we learn about place and about displacement. Laments for lost places and narratives of exile and return often inform, inspire, and incite the production of popular music. Songs build engagement among audiences at least in part through references that tap memories and hopes about particular places. Intentionally and unintentionally, musicians use lyrics, musical forms, and specific styles of performance that evoke attachment to or alienation from particular places.

Like other forms of contemporary mass communication, popular music simultaneously undermines and reinforces our sense of place. Music that originally emerged from concrete historical experiences in places with clearly identifiable geographic boundaries now circulates as an interchangeable commodity marketed to consumers all over the globe. Recordings by indigenous Australians entertain audiences in North America. Jamaican music secures spectacular sales in Germany and Japan. Rap music from inner-city ghettos in the U.S.A. attracts the allegiance of teenagers from Amsterdam to Auckland. Juke boxes and elaborate "sound systems" in Colombia employ dance music from West Africa as the constitutive element of a dynamic local subculture, while Congolese entertainers draw upon Cuban traditions for the core vocabulary of their popular music.

These transactions transform – but do not erase – attachments to place. Through the conduits of commercial culture, music made by aggrieved inner-city populations in Canberra, Kingston, or Compton becomes part of everyday life and culture for affluent consumers in the suburbs of Cleveland, Coventry, or Cologne. At the same time, electric-techno-art music made in Germany serves as a staple for sampling within African-American hip hop; Spanish flamenco and paso doble music provide crucial subtexts for Algerian rai artists; and pedal steel guitars first developed by country and western musicians in the U.S.A. play a prominent role in Nigerian juju.

This dynamic dialogue, however, does not necessarily reflect relations of reciprocity and mutuality. Inter-cultural communication does not automatically lead to inter-cultural cooperation, especially when participants in the dialogue speak from positions of highly unequal access to power, opportunity, and life chances. Citizens in advanced industrialized nations have long enjoyed the opportunity of consuming cultural commodities produced in colonized "hinterlands" both inside and outside of their national boundaries. Modernist literature, art, and music in Western countries has consistently spectacularized difference, titillating "respectable" audiences with sensational portrayals of "primitive," "exotic," and "oriental" outsiders.

(The cross-cultural communication carried on within today's contemporary popular music retains residual contradictions of centuries of colonialism, class domination, and racism.) But it also speaks to currents of culture and politics emerging from fundamentally new geopolitical and economic realities. The rapid mobility of capital and populations across the globe has problematized traditional understandings of place and made displacement a widely shared experience. Under these conditions, dispersed populations of migrant workers, emigrants, and exiles take on new roles as cross-cultural interpreters and analysts. As transnational corporations create integrated global markets and the nation state recedes as a source of identity and identification, popular culture becomes an ever more important public sphere.

In an innovative and original analysis, Arjun Appadurai argues that we need to draw a new cognitive map of the global cultural economy. Instead of dividing the world by continents or countries, Appadurai proposes that we think less of landscapes and more of the presence of concurrent ethnoscapes, mediascapes, technoscapes, finanscapes, and ideoscapes. In other words, the dynamic movement of ethnic groups, images, technology, capital, and ideologies allows us all to inhabit many different "places" at once.[1]

Yet, even under these circumstances of global integration, local identities and affiliations do not disappear. On the contrary, the transnational economy often makes itself felt most powerfully through the reorganization of spaces and the transformation of local experience – especially within and across urban areas. A century ago, the combined effects of state building, urbanization, and industrialization transformed popular perceptions about change over time, making *history* the constitutive problem of the age of industrialization. Today, the ever expanding reach and scope of electronic, computer chip, fiber optic, and satellite communication imposes a rationalized uniformity on production and consumption all over the world, making *place* the constitutive problem of the post-industrial era.

For more than a hundred years, struggles for social justice and equality have been waged as battles over the control of places – countries, cities, factories, and neighborhoods. But the division of labor and distribution of population within cities that characterized the industrial age has been supplanted by circuits and flows across cities in our post-industrial age. New technologies that separate management from production, flexible forms of capital accumulation that discourage investments in infrastructure, and increased emphasis on consumption rather than on production in metropolitan centers, all increasingly make urban identity a matter of connections between places. The export of industrial production to poorer countries extends across continents the class conflicts that previously took place largely within individual cities and states. Allegiances to place honed by centuries of successful struggles to extract concessions from capital now start to erode as the mobility of capital renders such strategies obsolete. But the circuits and flows of commerce created in the wake of flexible capital accumulation create new circuits and flows for culture and politics as well.[2]

The social movements of the industrial era tried to trap capital in one place – to extract concessions from capital by withholding labor, stopping production, or using the power of government to regulate and tax corporations and individuals. Their physical presence in factories or their numbers among the electorate provided them with leverage in struggles for power, but they also invariably resorted to cultural creativity to build public spheres and shared spaces that reflected their values and interests.

Today, shared cultural space no longer depends upon shared geographic place. What Henri Lefebvre called "theatrical or dramatized space" becomes increasingly important as a substitute for the lost public sphere of the industrial city.[3] New discursive spaces allow for recognition of new networks and affiliations; they become crucibles for complex identities in formation that respond to the imperatives of place at the same time that they transcend them. The interdependence of people throughout the world has never been more evident. From popular culture to politics, from the adoption market to the drug trade, new technologies and trade patterns connect places as well as people, redefining local identities and identifications in the process.

Video tapes made in Paris help Islamic fundamentalists seize power in Iran. Iranian exiles in Los Angeles publish telephone directories in Farsi, helping bring an influx of capital to southern California banking institutions. Hollywood films intended to assuage the effects of the American defeat in Vietnam become icons for anti-American militia fighters in Beirut. Civil war in Lebanon leads to Western repression against Islamic countries, which in turn helps provoke terrorist violence against French nationals and other foreigners living in Algeria as well as state terrorism against Islamic fundamentalists challenging their exclusion from the Algerian state.

As people in different places around the world face similar and interconnected kinds of austerity, inequality, and social disintegration, a transnational culture speaking to shared social realities starts to emerge. Yet the things that divide people remain as important as those that bring them together. The uneven distribution of resources, opportunities, and life chances in the world makes communication between places more instructive and more urgent than ever before. A peculiar inversion takes place as people from colonized countries long connected to global migrations emerge as experts about displacement and the qualities needed to combat it. (Music from aggrieved communities still serves traditional purposes of novelty, diversion, and exoticism for many consumers, but a poly-lateral dialogue among aggrieved populations and a crisis of confidence in declining industrialized nations gives new valence to the cultural creations emanating from aggrieved communities, making the relationship between "margins" and "center" dramatically different.

The promise and peril of popular music's new role in the world's economic, cultural, and political life appears dramatically in the actions of Boukman Eksperyans, a musical ensemble from Haiti. In May 1992, the six men and three women in the group gathered at the Audiotek Studios in Port-au-Prince to record an album featuring "Kalfou Danjere" ("Dangerous Crossroads"), the song that they had written especially for that year's carnival celebration. The Creole lyrics of their song warned "deceivers," "liars," "cheaters," and "assassins" of the dangers that awaited them at the "crossroads of the Congo people."[4]

In the wake of the military coup that had toppled the democratically-elected government of Jean-Bertrand Aristide in September 1991, "Kalfou Danjere" held unmistakable meaning for most Haitians. It drew upon the ideology and terminology of popular "voudou" religion to rebuke the corruption and brutality of the military dictatorship. Blending infectious indigenous voudou and rara rhythms with imported funk-rock and dance music, the musicians in Boukman Eksperyans used their time in the studio to produce an album that served as a vehicle for education and agitation among the Haitian people.

The song "Kalfou Danjere" invoked ancestral spirits, natural forces, minor deities, and the Supreme Being to predict a dangerous future for those who abused the Haitian people. By threatening trouble at the "crossroads," the song highlighted a place of crucial importance in African folklore and Caribbean voudou. Collisions occur at the crossroads; decisions must be made there. But the crossroads can also provide a unique perspective, a vantage point where one can see in more than one direction. In "Kalfou Danjere," Boukman Eksperyans described the crossroads as dangerous for the "deceivers," because there they would be called to judgment by the deities who protect the farmers, villagers, mountain dwellers, and urban poor who practice voudou.

In announcing the dangerous fate awaiting their enemies at the crossroads, the members of Boukman Eksperyans courted danger themselves. The Haitian government banned "Kalfou Danjere" from official carnival celebrations, and issued an order forbidding radio stations from broadcasting it. Military officials contended that the song posed a threat to public order, that it was "too violent" for people to hear – even though the lyrics of "Kalfou Danjere" expressly rejected violence. (At one point the lyrics affirm "we're not doing any killing, we're not going to play that game.") Unfortunately, the military's new-found, sudden, and decidedly short-lived aversion to "violence" – as expressed in this song – did not lead the government to curtail any of *its own* extensive repression, brutality, and terrorism against potential opponents. On the contrary, the military dictatorship increased its efforts at intimidation through a broad range of repressive measures including assassination and imprisonment.

Ever since their recording debut in 1989, the members of Boukman Eksperyans have been making music rendering them both dangerous and endangered. They won the Haitian Konou Mizik competition in 1989 with their song "Wet Chen" ("Break the Chain"). Their 1990 carnival song, "Ke'-m Pa Sote" ("My Heart Doesn't Leap, You Don't Scare Me") played a part in the popular revitalization of voudou, helping to spark the *Lavalas* movement ("the cleansing flood") – the mass mobilization that swept Aristide to power.[5] By connecting the dance hall with the voudou temple, "Ke'-m Pa Sote" also united town dwellers and rural peasants in opposition to the corruption that permeates Haitian politics. Its powerful polyrhythms and anthemic chorus enlisted listeners in an exciting and joyous collectivity that called into being through performance the kind of confident communality described by the song's lyrics.

Boukman Eksperyans, and the insurgent movement it helped inspire, sought to transform voudou from primarily an instrument of state repression to a vehicle for popular power. Under the dictatorial regimes of "Papa Doc" Duvalier, his son "Baby Doc," and their successors from the 1950s to the present, the Haitian government has used local voudou priests to recruit paramilitary forces known as *tontons macoutes*, creating an extra-legal network of loyalty and intimidation parallel to the state. Through its music, Boukman Eksperyans inverted, subverted, and reappropriated for revolutionary ends the rituals and symbols long employed by the *tontons macoutes* to preserve tyrannical rule. By the same token, they attempted to use the commodity culture brought to Haiti over centuries by foreign investment and foreign invasion as a focal point of resistance to the exploitation and oppression perpetrated on the people by outside powers and the country's own comprador elite.

Haitian military commanders dispatched soldiers, *tontons macoutes*, and civilian thugs (known as *attachés*) to Boukman Eksperyans concerts to prevent the group from performing "Ke'-m Pa Sote" and "Kalfou Danjere." The government subsequently banned "Innocent Christmas," another song from the *Kalfou Danjere* album, as well, because its lyrics asked listeners to "look at the route they want us to take to lose our freedom," to look "how they don't want us to say what we think."[6] But Boukman Eksperyans and its fans effectively foiled the government's strategy of silencing all opposition by circulating compact discs and cassettes (often copied on home recorders) throughout Haiti – as well as in exile communities in Miami, Montreal, New York, and Paris – helping to make "Kalfou Danjere" and "Ke'-m Pa Sote" ineradicable parts of the popular movement for democracy and justice in Haiti.[7]

Celebrating a legacy of insurgency and struggle deeply rooted in Haiti's history, Boukman Eksperyans adopted its name as a tribute to Joseph Boukman, the ex-slave and voudou *papaloi* (high priest) who played a prominent role in instigating the slave uprising and war for national independence in Haiti at the end of the eighteenth century. Described by C.L.R. James as "the first of that line of great leaders whom the slaves were to throw up in such profusion and rapidity in the years which followed," Boukman holds a special place in the hearts of Haitians as part of the pantheon of dark-skinned revolutionary heroes (along with Toussaint and Dessalines) who helped win independence for the nation. At the start of the 1791 insurrection, Boukman gathered his followers in the forests of Morne Rouge to assure them that unlike the god of the whites who sanctioned oppression, the god of the slaves "orders us to revenge our wrongs."[8] When Boukman died in battle, colonial officials had his head cut off and displayed in public as a warning to other potential rebels. But the brutality of their rulers only convinced the masses that they had no alternative to rebellion; their numbers grew to nearly 100,000 after Boukman's death.[9]

Two hundred years later, Boukman's name still serves as a impetus for insurgency in Haiti, in part because of the popularity of the musical group named after him. "We belong to the revolution," claims Theodore "Lolo" Beaubrun, Jr., the group's lead singer and keyboard, piano, and tambou player. "We have to find an alternative to the capitalism and the communism."[10] Lyrics in Boukman Eksperyans songs emphasize the African presence within Haiti's culture through mention of the *ginen* people – a reference to Guinea in West Africa, to the idea of an African homeland where voudou gods live, and to the state of spiritual awareness attained by those who practice voudou. By deploying signs and symbols from voudou, and by honoring Boukman, the group identifies itself with the dark-skinned masses and their heroes Toussaint and Dessalines, rather than with the tradition of the Catholic Creole elite and their historical heroes like Petion and Rigaud.[11]

But Boukman Eskperyans is a business as well as a political force. Its music circulates as a commodity in a global market. It serves as a source of speculative investment for multinational corporations engaged in marketing music all over the world. The group's historical references, Creole lyrics, and voudou metaphysics speak to distinctly Haitian realities, but its finished products also circulate as nodes in a network of global cultural commerce.

Boukman Eskperyans got started in the music business with the help of an American who owns a hotel in Haiti.[12] The group's manager lives in Montreal, and its British-based recording label arranged for post-production work on *Kalfou Danjere* in London and Miami. The members of the group blend Haitian voudou and rara drumming with Afro-American funk rock and South African dance music. Critic Jon Pareles described the group's sound as a mixture of "the cutting guitar of Santana" (the Mexican-born rock guitarist who moved to the U.S.A. as a teenager and found fame in the 1960s playing blues licks and Afro-Cuban rhythms) and "the three-chord bounce" of mba-qanga (the popular South African dance music).[13] Although its name honors one of Haiti's greatest heroes, it also offers a Creole rendering of "experience" – a name more likely to make international audiences think of Jimi Hendrix (who named his band the Jimi Hendrix Experience) than Joseph Boukman.[14]

Yet internationalism is hardly new to Haiti. U.S. marines occupied the country for almost two decades, and Franklin Delano Roosevelt wrote the country's constitution when he was Under-Secretary of the U.S. Navy. Sugar companies owned by American and other foreign investors have profited from low wages and low taxes on business in Haiti, and the U.S. government has been a perpetual source of direct and indirect support for totalitarian rule in the country.[15] The same circuits of investment and commerce that bring low-wage jobs to Haiti's factories and fields carry the music of Boukman Eskperyans to a wider world audience. The same connections between U.S. multinationals and Haitian poverty that insures a perpetual presence on the island by the American security state also makes the visibility of Boukman Eskperyans in the U.S.A. a strategic resource for the group as they try to criticize their government and still stay alive.

In "Kalfou Danjere," the members of Boukman Eksperyans warn their enemies about a dangerous crossroads – and consequently subject themselves to danger as well. But their own fusions of politics and popular culture, of nationalism and international-ism, of religion and revolution demarcate other crossroads and other dangers. Boukman Eksperyans lead singer Lolo Beaubrun claims that the group wants to help Haiti find an alternative to capitalism and socialism, but it still sells its songs as commodities in a capitalist market structure. Boukman Eksperyans tries to educate and agitate Haitians for social change, yet still serve the tastes of international audiences. The group attempts to use the traditions of voudou and nationalism for democratic ends, but runs the risk of being used by those traditions as well, of substituting superstition and fear for analysis and action.

The musicians in Boukman Eksperyans face serious contradictions as they attempt to address the volatile political and social conditions in Haiti at the same time that they address consumers around the globe as prospective customers. The influence of South African mbaqanga music on Boukman Eksperyans may testify to a dialogue between liberation struggles on different continents, but it also reflects the ability of commercial culture to collapse boundaries and render historically specific cultural expressions little more than fashions to be appropriated far from their conditions of creation. Music fans who may know nothing about Haitian history, voudou metaphysics, or Creole speech still "enjoy" the music of Boukman Eksperyans. They might use this music to become informed and connected to the life-and-death issues of revolutionary struggle in an impoverished Third World country, but they are just as likely to use the music of Boukman Eksperyans to turn the pain and strife in Haiti into just one more exotic spectacle, one more novelty, one more diversion for jaded consumers living in wealthy Western countries.

Yet, the international visibility enjoyed by the members of Boukman Eksperyans also helps protect them from repression by a government that has shown little reluctance to imprison and even assassinate its opponents. Their role in the global economy enables them to sharpen consciousness within their country about what it means to be Haitian. At the same time, U.S. hegemony over Haiti changes the U.S.A. as well.

Haitians fleeing poverty and oppression flock to Miami and New York, where their presence and impact on local employment and culture changes what it means to be Black, Cuban, Puerto Rican, and white in those cities. Incarceration of refugees from Haiti exposes the racist biases still permeating U.S. immigration policy, offending African Americans and discomforting other immigrant communities of color. The special health needs of Haitian immigrants expose the inequities and injustices of federal policies for the testing and treatment of AIDS, creating coalitions between immigrants and activists from gay and lesbian communities in some American cities. All of the populations held together by the presence of foreign capital in Haiti do not enjoy equal relations to one another or to power, but their destinies are linked in ways that become very visible once we start looking into the conditions that make the production of recorded music by Boukman Eksperyans possible.

The members of Boukman Eksperyans are not the only contemporary musicians whose work takes them to these dangerous crossroads. For many musicians around the world, the "popular" has become a dangerous crossroads, an intersection between the undeniable saturation of commercial culture in every area of human endeavor and the emergence of a new public sphere that uses the circuits of commodity production and circulation to envision and activate new social relations.

For example, Thomas Mapfumo's chimurenga music played a vital role in the struggle for national liberation in Zimbabwe in the 1970s and 1980s at the same time that it won a global following as a form of "world beat" music.[16] Rock singer and songwriter Freddie Aguilar encouraged opposition to the dictatorship of Ferdinand Marcos in the Philippines with his recording of "Katarungang" ("Justice"), and his version of a traditional patriotic tune, "Bayan Ko," served as the theme song of anti-Marcos opposition in the 1986 election campaign.[17] Soul Vibrations – a calypso/reggae/salsa band composed of English-speaking Black Nicaraguan Indians – emerged on the world market in the late 1980s with songs that praised their country's government for its solidarity with Mozambique, but at the same time condemned it for denying autonomy to the indigenous population along the Atlantic coast.[18]

In Germany in 1992, Jens Muller, a twenty-one-year-old rap singer calling himself "J," used his $40,000 advance from a recording company to finance *Germany Alert*, an anti-racist newsletter designed to combat growing violence in his country against people of Turkish, Vietnamese, and African ancestry.[19] Like the music of Fela Kuti in Nigeria, Ruben Blades in Panama, or Yothu Yindi in Australia, the music of Mapfumo, Aguilar, Soul Vibrations, J, and Boukman Eksperyans illustrates the emergence of a kind of politics that takes commodity culture for granted and the emergence of a kind of cultural practice that aspires to political significance. They evidence the early stirrings of efforts to theorize the emerging world order from the grass roots, to speak *to* and *through* the systems of communication and commerce that signal the emergence of fundamentally new opportunities and dangers.

In some cases, the politics of contemporary popular music emerge as much from the reception strategies of audiences as from the intentions of artists. People fight with the means at their disposal; in a world characterized by the circulation of commodities, commercial culture can provide an effective means of receiving and sending messages in unexpected ways. Jamaican reggae singer Bob Marley's visit to Australia in 1979 helped launch a "Black power" movement among that country's indigenous activists. They interpreted Marley's message that "all Black men are brothers" as meant for them. Consequently, when indigenous bands including Kuckles, No Fixed Address, and Coloured Stone began to record protest songs against their mistreatment by white Australians, they used reggae as a prominent means of expression.[20]

Similarly, a massive anti-racism movement (SOS-Racisme) in France in the mid-1980s promoted Algerian rai music – a synthesis of North African and European popular musics – as an emblem of inter-cultural cooperation. Subsequent anti-government rioters in Algiers in 1988 took rai singer Cheb Khaled's "El Harba Wine" ("Where to Flee?") as their anthem, even though the song itself had no intentional political content.[21] Nicaraguans disgusted with the Sandinista government's glorification of Cuban socialism in the late 1980s rejected the didactic folk revival sponsored by their own government in favor of a commercial recording. This recording, "Juana, La Cubana," is a Mexican version of a Colombian song that made fun of Cubans, and became popular because it provided disgruntled Nicaraguans with an opportunity to express some not very covert resentments against their leaders.[22]

When indigenous Australians draw their forms of cultural resistance from diasporic Africans in Jamaica, when French anti-racists use music initially created by the collision between French imperialism and Arab cabaret singers in Algeria, when Algerian rebels take up rai music popular in Paris as an emblem of modernization, when Nicaraguans shun a government-sponsored "new song" movement and instead use the salacious lyrics of an international popular song as an expression of "their" politics, they illustrate the many kinds of crossroads and the many kinds of dangers embedded in the cultural conduits of our time. If political activity could ever have been seen simply as the province of the nation state, it can be seen that way no longer.

New technologies, mass migrations, and the rapid movement of ideas, images, and expressions across the globe have created new networks of identification and affiliation that render obsolete some traditional political practices and identities while creating complicated and complex new cultural fusions with profound political implications. For example, one of the leading traditional taiko drummers in Japan recently was a Chicano from East Los Angeles named Maceo Hernandez-Delgado. He learned about Japanese cultural traditions while growing up in multi-cultural Los Angeles, and traveled to Japan to study music as a kind of return to a homeland that he had never known.[23] At the same time, one of the world's most accomplished Afro-Caribbean salsa bands, Orquesta de la Luz, comes from Japan. The cover of one of the band's compact discs presents a portrait of the Orquesta members' distinctly Japanese faces juxtaposed against the album's title: *Somos Diferentes (We Are Different)*. Reggae music from Jamaica and Elvis Presley songs from the U.S.A. enjoy popularity in Japan, in part because Japanese listeners hear reggae as similar to Japanese O-Bon festival music, and they interpret Presley's songs as a variant of Japanese enka music.[24] Koreans listening to African-American rap music compare it to sasui, a Korean lyrical form within folk dramas known as pansori.[25] Leila K, a Moroccan teenager who records dance-hall rap music in Sweden, had a U.S. hit with "Got to Get" in 1990, while "Sadeness" became a 1991 international hit as a song based on Gregorian chants put together in a Spanish studio by a producer born in Rumania.[26] In Los Angeles, one of the most important producers of Chicano artists creating African-American-based rap music is Steve Yano, a Japanese American raised in a Chicano neighborhood, who began his business selling rap cassettes at Chicano swap meets and whose recording studio occupies an office that previously housed a Chinese-language cable television company.[27]

The inter-cultural communication encoded in these musical performances has complicated origins and implications. In an era when every continent seems convulsed by ethnic, religious, and racial violence, examples of cross-national and multi-racial music offer hope for a better future. Yet, certain kinds of multi-culturalism and internationalism are also essential elements in the project of transnational capital to erase local differences and distinctions in the hope of making all cultural and political units equally susceptible to investment, exploitation, and the sale of mass-produced commodities that make the love of gain and the lure of accumulation the only cultural qualities that count. But while very much a product of the ever expanding reach and scope of capital, these cultural creations also testify to the ways in which artists from aggrieved communities can use the very instruments of their displacement and dispossession to forge a new public sphere with emancipatory potential.

In 1993, audiences around the world began hearing the music of an artist calling himself "Apache Indian." Because of his stage name and the title of his first album, *No Reservations*, some speculated that he might be an American Indian. But his music had the hard edge of Jamaican raggamuffin dance-hall rap, suggesting that he might be West Indian. In fact, Apache Indian turned out to be Steve Kapur, a former welder from Handsworth in England whose parents were Punjabi immigrants from the southwest Asian nation of India. Kapur grew up in the same racially-mixed neighbor-hood that produced the inter-racial reggae band UB40, and took his stage name in honor of his idol, the West Indian artist Wild Apache, aka Super Cat, both because Kapur admired his music and because Wild Apache himself included Caribbean East Indians among his ancestors.[28]

Apache Indian's music mixes hip hop, reggae, and Anglo-American pop styles with the Asian-Indian dance music bhangra, leading some commentators to call his music bhangramuffin. "I grew up in a very multi-cultural place," he explains, "where you can't get away from the reggae sound, and as an Asian, you can't get away from the bhangra sound, and living in this country, you can't get away from pop. All these flavors just came out."[29] Kapur developed an early interest in music as a fan of Elvis Presley; he met his girlfriend Harj at a swap meet organized by an Elvis Presley fan club. But he was also strongly influenced by the music and Rastafarian religion of Bob Marley, in part because of the Jamaican's success as an artist of color in attracting an international audience, but also because Marley's philosophy and values spoke power-fully to Kapur's life as a diasporic Indian in Britain. As a teenager, Kapur wore his hair in dreadlocks and painted his bedroom red, gold, and green – the colors of Black nationalism popularized by Marley and other Rastafarians.[30]

Apache Indian's recordings enjoyed phenomenal sales among the diasporic Indian community in Toronto, largely because young Indian Canadians saw his use of bhangra as a sign of respect for Indian traditions. But when Kapur toured India he found that he had an image as a rebel because of songs like "Arranged Marriage" that criticized the caste system, because he lived with but did not marry his Sikh girlfriend, and because his music adhered to Western rather than to traditional Indian standards of excellence. In England, Apache Indian's music became an important icon of unity between Afro-Caribbeans and Afro-Asians who had long been divided despite their common identification as "Black" Britons. Reggae musicians in Jamaica welcomed Apache Indian as an artist worthy of respect and as an ally in their cultural and political projects. The Jamaican singer Maxi Priest contributed to Apache Indian's recording session at Tuff Gong studios in Kingston by singing in Punjabi. "He doesn't have to tap into the Indian market," commented a grateful and admiring Apache Indian in respect of Priest's efforts, "he just wanted to do it."[31]

The emergence of an artist like Apache Indian underscores some important aspects of the relationship between cultural space and physical place in our time. The exchange of populations and cultural commodities across the globe creates an inter-connectedness with enormous implications for culture and politics. Constance Sutton describes New York as "the Caribbean crossroads of the world," because it has a Caribbean population larger than the combined populations of Kingston (Jamaica), San Juan (Puerto Rico), and Port-of-Spain (Trinidad). Islanders who identify themselves as from Barbados or Grenada at home become something new – "Caribbean" or "West Indian" – in New York, Miami, Toronto, Montreal, London, and Paris.[32] One reason why carnival celebrations in London have become important to that city's Afro-Caribbean population is that they have emerged as important sites for creating a composite "West Indian" identity that transcends affiliations to individual islands.[33] Similarly, Paris now serves as a more convenient meeting place for African intellectuals and artists than any city on the African continent.

Of course, imperial capitals have always served as important sites for diasporic colonial populations, but never before have diasporic immigrants played such a vital role in global economy and culture. As the pernicious effects of global capitalism come home, as the austerity imposed on the Third World by the International Monetary Fund and other agents of transnational capital continues to destroy life chances around the globe, diasporic populations speak powerfully about realities that are all too familiar to them but relatively novel to inhabitants of advanced industrialized countries. This is one reason why music from Asia, Africa, and Latin America is more than a novel diversion in Europe and North America these days; its affect and power and lyrical eloquence stems in part from the understandings it conveys about capitalism and coercion. A peculiar prestige from below accompanies the rise of "world beat" music, in part because it seems as complicated as the rest of contemporary cultural life and to reflect the insights of artists who appear "a day older in history than everybody else."[34]

Models of cultural imperialism based on binary oppositions between a metropolis and its periphery inadequately describe the poly-lateral relations across countries and cultures that characterize contemporary cultural production. Political strategies based solely on seizing state power underestimate the interconnectedness of the global economy and the capacity of capital to neutralize the nation state. Concepts of cultural practice that privilege autonomous, "authentic," and non-commercial culture as the only path to emancipation do not reflect adequately the complexities of culture and commerce in the contemporary world.

Long histories of avant-garde art and vanguard politics demonstrate the overwhelming failure of efforts to transform society by imagining that we can stand outside it, by seeking transcendent critiques untainted by dominant ideologies and interests. The strategies that emerge from today's global realities point to another path, to the efforts by Boukman Eksperyans, Apache Indian, and others to produce an immanent critique of contemporary social relations, to work through the conduits of commercial culture in order to illumine affinities, resemblances, and potentials for alliances among a world population that now must be as dynamic and as mobile as the forces of capital.

The dangerous crossroads created constantly within contemporary cultural production, distribution, and exchange require neither simple celebration nor surrender masquerading as cynical critique. Instead, we need to think through the promise and peril of the present situation. Faced with what Nestor Garcia Canclini astutely identifies as "hybrid transformations generated by the horizontal coexistence of a number of symbolic systems,"[35] we need to think realistically about the ways in which the world's population has been divided and segmented into very different relationships with a centralized global economy. Moreover, we need to explore the potential of popular culture as a mechanism of communication and education, as a site for experimentation with cultural and social roles not yet possible in politics.

This book is an effort to take advantage of the unique perspectives afforded by the many crossroads of contemporary culture, but to face up to their dangers as well. In it, I examine a plurality of practices within popular music to understand how popular culture contains different meanings in different countries. But I also examine how the interconnectedness of capitalist culture might help create collective solutions to the systematic and unrelenting injustice and austerity which characterizes life for so many people on this planet. The book is based on the premise that the power of transnational capital means that all of us must become transnational too.

In writing a book about dangerous crossroads, I inevitably run the risk of making dangerous distortions and errors of my own. As a North American limited by the parochialism and prejudices of my life and my culture, I know that my efforts to interpret and analyze political and cultural practices from contexts far different from my own are likely to fall short in ways that I can not anticipate. Readers interested in a comprehensive survey of world music or a guide to its appreciation and interpretation will surely be disappointed by my choice to study music as a social force. Many dimensions of music's local and global uses and effects remain outside my purview as well, since I focus on issues of place and politics. But the most important thing is to begin to recognize the voices that already exist in the world expressing important theoretical insights into the crises that bind us all, albeit to different degrees and with different consequences. For cultural creators, critics, and consumers alike, risks are necessary; continuing to address only familiar issues and questions posed solely within ethnocentric national categories would be far worse than the possibility of making a few errors while asking questions that address appropriately the complexity of the cultural and political tasks facing us. These crossroads are dangerous for all of us, but the greatest danger would come from pretending that we can ignore them. As Charles Péguy once observed, "No one could suspect that times were coming . . . when the man who did not gamble would lose all the time, even more surely than he who gambled."[36]

In an incisive formulation that illumines powerfully the poetics and politics of place in our time, Deborah Pacini Hernandez explains that the spread of "international" music paradoxically often encourages "deeper exploration of national musics"; when music travels across cultures, artists and audiences notice peculiarities of place that would otherwise remain hidden from them without the opportunity for comparison.[37] Consequently, international music can make local and national knowledge *more* important rather than less. The reach and scope of transnational capital makes indigenous Haitian traditions all that much more powerful as forms of resistance for Boukman Eksperyans. The disintegration of the Canadian nation state as a consequence of the disastrous North American Free Trade Agreement and the abandonment of the social wage by the Mulroney government, gives renewed hope to Québécois nationalists because their province enjoys distinct cultural differences from Canada *and* from the U.S.A. History does not disappear in our age of simultaneity. Often, repressed elements of the past surge to the surface as part of the present.

Just as the internationally-inflected music of Boukman Eksperyans helped them rediscover the specificities of Haitian culture and history, many of the fusions that seem to be recent developments made possible only by global economy and culture actually reflect enduring traditions and legacies firmly rooted in the inequalities and inequities of the histories of particular places. They are not postmodern fusions, but present manifestations of the long history of inter-cultural communication among the world's peoples over hundreds of years. Some of the novel combinations that characterize contemporary culture (like the popularity of Nigerian highlife music in Hamburg, Germany or the importance of Brazilian samba music in Lagos, Nigeria) reflect real historical connections and affinities, not just a serendipitous exchange of signs and symbols across cultures.

For example, consider the importance to the emergence of postmodern fusion music all around the world of cities that have been seaports. Algerian rai music comes from Oran, long a center for cross-cultural communication among Arab, Black, French, and Spanish people and cultures. The Australian indigenous bands Kuckles and Sunburn that mixed calypso, reggae, pop, and indigenous musics so effectively in the 1980s began playing music in Broome, a pearling center known for its demographic mixture of European, Japanese, Filipino, and indigenous residents.

Manu Dibango from Cameroon first developed his eclectic combination of African, American, European, and Cuban music in his home town of Douala, a port serving sailors from all over the world. Black musicians in New Orleans regularly turned to Cuban, Haitian, Trinidadian, and Jamaican musical forms in part because of the extensive sea traffic between their city and Mantanzas, Havana, Port-au-Prince, Port-of-Spain, and Kingston. Similarly, it is no accident that seaport cities like Cartagena (Colombia) and Hamburg (Germany) became centers for African musical influences or that the Beatles would come from Liverpool, the British port most involved in the slave trade with Africa and the Caribbean.[38] (Much that seems new in contemporary culture carries within itself unresolved contradictions of the past.) The solutions to what seem like our newest problems may well be found in communities that have been struggling with them for centuries. The most "modern" people in the world that is emerging may be those from nations that have been considered "backward."

The crossroads we confront contain both residual and emergent elements; they encompass both dangers and opportunities. Following Nestor Garcia Canclini we can see that the nation states and social movements that have traditionally been patrons of culture have lost power and influence in the age of transnational capital, while cultural activity "linked to the expanding modes of capitalist development" (like corporations and cultural foundations) is ascendant.[39] These developments call for new forms of social theory capable of explaining new connections between culture and politics, as well as for new forms of cultural criticism suited to seeing beyond the surface content of cultural expressions to understand and analyze their conditions of production. The aim here is not to produce another theory for interpreting culture, but rather to come toward a better theorized understanding of social relations by understanding the interplay of art, culture, and commerce within them.

The violence that emerged with such destructive fury in the Los Angeles rebellion of 1992, in murderous attacks on "foreigners" in Germany during 1992–1993, and in racial, religious, and ethnic conflicts across the globe in recent years dramatize the dangers emerging at various crossroads of commerce and culture. Anxiety and xenophobia fueled by a sense of cultural loss, the very real deprivation of displaced populations, anger emanating from a permanent austerity economy, and the surveillance and suppression necessary for the perpetuation of privilege provide preconditions for explosions everywhere. The interconnectedness of cultures displayed by world music is not without utopian possibilities, but the ravages of unimpeded capital accumulation create grave dangers as well. These crossroads are dangerous for all of us; how well we negotiate them may determine what kind of future we will face – or whether we will face any future at all. Dangers await at the crossroads, but never with more peril than when we refuse to face them.

NOTES

1. Arjun Appadurai, "Disjuncture and Difference in the Global Cultural Economy," *Public Culture* vol.2 no.2 (1990), 1–24.

2. For descriptions of these new spatial and social relations see Joseph Kling, "Complex Society/Complex Cities: New Social Movements and the Restructuring of Urban Space," in Robert Fisher and Joseph Kling, eds, *Mobilizing the Community: Local Politics in the Era of the Global City* (Newbury Park, London, New Delhi: Sage Publications, 1993), 28–51.

3. Quote by Lefebvre from Joseph Kling, "Complex Society/Complex Cities," 36.

4. Boukman Eksperyans, *Kalfou Danjere*, liner notes, Mango Records 162-539-927-2, 1992.

5. Chris Tilly, "Haiti's Agony," *Dollars and Sense* no.192 (March/April) 1994, 16.

6. "Innocent Christmas," Boukman Eskperyans, *Kalfou Danjere*, liner notes.

7. Larry Birnbaum, "Boukman Eksperyans," *Down Beat* (March) 1993, 45; Gene Santoro, "South of the Border," *Nation*, February 1, 1993, 139; Jon Pareles, "Boukman Eksperyans," *New York Times*, November 19, 1992.

8. C.L.R. James, *The Black Jacobins* (New York: Vintage, 1963) 86, 87.

9. C.L.R. James, *The Black Jacobins*, 96.

10. Jon Pareles, "Boukman Eksperyans."

11. James Ferguson, "Voodoo and Haitian Politics," *Race and Class*, p.95; C.L.R. James, *The Black Jacobins*, 147–8, 369–70, 372, 54, 58, 411, 99, 108, 234–5.

12. Philip Sweeney, *The Virgin Directory of World Music* (New York: Henry Holt, 1991), 214.

13. Jon Pareles, "Boukman Eksperyans."

14. Because Hendrix named his band "The Jimi Hendrix Experience" and is known for his song "Have You Ever Been Experienced?"

15. Chris Tilley, "Haiti's Agony," 16–19, 36, 37.

16. Julie Frederikse, *None But Ourselves: Masses vs. Media in the Making of Zimbabwe* (Exeter, NH: Heinemann, 1992); Don Snowden, "Zimbabwe Singer's Dream Helps Make the Revolution," *Los Angeles Times*, October 21, 1989, F6.

17. Philip Sweeney, *The Virgin Directory*, 167, 168.

18. Greg Landau, *Rock Down Central America*, 1989. Produced by Senal S.A.

19. Mike Hennessey, Ken Terry, Paul Verna, "German Rapper Takes Aim at Fascism," *Billboard*, September 26, 1992, 1.

20. Marcus Breen, ed., *Our Place, Our Music: Aboriginal Music* (Canberra: Australian Aboriginal Press, Australian Popular Music in Perspective, volume 2, 1989), 121.

21. David McMurray and Ted Swedenburg, "Rai Tide Rising," *Middle East Report* (March–April) 1991, 42.

22. Greg Landau, personal communication, February 10, 1994.

23. John Esaki, *Maces: Demon Drummer from East L.A.*, 1993. Produced by Visual Communications.

24. Dean W. Collingwood and Osamu Kusatsu, "Japanese Rastafarians: Non-Conformity in Modern Japan," unpublished paper 1991, 8; Ayako Maeda, "Elvis Presley in the Land of the Rising Sun," presentation at American Studies Association meetings, Boston, MA, November 6, 1993.

25. Byung Hoo Suh, "An Unexpected Rap Eruption Rocks a Traditional Music Market,' *Billboard*, August 22, 1992, S6.

26. David McMurray and Ted Swedenburg, "Rai Tide Rising," 41; Dave Laing, " 'Sadeness', Scorpions and Single Markets: National and Transnational Trends in European Popular Music," *Popular Music* vol.11 no.2 (May) 1992, 127.

27. Lorraine Ali, "Latin Class: Kid Frost and the Chicano Rap School," *Option* no.53 (November– December) 1993, 70.

28. Brooke Wentz, "Apache Indian," *Vibe* (November) 1993, 86.

29. Thom Duffy, "Apache Indian's Asian-Indian Pop Scores U.K. Hit," *Billboard*, February 20, 1993, 82.

30. Paul Bradshaw, "Handsworth Revolutionary," *Straight No Chaser* no.23 (Autumn) 1993, 26.

31. Paul Bradshaw, "Handsworth Revolutionary," 29.

32. Winston James, "Migration, Racism, and Identity: The Caribbean Experience in Britain," *New Left Review* no.193 (May–June), 1992, 37, 36.

33. Abner Cohen, *Masquerade Politics* (Berkeley: University of California Press, 1993), 40.

34. I appropriate this phrase from another context, from Robert Warshow's "Clifford Odets: Poet of the Jewish Middle Class," in Robert Warshow, *The Immediate Experience* (New York: Atheneum, 1979), 63.

35. Nestor Garcia Canclini, "Cultural Reconversion," from George Yudice, Jean Franco, and Juan Flores, eds, *On Edge: The Crisis of Contemporary Latin American Culture* (Minneapolis: University of Minnesota Press, 1992), 32.

36. Quoted in C. Wright Mills, *White Collar: The American Middle Classes* (New York: Oxford University Press, 1951), viii.

38. Deborah Pacini Hernandez, "Bachata: From the Margins to the Mainstream," *Popular Music* vol.11 no.3 (1992), 360. See also the eloquent formulation advanced by Jocelyne Guilbault in "On Redefining the 'Local' Through World Music," *Popscriptum* (forthcoming).

38. Paul Gilroy notes that the German edition of Frederick Douglass's *My Bondage, My Freedom* was published in Hamburg in 1860: Paul Gilroy, *The Black Atlantic: Modernity and Double Consciousness* (Cambridge, MA: Harvard University Press, 1993), 60.

39. Nestor Garcia Canclini, "Cultural Reconversion," 33.

2

Diasporic Noise: History, Hip Hop, and the Post-colonial Politics of Sound

AFRICA BAMBAATAA

In 1989, a nineteen-year-old African-American woman from Irvington, New Jersey performing under the name Queen Latifah starred in a music video promoting her rap song "Ladies First." At a time when politicians, journalists, and even most male rappers presented few positive images of Black women, Queen Latifah drew upon the diasporic history of Black people around the world to fashion an affirmative representation of women of African descent. Assisted by Monie Love, an Afro-Caribbean rapper from London, as well as Ms. Melody and a chorus of other Black female rappers from the U.S.A., Latifah appeared in a video that interspersed still photos of Angela Davis, Sojourner Truth, and Madame C.J. Walker with newsreel films of women prominent in the struggle against apartheid in South Africa. Uniting Black people across generations and continents, the young rap artist from New Jersey situated claims about her prowess with rap rhythms and rhymes within a broader story of diasporic struggle.

In telling its story about the achievements, ability, and desirability of Black women, "Ladies First" inverted and subverted existing representations with wide circulation in mass media and popular culture. During a decade when politicians and journalists in the U.S.A. regularly depicted Black women as unwed mothers and "welfare queens," Latifah's video presented them as "queens of civilization" and "mothers" who "give birth" to political struggle. At a time when "gangsta rap" glamorized the aggression and violence of street criminals, "Ladies First" celebrated the militancy of collective strug gles for social change. In an era when some Black nationalists belittled the gains made by Black women as detrimental to the community as a whole and urged them to accept subordinate places behind Black men, Latifah hailed the historic accomplishments of African-American women and emphasized the need for equal dedication and commitment from Black men and Black women in their common struggle against racism. Most important, in an American culture increasingly dismissive of African-American appeals for justice, dignity, and opportunity as "minority" concerns, Latifah's deployment of images from the African diaspora demonstrated that the "minority" populations of the U.S.A. are part of the global majority who have been victimized and oppressed by Euro-American racism and imperialism.

Queen Latifah's effort to map out discursive and political space through the trope of the African diaspora builds on historical practices within hip hop culture as well as within the broader history of Afro-America. The first visible manifestations of what we have come to call hip hop culture (rap music, break dancing, graffiti, B Boy and wild style fashions) appeared in the early 1970s when a member of a New York street gang (The Black Spades) calling himself Afrika Bambaataa organized "The Zulu Nation."

Confronted by the ways in which displacement by urban renewal, economic recession, and the fiscal crisis of the state combined to create desperate circumstances for inner-city youths, Bambaataa tried to channel the anger and enthusiasm of young people in the South Bronx away from gang fighting and into music, dance, and graffiti. He attracted African-American, Puerto Rican, Afro-Caribbean, and Euro-American youths into his "nation." He staged dances featuring his estimable talents as a "mixer" and sound system operator capable of providing a non-stop flow of danceable beats from an enormous range of musical styles. In 1982, he recorded "Planet Rock" under the name Afrika Bambaataa and Soulsonic Force, and sold more than a million copies on twelve-inch vinyl of his song "Planet Rock."

Part of a generation of inner-city youths who found themselves unwanted as students by schools facing drastic budget cuts, unwanted as citizens or users of city services by municipalities imposing austerity regimens mandated by private financial institutions, and even unwanted as consumers by merchants increasingly reliant on surveillance and police power to keep urban "have-nots" away from affluent buyers of luxury items, Bambaataa and his Zulu nation used their knowledge as consumers of popular music to become skilled producers of it. They used the conduits of popular culture to bring the expressive forms of their isolated and largely abandoned neighborhoods to an international audience. Hemmed in by urban renewal, crime, and police surveillance, and silenced by neglect from the culture industry, the school system, and city government, they found a way to declare themselves part of a wider world through music. "You can go do anything with rap music," Bambaataa has argued, "you can go from the past to the future to what's happening now."[1]

Bambaataa named his "Zulu Nation" after the 1964 British film *Zulu* directed by Cy Endfield and starring Michael Caine. The motion picture clearly intended to depict the Zulus as predatory savages opposed to the "civilizing mission" of the British empire. But as an American Black whose mother and aunts had migrated to New York from Barbados, Bambaataa saw it another way. In his eyes, the Zulus were heroic warriors resisting oppression. He used their example to inspire his efforts to respond to racism and class oppression in the U.S.A. "Planet Rock" reached a world audience through the same mechanisms of commercial culture that brought *Zulu* from Britain to the Bronx twenty years earlier, but instead of celebrating Western imperialism, the song hailed the utopian potential of Black music to transform the entire world into "a land of master jam."[2]

In lyrics written and rapped by MC Globe, "Planet Rock" celebrated the ability of music to take listeners to the past and to the future, but it also urged them to enjoy the present, to "chase your dreams" and "live it up," because "our world is free." The song located listeners and dancers "on this Mother Earth which is our rock," and combined new styles of rapping with a wide variety of Bambaataa's samples, including the theme music from the film *The Good, the Bad, and the Ugly*, sounds from the German techno band Kraftwerk, and cuts from the British band Babe Ruth over a Roland TR 808 drum synthesizer. Bambaataa and his nation inserted themselves into international commercial culture through "Planet Rock," which one perceptive reviewer described as "an unlikely fusion of bleeping, fizzing, techno-rock, Zulu surrealism, and deep-fried funk."[3]

Afrika Bambaataa's "Planet Rock" and Queen Latifah's "Ladies First" testify to the vitality of what Paul Gilroy calls "diasporic intimacy" in the Black Atlantic world. Their efforts are only a small part of an international dialogue built on the imagination and ingenuity of slum dwellers from around the globe suffering from the effects of the international austerity economy imposed on urban areas by transnational corporations and their concentrated control over capital. In recent recordings, Jamaican toaster Macka B raps an English-language history of Senegal over the singing of Baaba Maal, who speaks the Pulaar language of his native land. Cameroon expatriate Manu Dibango has recorded jazz albums with British rapper MC Mello and Parisian rapper MC Solaar. Solaar appeared on the recent hip hop–jazz fusion recording by Guru of the U.S. rap group Gang Starr, while local rap artists in South Korea, Japan, Germany, France, and New Zealand have found significant popularity imitating the African-American styles mastered by Afrika Bambaataa and Queen Latifah.[4]

The significance of these seemingly ephemeral works of popular culture goes far beyond their role as commodities. The diasporic conversation within hip hop, Afrobeat, jazz and many other Black musical forms provides a powerful illustration of the potential for contemporary commercialized leisure to carry images, ideas, and icons of enormous political importance between cultures. Whatever role they serve in the profit-making calculations of the music industry, these expressions also serve as exemplars of post-colonial culture with direct relevance to the rise of new social movements emerging in response to the imperatives of global capital and its attendant austerity and oppression.

In *Postmodernism, or the Cultural Logic of Late Capitalism*, Fredric Jameson challenges us to imagine a political form suited to "the invention and projection of a global cognitive mapping on a social as well as a spatial scale."[5] That form already exists in hip hop culture as well as in many other forms of global cultural practice. The existence of the African diaspora functions throughout the world as a crucial force for opening up cultural, social, and political space for struggles over identity, autonomy, and power. When properly contextualized as a part of post-colonial culture and of the rise of new social movements, the musical productions of the African diaspora provide one answer to Jameson's challenge with a cultural politics already underway.

POST-COLONIAL CULTURE

During the great global struggle against colonialism in the years following World War II, national self-determination and anti-colonialist internationalism engaged the attention of intellectuals throughout Africa, Asia, and Latin America. From Che Guevara's *Reminiscences of the Cuban Revolution* to Sembene Ousmane's *God's Bits of Wood*, from Chairman Mao's *Yenan Program* to Frantz Fanon's *The Wretched of the Earth*, nation building occupied center stage as the crucial element in anti-colonial emancipation. Although often somber and self-critical, anti-colonial expressions nonetheless contained an irrepressible optimism about the inevitability of liberation and about the potential achievements of post-colonial nationalism.

Forty years later, a literature of disillusionment and despair calls attention to conditions of austerity and oppression operative everywhere in the Third World. This "post-colonial" literature seems to confirm in the sphere of culture the failure of nationalist anti-colonial movements around the globe to translate national independence into something more than neo-colonial economic, cultural, and even political dependency. Defenders of colonialism point to the pervasive poverty and political problems of post-colonial countries as proof that independence came too soon. Anti-colonialists generally charge that colonialism itself continues to be the problem, that colonial practices did little to prepare people and institutions for independence. Yet bothof these arguments hinge on outdated premises with little relevance for the present.

In this debate, anti-colonialists and neo-colonialists both presume that the nation state still holds the key to self-determination, that the "quality" of government officials determines the well-being of the nation. But a combination of political, technological, and cultural changes since the 1970s has undermined the authority of the nation state while making multinational corporations, communications networks, and financial structures more powerful than ever before. In an age when capital, communications, and populations travel across the globe at an accelerated pace, the ability of any one nation state to determine its people's life chances has become greatly constrained.

Capitalist transnational corporations have gained great advantages by separating management from production with the aid of computer-generated automation, containerization in shipping, and the new technologies ushered in through fiber optics, computer chips, and satellites. Strategies to extract concessions from capitalists through taxation and regulation fail because of the extraordinary mobility of capital that makes it easy to play one country or region against another. At the same time, the need for capital compels formerly colonized nations to accept the compulsory austerity measures required by the International Monetary Fund and the World Bank as the price of securing loans. In rare cases when these forces fail to bring about desired results, the former imperial powers have shown little reluctance to bring direct or indirect military pressures to bear against nation states deviating from the dictates of this comprehensive world system.[6]

Thus, the failures of newly independent regimes that pervade post-colonial literature stem as much from fundamentally new conditions in world politics, economics, and culture as they do from the legacy of colonialism or the shortcomings of the struggles against it. Without denying the very important critiques of corruption and political oppression that appear in post-colonial culture, it is also important to understand that post-colonial expressions address emerging problems in the present as well as the failures of the past. The post-colonial era is one of displacement and migration, of multi-culturalism and multi-lingualism, of split subjects and divided loyalties. Post-colonial culture exposes the impossibility of *any* national identity incorporating into a unified totality the diverse and diffuse elements that make up a nation. While valuable for its insights into the failures of particular anti-colonial liberation movements, post-colonial art also exposes the inadequacy of national "imagined communities" to monitor, regulate, and remedy the explosive contradictions of global structures of economic, political, and cultural power. Indeed, the popularity of post-colonial writing and film in advanced industrial nations as well as in formerly colonized states stems from its relevance to conditions in metropolitan nations as well to those in the Third World.[7]

The crisis signaled by the emergence of post-colonial literature, art, and music is the crisis confronting movements for progressive social change all around the world. For more than a century, aggrieved populations have pinned their hopes on seizing control of the nation state, or at least on using its mechanisms to extract concessions from capital. But these traditional strategies for social change have been confounded by the emergence of "fast capital" and the equally rapid mobility of ideas, images, and people across national boundaries.

Yet new forms of domination also give rise to new forms of resistance. Rather than viewing post-colonial culture as a product of the *absence* of faith in yesterday's struggles for self-determination, it might be better to view it as product of the *presence* of new sensibilities uniquely suited for contesting the multinational nature of capital. The disillusionment and despair with politics in post-colonial writing may prove extraordinarily relevant beyond the former colonies; it may in fact be a strategically important stance for people around the globe in an age when centralized economic power has rendered many of the traditional functions of the nation state obsolete. As sociologists Harvey Molotch and John Logan argue, "when the state becomes unable to serve as a vehicle for trapping capital (and perhaps redistributing it), it places more than its legitimacy at risk; it loses some of its very meaning."[8] Of course, the state still serves as a source of repression, and still serves as an important instrument for people interested in using politics to address the rampant austerity and injustice of our time. But the state can no longer serve as the sole site of contestation for movements that find they have to be cultural as well as political, global as well as local, transnational as well as national.

One reason for the popularity of post-colonial art among readers in post-imperial countries comes from a shared disillusionment with the nation state and its failed promises. Similarly, stories of exile and return often employ the historical displacement of formerly colonized populations to express a more general sense of cultural displacement engendered everywhere by mass communications, population migrations, and the destructive effects of "fast capital" on traditional communities. Of course consumers of post-colonial cultural artifacts have many different motivations. A search for novelty, boredom with familiar paradigms, and traditional European and American practices of fascination with (but not respect for) the "exotic" also account for the recent "emergence" of post-colonial art in Western consciousness. But while it would be a mistake to ever underestimate the venal intentions and effects of Euro-American appropriations of the cultures of Asia, Africa, and Latin America, it would also be a major error to overlook the strategic importance of post-colonial perspectives for theorizing the present moment in world history.

The strategies of signification and grammars of opposition developed among post-colonial peoples speak powerfully to the paradoxically fragmented and interconnected world created by new structures of commerce culture and technology. The populations best prepared for cultural conflict and political contestation in a globalized world economy may well be the diasporic communities of displaced Africans, Asians, and

Latin Americans created by the machinations of world capitalism over the centuries. These populations, long accustomed to code switching, syncretism, and hybridity may prove far more important for what they *possess* in cultural terms than for what they appear to *lack* in the political lexicon of the nation state.

For example, throughout the Black Atlantic world, one function of "Black nationalism" has always been to elide national categories – to turn national minorities into global majorities by affirming solidarity with "people of color" all around the globe. But Black populations have been open to other kinds of internationalism as well. In his excellent book on Black communists in Alabama in the 1930s, Robin D.G. Kelley shows how envisioning themselves as part of an international communist movement emboldened workers who might otherwise have been intimidated by the forbidding equation of power in their own country. They liked to hear that Stalin was on their side, certainly not because of Stalin's actual record on national self-determination or on racism, but because Stalin's existence made the world bigger than Alabama, and it seemed to render the racism in that state relative, provisional, and contingent.[9] Similarly, as Robert A. Hill demonstrates, the emergence of Rastafarianism as an important force within Jamaican politics depended upon antecedents in the "Holy Piby" or "Black Man's Bible" that connected it to the experiences and perspectives of Jamaican migrant workers in diverse sites, from Perth Amboy, New Jersey to Cape Town, South Africa to Colón, Panama. Everywhere, diasporic Africans have used international frames to remedy national frustrations.[10] Their strategies have proved crucial to the success of anti-racist movements on many continents, but they now also hold significance as a model of transnational mobilization for other aggrieved populations.

The present moment in world history is marked by the failure of two grand narratives – the liberal faith in progress, modernization, and the bureaucratic state, and the conservative faith in free trade, de-regulation, and the "free market." The global struggles for democratic change and national independence that reached their apex in the 1960s seriously discredited social theories associated with social democracy and liberal capitalism. There was a rapid unraveling of the post-war "consensus" in industrialized nations that posited a universal stake in the advance of technology, Keynesian economics, and bureaucratic rationality. From "modernization" theory in sociology to "modernism" in the arts, ways of explaining the world that had seemed incontrovertible in the 1950s suddenly seemed totally inadequate for explaining the revolutionary ruptures, clashes, and conflicts of the 1960s. But the inadequacy of existing liberal social theory, coupled with the inability among aggrieved groups to propose or implement credible radical alternatives, created an opportunity for conservatives and plutocrats.

De-industrialization and economic restructuring in capitalist countries in the 1970s and 1980s caused the re-emergence of theories lauding the free market (which themselves had been discredited since the Great Depression) as a frame for interpreting world politics and culture. Neo-conservative policies in all industrialized countries encouraged and subsidized the creation of a world economy under the control of multinational corporations and institutions. The dismantling of social welfare structures in the metropolis and the externalization of class tensions onto unprotected workers and consumers at the periphery served to unite capital while fragmenting its potential opponents. The ideology of free market economics appears to have triumphed all around the world, but rather than prosperity and freedom for all, it has produced extravagant wealth for the few and mostly austerity, corruption, and instability for the many.

Yet the relentlessness of capital in seeking new areas for investment has also led to unexpected emergences and convergences in the field of culture. The reach and scope of commercial mass media unite populations that had previously been divided. The spread of commodities into new areas often creates new economies of prestige and undermines traditional hierarchies. The accelerated flow of commerce, commodities, and people across national boundaries creates new social and political realities that enable some people in colonized countries to create new opportunities and alliances. Moreover, the very obsolescence of previous theories of social organization serves as an impetus for creating new ways of looking at the world.

The contemporary crisis of social theory comes largely from the inability of either the nation state or the free market to address adequately the grim realities of the emerging global economy and culture. Post-colonial culture has emerged in the context of this stalemate between two discredited theories. Important on its own terms as art, it also holds significance because of its potential to become one of the sites where social theory becomes reconstituted on a global scale. Post-colonial cultural expressions are based in the experiences of people and communities, rather than on the master narratives of the nation state. They foreground questions of cultural and social identity, rather than direct struggles for political power. They are pragmatic, immediate, and non-ideological, seeking to change life but putting forth no single blueprint for the future. In short, post-colonial culture contains all of the aspects identified by social theorists as characteristic of the "new social movements."

THE NEW SOCIAL MOVEMENTS

Theorists Manuel Castells and Alain Touraine stress that new social movements are often locally based and territorially defined. Hip hop and other forms of diasporic African music participate in constructing these local identities, but they bring to them a global consciousness.[11] They play out local rivalries (for example between New York and Los Angeles rappers) and speak powerfully to local politics (in the Caribbean, Europe, Africa, and North America), but they also situate themselves within international concerns. They have inverted prestige hierarchies around the world, and established new centers of cultural power from Kingston, Jamaica to Compton, California. But hip hop and reggae have also played roles in political movements opposed to apartheid in South Africa, in struggles for educational and curricular reform, and in battles against police brutality around the globe.

Certain Afro-centric theorists might claim that the extraordinary capacity of African musical systems to "capture" the cultures of their colonizers proves the existence of a trans-cultural trans-historical essential culture within the bodies of Africans. But more accurate is Paul Gilroy's analysis that "the African diaspora's consciousness of itself has been defined in and against constricting national boundaries," – forcing a transnational consciousness. Gilroy notes Ralph Ellison's argument in *Shadow and Act* that the amalgamated cultures formed by the fusion of African identities with European, American, and Asian circumstances mean that "it is not culture which binds the people who are of partially African origin now scattered throughout the world but an identity of passions."[12] The ability to find that identity of passions and turn it into a diasporic conversation informing political struggles in similar but not identical circumstances has enabled peoples of African descent to survive over the centuries; it may now also hold the key to survival for the rest of the world as well.

Like the influence of Central American magic realism on novels by African-American women, like the importance of novels questioning categories of identity by Asian-American and Native American women for feminists from many ethnicities, or like the growing recognition by indigenous populations of congruent realities in diverse national contexts, the music of the African diaspora testifies to the capacity of post-colonial culture to illumine families of resemblance illustrating how diverse populations have had similar although not identical experiences. By virtue of a shared skepticism about the nation state, an identification with the lived experiences of ordinary people, and an imaginative, supple, and strategic reworking of identities and cultures, post-colonial culture holds great significance as a potential site for creating coalitions to pose alternatives to the discredited maxims of conservative free-market capitalism or liberal social democracy.

The terrain of culture has emerged as a privileged site for transnational communication, organization, and mobilization at a time when the parochialism of trade unions and political parties leaves those institutions locked into national identities that seem to render them powerless to confront the inequities and injustices of the new global economy. Jamaican reggae singer Bob Marley's music of the 1970s played an important role in the formation of a "Black Power" movement in Australia, influenced liberation movements in Southern Africa, and formed a focal point of unity between diasporic Blacks and working-class whites in Britain.[13] More recently, Thomas Mapfuzmo's music deployed traditional cultural forms to fuse a new political unity during and after the chimurenga war in Zimbabwe, while Boukman Eksperyans has created music capable of connecting opponents of Haiti's dictatorial governments to popular traditions of slave rebellion and voudou religion. Popular music has also played an important role in movements against police brutality in the United Kingdom and the United States, and in campaigns building pan-ethnic anti-racist alliances in France and Germany.[14]

Among diasporic communities especially, traditional aesthetic, philosophical, moral, and political principles serve as resources in struggles against centralized systems of power. For these populations there have never been any "old social movements," because questions of identity and community always superseded the potential for making claims on the state through ideological coalitions. Their distance from state power and their experiences with cultural exclusion forced upon diasporic communities political practices rooted in the realities of what we have now come to call the "new social movements."[15]

Oppositional practices among diasporic populations emerge from painful experiences of labor migration, cultural imperialism, and political subordination. Yet they are distinguished by an ability to work within these systems. In contemporary culture, artists from aggrieved communities often subvert or invert the very instruments of domination necessary for the creation of the new global economy – its consumer goods, technologies, and images. Post-colonial literature, Third Cinema, and hip hop music all protest against conditions created by the oligopolies who distribute them as commodities for profit. They express painful recognition of cultural displacements, displacements that their very existence accelerates. Yet it is exactly their desire to work *through* rather than *outside* of existing structures that defines their utility as a model for contemporary global politics.

One might conclude that this reliance of post-colonial culture on existing economic and cultural forms can at best lead only to subordinate rather than autonomous reforms. That possibility certainly exists. But the desire to work through existing contradictions rather than stand outside them represents not so much a preference for melioristic reform over revolutionary change, but rather a recognition of the impossibility of standing outside totalitarian systems of domination. Attempts to create liberated zones, cooperatives, "socialism within one country," and counter-cultural communes have all failed because of the hegemonic power of capitalists within the world economic system. Although still useful as a means of raising consciousness, these strategies have been largely superseded by forms of struggle that engage in what Gramsci called the war of position (an effort to build a counter-hegemonic alliance) rather that what he termed the war of maneuver (the effort to seize state power).

Throughout the twentieth century, Leninist vanguard parties and artistic avant-gardes alike have attempted to position themselves outside dominant systems. They sought "free spaces" and "liberated zones" as prerequisites for the kinds of ideological mobilization that they felt would be necessary for radical change. But the Leninist parties always replicated the very structures of hierarchy and exploitation that they presumed to challenge (even after they seized state power), and attempts by artistic avant-gardes to confound the logic of the art market only produced newer and more lucrative objects for collection and exchange.

The cultural politics of post-colonialism flow from experiences resonant with the histories of Leninist parties and artistic avant-gardes, from struggles for independence and autonomy which also proved illusory even when they seemed to have won their goals. Rather than stand outside of society, the new social movements and their cultural corollaries immerse themselves in the contradictions of social life, seeking an immanent rather than a transcendent critique.

Thus, although they seem "new" to theorists of the new social movements, the techniques of immanent critique have a long history among aggrieved populations. People can take action only in the venues that are open to them; oppressed people rarely escape the surveillance and control of domination. Consequently they frequently have to "turn the guns around," to seize the instruments of domination used to oppress them and try to put them to other uses. For example, slave owners in the nineteenth-century South brought the Christian bible to their slaves to teach that true rewards come only in heaven; the slaves inverted their message by embracing Old Testament stories about Moses, Daniel, and Samson who secured deliverance in this world.[16] Similarly, imperialistic oil companies brought forty-five-gallon oil drums to

Trinidad in the 1940s and left them discarded and dented; but Black workers discovered that the dents made it possible to turn the barrels into complete melodic and harmonic instruments. By combining rhythmic drumming and systemized pitch into the same instrument, they created a vehicle perfectly suited for expressing their situatedness in both European and African musical traditions.[17] Rastafarians and reggae musicians in Jamaica in the 1960s and 1970s seized the Judeo-Christian bible, English language, and commercial popular music only to reveal them as fabricated artifacts reflective of social hierarchies by "flinging them back rude" through inversions and subversions that de-naturalized religion, language, and music.[18]

The global popularity of hip hop culture – rap music, graffiti, break dancing, B Boy fashion etc. – has been perhaps the most important recent manifestation of post-colonial culture on a global scale. The "diasporic intimacy" linking cultural production and reception among people of African descent in the Caribbean, the United States, Europe, and Africa has resulted in a cultural formation with extraordinary political implications. Although hip hop circulates as a commodity marketed by highly central-ized monopolies from metropolitan countries, it also serves as a conduit for ideas and images articulating subaltern sensitivities. At a time when African people have less power and fewer resources than at almost any previous time in history, African culture has emerged as the single most important subtext within world popular culture. The popularity of hip hop reflects more than cultural compensation for political and economic domination, more than an outlet for energies and emotions repressed by social power relations. Hip hop expresses a form of politics perfectly suited to the post-colonial era. It brings a community into being through performance, and it maps out real and imagined relations between people that speak to the realities of displacement, disillusion, and despair created by the austerity economy of post-industrial capitalism.[19]

HIP HOP AND THE POLITICS OF SOUND

Hip hop culture brings to a world audience the core values of music from most sub-Saharan African cultures.[20] It blends music and life into an integrated totality, uniting performers, dancers, and listeners in a collaborative endeavor. As ethnomusicologist John Miller Chernoff observes, "the model of community articulated in an African musical event is one that is not held together by ideas, by cognitive symbols or by emotional conformity. The community is established through the interaction of individual rhythms and the people who embody them."[21] African music is participatory, collective, and collaborative. Rhythms are layered on top of one another as a dialogue – hearing one enables the others to make sense. The incorporation of these African elements into hip hop raises challenges to Western notions of musical (and social) order. As the great jazz drummer Max Roach explains,

> The thing that frightened people about hip hop was that they heard rhythm – rhythm for rhythm's sake. Hip hop lives in the world of sound – not the world of music – and that's why it's so revolutionary. What we as black people have always done is show that the world of sound is bigger than white people think. There are many areas that fall outside the narrow Western definition of music and hip hop is one of them.[22]

While clearly grounded in the philosophies and techniques of African music, the radical nature of hip hop comes less from its origins than from its uses. The flexibility of African musical forms encourages innovation and adaptation – a blending of old and new forms into dynamic forward-looking totalities. In her important scholarship on rap music, Tricia Rose has argued against reducing hip hop to its origins in African music or African-American oral traditions, but instead calls for an understanding of hip hop as "secondary orality," the deployment of oral traditions in an age of electronic reproduction.[23] As a cultural discourse and political activity, it thus speaks to both residual and emergent realities.

Digital sampling in rap music turns consumers into producers, tapping consumer memories of parts of old songs and redeploying them in the present. It employs advanced technology to reconstruct the human voice, and features robot-like movements and mechanical vocals that simulate machines.[24] Sampling foregrounds the fabricated artifice of machine technologies, calling attention to them through repetition, scratching, and mixing. But at the same time, these tactics humanize the machine by asking it to do the unexpected, and they allow for human imitations of machine sounds – as in the vocals by Doug E. Fresh, "the original human beat box."[25] Hip hop calls into question Western notions of cultural production as property through its evocation, quotation, and outright theft of socially shared musical memories. Yet it also illumines the emancipatory possibilities of new technologies and the readiness of marginalized and oppressed populations to employ them for humane ends – for shedding restricting social identities and embracing new possibilities of a life without hierarchy and exploitation.

Kobena Mercer and others have warned us against the folly of thinking that some cultural forms are innately radical – that the right combination of notes or colors or words can be socially or politically radical by themselves. Culture functions as a social force to the degree that it gets instantiated in social life and connected to the political aspirations and activities of groups.[26] It is here that hip hop holds its greatest significance and its greatest challenge to interpreters.

For example, in the mid-1980s, the New York graffiti artist, style leader, and hip hop entrepreneur Fab Five Freddy learned an important lesson about the politics of sound from Max Roach, the great jazz drummer from the bebop era.[27] Separated by decades and musical styles (Fab Five Freddy's father was once Max Roach's manager), the two men shared a common admiration for the energy and artistry of rap music. But one day Roach baffled his young friend by describing LL Cool J's music as "militant." Freddy later recalled, "I thought it was funny he should say that because I thought LL was an ego rapper, and political rap seemed out of fashion." But Roach persisted, claiming that:

> The rhythm was very militant to me because it was like marching, the sound of an army on the move. We lost Malcolm, we lost King and they thought they had blotted out everybody. But all of a sudden this new art form arises and the militancy is there in the music.

Once Roach had directed his attention away from the lyrics and toward the rhythm, Fab Five Freddy understood the drummer's point. "LL Cool J doesn't seem to like political music," he later explained in describing the incident, "but the politics was in the drums."[28]

The "politics in the drums" that Max Roach disclosed to Fab Five Freddy pervade hip hop. They express the restlessness and energy described by Frantz Fanon in his now classic anti-colonial text, *The Wretched of the Earth*. Speaking about times when desires for radical change permeate popular culture even though no political movement has yet arrived to challenge the established order, Fanon argues:

> Well before the political fighting phase of the national movement, an attentive spectator can thus feel and see the manifestation of a new vigor and feel the approaching conflict. He [sic] will note unusual forms of expression and themes which are fresh and imbued with a power which is no longer that of an invocation but rather of the assembling of the people, a summoning together for a precise purpose. Everything works together to awaken the native's sensibility and to make unreal and unacceptable the contemplative attitude or the acceptance of defeat.[29]

Hip hop's energy originates in many sources, but a crucial component of its power comes from its ability to respond to the realities of the African diaspora. Most commentators in the U.S.A. have portrayed diasporic consciousness as essentially a one-way process of preserving African elements in America or maintaining Afro-Caribbean traditions in New York. To be sure, African and Caribbean elements appear prominently in U.S. hip hop, and many of the originators of hip hop in New York during the 1970s had Caribbean backgrounds. (Grandmaster Flash's parents and Afrika Bambaataa's mother and two aunts came to New York from Barbados; Kool DJ Herc aka Clive Campbell was born in Jamaica.)[30] But these claims place a value on origins that distorts the nature of Black Atlantic culture. The flow of information and ideas among diasporic people has not been solely from Africa outward to Europe and the Americas, but rather has been a reciprocal self-renewing dialogue in communities characterized by upheaval and change. The story of the African diaspora is more than an aftershock of the slave trade, it is an ongoing dynamic creation. The radicalism of diasporic African culture comes not only from the contrast between African and Euro-American values, but also from the utility of exploiting diasporic connections as a way of expanding choices everywhere – in Africa as well as in Europe, the Caribbean, and the Americas. Just as American and European Blacks have drawn on African traditions to contest Euro-American power relations, Africans have drawn upon cultures of opposition and strategies of signification developed by diasporic Africans as a form of struggle on the African continent.

For example, Fela Kuti, the founder of Nigeria's radical Afro-beat music subculture, learned part of his political radicalism in Los Angeles. His mother had been an activist, a friend of Ghana's President Kwame Nkrumah, and a founder of the Nigerian Women's Union and a leader in the successful struggle to gain the right to vote for women in her country.[31] For ten months in 1969–1970, Fela played music in Los Angeles at the Citadel de Haiti night club on Sunset Boulevard (owned by Black actor Bernie Hamilton, later featured in the television program "Starsky and Hutch"), but his main focus was on learning about Black nationalism. Sandra Smith (now Sandra Isidore), a woman active in the Black Panther Party, gave Fela a copy of *The Autobiography of Malcolm X* which introduced him to ideas about Pan-Africanism that had been censored in Nigeria.[32] "Sandra gave me the education I wanted to know," he recalled years later. "I swear man! She's the one who spoke to me about . . . Africa! For the first time I heard things I'd never heard before about Africa! Sandra was my adviser."[33]

Fela told friends he learned more about Africa in Los Angeles that he had in Lagos, and insisted that "The whole atmosphere of Black Revolution changed me, my consciousness, my thinking, my perception of things. I was educated."[34] Sandra Smith recalls that she introduced him to poems by Nikki Giovanni and the spoken-word art of The Last Poets, as well as to writings by Angela Davis, Jesse Jackson, Stokely Carmichael, and Martin Luther King. In addition, she introduced him to music by Nina Simone and Miles Davis, and connected him with a circle of friends that included singer Esther Phillips, actors Melvin van Peebles and Jim Brown, and the comedian Stu Gilliam.[35] "For the first time, I saw the essence of blackism," he later told an interviewer. "I was exposed to awareness. It started me thinking. I saw how everything worked there. I realized that I had no country. I decided to come back and try to make my country African."[36]

Experiences in the U.S.A. made Fela Kuti more radical politically, but they also changed his music by informing it with a diasporic consciousness. As he explained, "Most Africans do not really know about life. They think everything from overseas is greater, but they do not know also that everything from overseas could have gone from here to overseas and come back to us. America gave me that line of thought."[37] Kuti has subsequently collaborated with Black American musicians including trumpeter Lester Bowie and vibraphonist Roy Ayers. Bowie went to Nigeria and lived with Fela during a particularly difficult time in his life, and admired both the music and politics that the Nigerian produced. "Fela's stubborn about the right things," Bowie explained to an interviewer. "He wants freedom, he wants to get away from oppression. The inequality of wealth in his country is unbelievable, and he's trying to address that. So did Martin Luther King, Jr., so did Malcolm X and so did the founding fathers of America."[38]

Similarly, Roy Ayers credits Fela for deepening his understanding of Africa during their collaborations. Kuti and Ayers toured Africa and recorded together in 1979. Ayers had been a frequent visitor to Africa, but even in the U.S.A. his deep interest in Afro-Cuban jazz gave his music a diasporic flavor. The recordings made by Fela Kuti and Roy Ayers showed traces of the Afro-Cuban influences on North American jazz as well as of Cuban "rhumba" bands on African, especially Congolese, music.[39] In turn, Ayers's 1970s jazz-funk albums (especially his Black nationalist *Red, Black, and Green* from 1973) have been a prime source of samples in recent years for hip hop djs and producers. "I've had about eight hit records on re-releases – rappers who have sampled my music," Ayers told an interviewer recently. "I was very happy because they give you a percentage, but more than that, I was honored that they dig my music. I went from swing to bebop to Latin, disco, funk, and fusion, so I respect all styles of music."[40]

Sojourns in North America and collaborations with African-American artists have been important to other African musicians as well. Aster Aweke sang for exiled

Ethiopians in Washington, D.C. during the 1980s, creating a fusion music that turned Ethiopian wind and string parts into horn riffs and vocals in a style clearly influenced by Aretha Franklin and Anita Baker.[41] When Ali Farka Toure of Mali first heard records by Mississippi blues guitarist and singer John Lee Hooker he told a friend, "Listen, this is music that has been taken from here."[42] Toure eventually met Hooker and played music with him in Paris during the 1970s.[43] Expressing a preference for music by Hooker, Albert King, Otis Redding, James Brown, Wilson Pickett, Jimmy Smith, and Ray Charles, Toure explains, "If you listen to them for sixteen hours, you can no longer locate the stars, the sky and the clouds!"[44]

Abdullah Ibrahim left South Africa to tour Europe in 1962 and met Duke Ellington in Zurich. Ellington liked his music and arranged a recording contract for Ibrahim and his trio. When asked by an interviewer if he was surprised to be helped in that way by an American Black, Ibrahim replied that he did not really think of Ellington as an American or as a citizen of any country, but more as "the wise old man in the village – the extended village."[45] James Brown's tour of Zaire in 1969 had a major impact on African music, especially in helping promote the "Congo soul" sound of Trio Madjeski.[46] In the 1970s, songs by U.S. rhythm and blues artists including Harold Melvin and the Blue Notes and the Staples Singers became anthems for township youths in South Africa because the songs enabled them to voice "cries for justice, recognition, and social action" denied them in the rest of their lives.[47]

Diasporic dialogue has also extended far beyond binary exchanges between Africa and North America. For example, Alpha Blondy from Côte d'Ivoire in Africa learned French reading the bible and mastered English from his school lessons and from playing American rock'n'roll in high school.[48] He went to Columbia University in New York in 1976 to study world trade. There he discovered a Jamaican-American reggae band, Monkaya, which he joined, singing his native Mandinka lyrics to the reggae beat. Blondy has become one of the best-selling reggae artists in the world, having recorded reggae songs in English, French, Dioula, and Mandingo. Explaining his interest in what most would consider West Indian music, Blondy argues: "In Africa, the new generation, my generation, is a mixture of Western and African culture. Reggae has succeeded in a musical unification, it's a good therapy to bring people together."[49] As part of this "therapy," Blondy's band includes musicians from Africa and the Caribbean, and he has performed songs in Arabic during concerts in Israel and songs in Hebrew during concerts in Arab countries. He played a concert in 1986 dedicated to encouraging good relations between Mali and Burkina-Faso, and drew 10,000 fans at the Moroccan International Festival of Youth and Music in Marrakech that same year to hear him play reggae.[50]

Reggae itself originated in Afro-Jamaican religious Burru music, especially its bass, funde, and repeater drums, but the form also drew upon African-American soul music, on records smuggled back to the island by Jamaican migrant workers employed to cut sugar cane in the southern U.S.A. (including Coxsone Dodd, founder of Kingston's Studio One), as well as on broadcasts by U.S. radio stations including WINZ in Miami.[51] Africans like Alpha Blondy, who were familiar with American soul music, took to reggae in part because it contained elements of music they were already familiar with from America as well as from Africa.

On the other hand, when Jamaican singer Jimmy Cliff first heard the yelle music of Baaba Maal from Senegal, it struck him as structurally connected to the rhythms of reggae. Rap music's popularity in Korea stems in part from the close cultural connections built between the U.S.A. and that country since the mass exodus following the Kwangju uprising of the early 1980s, but also from the similarities between rap and traditional Korean sasui lyrics which are recited to the accompaniment of drums.[52]

Manu Dibango, a singer-composer-arranger-reed-piano player from Cameroon, moved to Paris in the 1960s where he started making records, including a tribute to the U.S. rhythm and blues saxophone player King Curtis. In 1972 Dibango's "Soul Makossa" became an international hit. He moved to New York in the early 1970s where he played the Apollo Theatre in Harlem along with the Temptations and Barry White, and he also collaborated there with Afro-Caribbean musicians including Johnny Pacheco and the Fania All-Stars.[53] By the mid-1980s Dibango brought Antillean musicians into his band and expanded his repertoire to include the zouk music of the Francophone West Indies.[54]

Of course Caribbean music had long been familiar in Africa. The British government stationed West Indian regiments in West Africa as early as the 1830s, and their syncopated brass band and gumbey musics gained immediate popularity. The adaba variety of Nigerian highlife bears traces of calypso, while that nation's juju music uses the Brazilian samba drum.[55]

Hip hop employs the legacy of similar instances of diasporic dialogue. Jazzie B of the British group Soul II Soul remembers the lessons he learned in his youth from African American artists. "People like Curtis Mayfield were a very strong part of my life," he remembers. "His songs weren't just songs to me. They were knowledge. I used to carry my records right along with my school books." But at the same time, Jazzie B also credits the "African" community in Britain for having a formative influence on his music.

"I don't just remember the music at the Africa Centre [dances], I also remember the people. It was like a religion, all those people sweating and dancing and partying together. It was very inspiring. That's what I tried to put on our album – that same sense of unity and spirit."[56]

The dynamism of diasporic interchanges in music confirms Peter Linebaugh's wry observation that long-playing records have surpassed sea-going vessels as the most important conduits of Pan-African communication.[57] But it is important to understand that diasporic dialogue in music builds on an infrastructure with a long history. For example, in the 1930s, Paul Robeson galvanized the black population of Britain (and other countries) with theatrical performances that complemented his role as a spokesperson for causes like the defense of the Scottsboro boys.[58] His films *King Solomon's Mines* (1937) and *Sanders of the River* (1934, featuring Jomo Kenyatta) brought certain aspects of African culture to world audiences accustomed to only the most caricatured views of the continent. Many Africans encountered Pan-Africanism the way Fela Kuti did, through the writings of diasporic Africans including Malcolm X, Aimé Césaire, Marcus Garvey, George Padmore, and W.E.B. DuBois.[59] As a foreign student, Kwame Nkrumah learned some lessons in politics attending Adam Clayton Powell's activist church in New York City, while Ghanaian activists used the U.S. abolitionist hymn "John Brown's Body" to protest Nkrumah's imprisonment during the struggle for independence.[60] These political connections had deep cultural roots; Manu Dibango remembers how important it was for him to hear Louis Armstrong on the radio when he was growing up in Cameroon. "Here was a black voice singing tunes that reminded me of those that I had learned at the temple. I immediately felt at one with the warmth of that voice and with what it was singing."[61]

More recently, post-colonial writers in Africa have expressed their indebtedness to African-American writers. Ngugi Wa Thiong'o asserts:

> There's a very vibrant connection between Afro-American traditions in literature and those from many parts of the third world. I know that African literature as a whole has borrowed quite heavily from the Afro-American literary tradition, and I hope vice-versa. Writers like Langston Hughes, Richard Wright, Amiri Baraka, and Alice Walker are quite popular in Africa.[62]

Nigerian writer Buchi Emecheta adds: "To me, the greatest writers who come from ethnic minorities writing in English come from America. I think the deep, the real deep thinkers now writing in the English language are the black women, such as Toni Morrison, Gloria Naylor, Alice Walker, etc."[63]

The dialogue of the African diaspora informs the politics and culture of countries across the globe. It draws upon ancient traditions and modern technologies, on situated knowledge and a nomadic sensibility. Generated from communities often criminally short of resources and institutions, it commands prestige from multinational corporations and other bastions of privilege. It flows through the circuits of the post-industrial austerity economy, and yet still manages to bring to light inequities and injustices.

From Queen Latifah's "Ladies First" with its images of Africa and the Americas to Thomas Mapfumo's "Hupenyu Wanyu" which appropriates the African-American "Bo Diddley" beat for radical politics in Zimbabwe, diasporic intimacy secures space for oppositional expressions obliterated by much of mass media and electoral politics. In a world coming ever closer together through the machinations of global capital, it displays a situated but not static identity. Rooted in egalitarian and democratic visions of the world, diasporic intimacy nonetheless embraces contradiction, change, and growth. It serves notice of the willingness and ability of millions of people to play a meaningful role in the world that is being constructed around us.

In culture and in politics, diasporic expressions constantly come back to what Frantz Fanon called "the seething pot out of which the learning of the future will emerge."[64] A sense of urgency about the future permeates the practices of popular music. Salif Keita of Mali locates his interest in making popular music as more than a matter of style. In his own performances he blends traditional Malian music with things he learned listening to Western artists ranging from Pink Floyd to Stevie Wonder, from James Brown to Kenny Rogers. Defending his eclecticism, Keita explains, "At home, we are traditionalists. It's an attitude I disapprove of. It's we who make the history, and if we refer only to what has passed, there will be no history. I belong to a century that has little in common with the time of my ancestors. I want society to move."[65]

Manu Dibango sums up the problem with characteristic eloquence (although with unfortunately sexist pronouns) in a statement that might serve as the motto of the post-colonial project. He asserts:

> People who are curious search for sounds; they seek out harmony and melody because they are curious. Your curiosity can be limited by your environment, or you can expand it to take in things from outside; a bigger curiosity for a bigger world. The extent of your curiosity should not be determined by the village, or the town, or a city in another continent. The musician moves in these circles, but he moves to break out of his limits.[66]

NOTES

1. Mark Dery, "Rap," *Keyboard* (November) 1988, 34.

2. David Toop, *Rap Attack 2: African Rap to Global Hip Hop* (London: Serpent's Tail, 1991), 19, 39, 37, 56–60; Lawrence Stanley, ed., *Rap: The Lyrics* (New York: Penguin, 1992), 8; Joel Whitburn, *Top R&B Singles, 1942–1988* (Menomonee Falls, WI: Record Research, 1988), 33.

3. Mark Dery, "Rap," 46.

4. Larry Birnbaum, "Baaba Maal Sings Blues from the Real Heartland," *Pulse* (September) 1993, 39; Jay Cocks, "Rap Around the Globe," *Time* October 19, 1992, 70; Michael Jarrett, "Guru," *Pulse* (September) 1993, 39.

5. Fredric Jameson, *Postmodernism, or the Cultural Logic of Late Capitalism* (Durham, NC: Duke University Press, 1991), 47.

6. For an eloquent summary of the role played by transnational corporations see Masao Miyoshi, "A Borderless World? From Colonialism to Transnationalism and the Decline of the Nation State," *Critical Inquiry* (Summer) 1993. See also Thomas J. McCormick, *America's Half Century* (Baltimore, MD: Johns Hopkins University Press, 1989).

7. Which, of course, is not to say that messages intended for one purpose in Asia, Africa, and Latin America would not be received with a very different meaning by readers in Europe or North America.

8. Harvey Molotch and John Logan, *Urban Fortunes: The Political Economy of Place* (Berkeley: University of California Press, 1987), 254.

9. Robin D.G. Kelley, *Hammer and Hoe* (Chapel Hill: University of North Carolina Press, 1990).

10. Robert A. Hill, "Dread History: Leonard P. Howell and Millenarian Visions in Early Rastafari Religions in Jamaica," *Epoche: Journal of the History of Religions at UCLA* (1981), 32–4; George Lipsitz, " 'How Does It Feel When You've Got no Food?' The Past as Present in Popular Music" in Richard Butsch, ed., *For Fun and Profit* (Philadelphia, PA: Temple University Press, 1990), 195–215; Paul Gilroy, *"There Ain't No Black in the Union Jack": The Cultural Politics of Race and Nation* (Chicago, IL: University of Chicago Press, 1987), 156.

11. Manuel Castells, *The City and the Grass Roots* (London: Edward Arnold, 1983); Alain Touraine, *The Voice and the Eye: An Analysis of Social Movements* (Cambridge: Cambridge University Press, 1981). See Paul Gilroy, *"There Ain't No Black in the Union Jack,"* esp. ch.6.

12. Paul Gilroy, *"There Ain't No Black in the Union Jack,"* 158, 159.

13. See Marcus Breen, "Desert Dreams, Media, and Interventions in Reality: Australian Aboriginal Music," in Reebee Garofalo, ed., *Rockin' the Boat* (Boston, MA: South End, 1992), 149–70.

14. See for example references to the Newham 7 in Winston James, "Migration, Racism, and Identity: The Caribbean Experience in Britain," *New Left Review* no.193 (May–June) 1992, 46; Nora Rathzel, "Germany: One Race, One Nation?" Race and Class vol.32 no.3 (1990). The role of the musical group Boukman Eksperyans and of a wide variety of visual artists in finding new meanings for voudou as part of the Aristide coalition in Haiti provides one of the best examples of these movements. Willie Apollon, "Voodoo and Visual Art," presentation at the University of California, San Diego, April 9, 1993.

15. For "new social movement" activity within old social movements see Robin D.G. Kelley, *Hammer and Hoe* and Vicki Ruiz, *Cannery Women, Cannery Lives* (Albuquerque: University of New Mexico Press, 1987).

16. Lawrence Levine, *Black Culture, Black Consciousness* (Berkeley: University of California Press, 1977); George Lipsitz, "The Struggle for Hegemony," *Journal of American History* vol.75 no.1 (June) 1988, 146–50.

17. Tom Chatburn, "Trinidad All Stars: The Steel Pan Movement in Britain," in Paul Oliver, ed., *Black Music in Britain: Essays on the Afro-Asian Contribution to Popular Music* (Buckingham: Open University Press, 1990), 120–1.

18. Dick Hebdige, "Reggae, Rastas, and Rudies" in Stuart Hall and Tony Jefferson, eds, *Resistance Through Ritual: Youth Subcultures in Post War Britain* (London: Hutchinson, 1976), 138–9; Robert A. Hill, "Dread History: Leonard P. Howell and Millenarian Visions in Early Rastafari Religions in Jamaica," *Epoche: Journal of the History of Religions at UCLA* (1981), 32–4; George Lipsitz, " 'How Does it Feel When You've Got No Food?' The Past as Present in Popular Music," 195–214.

19. For discussion of hip hop and the "new social movements" see Paul Gilroy, *"There Ain't No Black in the Union Jack,"* 223–50.

20. It is important not to assume one unified African system of thought, politics, or culture. But especially in comparison to Western music, certain social and stylistic features from West Africa provide a vivid contrast.

21. John Miller Chernoff, "The Rhythmic Medium in African Music," *New Literary History* vol.22 no.4 (Autumn) 1991, 1095. See also J.H. Kwabena Nketia, *The Music of Africa* (New York: Norton, 1974), 21–50.

22. Frank Owen, "Hip Hop Bebop," *Spin* vol.4 (October) 1988, 61.

23. Tricia Rose, "Orality and Technology: Rap Music and Afro-American Cultural Resistance," *Popular Music and Society* vol.14 no.4 (Winter) 1988, 35–44. See also her *Black Noise* (Hanover: Wesleyan/University Press of New England), 1994.

24. High-tech and science-fiction themes played an important role in 1970s African-American music as a way of imagining a space outside of Euro-American racism, especially in the work of George Clinton and Funkadelic.

25. Paul Gilroy, *"There Ain't No Black in the Union Jack,"* 214.

26. I thank Mercer for bringing this to the attention of the Minority Discourse Group at the University of California Humanities Research Institute many times during the Fall of 1992.

27. Fab Five Freddy (Braithwaite) had long known Roach because his father was an attorney who served at one time as Roach's manager. David Toop, *Rap Attack 2*, 140.

28. Frank Owen, "Hip Hop Bebop," 73.

29. Frantz Fanon, *The Wretched of the Earth* (New York: Grove Press, 1968), 243.

30. David Toop, *Rap Attack 2*, 18, 19; Robert Farris Thompson, "Hip Hop 101," *On Campus*, 98.

31. Rob Tannenbaum, "Fela Anikulapao Kuti," *Musician* no.79 (May) 1985, 30.

32. Born in Arkansas, Sandra Smith met Fela at an NAACP-sponsored performance featuring Fela's band and her own dance troupe that performed what they believed were African dances: Carlos Moore, *Fela, Fela: This Bitch of a Life* (London: Allison & Busby, 1982), 83, 91–2.

33. Carlos Moore, *Fela, Fela*, 85.

34. Tom Cheney, "Sorrow, Tears, and Blood: Q&A with Fela Anikulapo Kuti," *Los Angeles Reader* vol.8 no.41 (August 1, 1986), 1; Labinjog, "Fela Anikulapo Kuti," *Journal of Black Studies* (September) 1982, 126.

35. Carlos Moore, *Fela, Fela*, 95, 100.

36. John Darnton, "Afro-Beat: New Music with a Message," *New York Times*, July 7, 1986, 46.

37. Mabinuori Kayode Idowu, *Fela: Why Blackman Carry Shit* (Kaduna, Nigeria: Opinion Media Limited, 1985), 37.

38. Rob Tannenbaum, "Fela Anikulapao Kuti," 30.

39. Graeme Ewens, *Africa O-Ye! A Celebration of African Music* (New York: Da Capo, 1992), 32, 35; Kuti & Ayers, *Music of Many Colours*, Celluloid CD 6125, 1980, 1986.

40. Larry Birnbaum, "BeBop Meets Hip-Hop: Jazz for the Hip-Hop Nation," *Downbeat* vol.60 no.2 (February 1993), 35–6.

41. Graeme Ewens, *Africa O-Ye!* , 55; Ashenafi Kebede, "Aster Aweke," *Ethnomusicology* vol.35 no.1 (Winter), 1991, 157–9.

42. Ali Farka Toure, *African Blues*, liner notes, Shanachie Records 65002. From an interview with Ian Anderson in *Folk Roots*.

43. Graeme Ewens, *Africa O-Ye!*, 67.

44. Ali Farka Toure, *African Blues*, liner notes.

45. Karen Bennett, "An Audience with Dollar Brand," *Musician* (March) 1990, 41.

46. Graeme Ewens, *Africa O-Ye!*, 127.

47. David B. Coplan, *In Township Tonight! South Africa's Music and Theatre* (London: Longman, 1985), 195.

48. Don Snowden, "Alpha Blondy's Multicultural Universe," *Los Angeles Times*, February 21, 1988, calendar section, 76.

49. Jon Pareles, "African-Style Reggae Crosses the Atlantic," *New York Times*, March 22, 1988, C 13.

50. Stephen Davis, "Alpha Blondy," *The Reggae and African Beat* vol.7 no.1 (1987), 33.

51. Wendell Logan, "Conversation with Marjorie Whylie," *Black Perspective in Music* vol.10 no.1. (n.d.) 86, 88, 89, 92; Dick Hebdige, "Reggae, Rastas, and Rudies," in Stuart Hall and Tony Jefferson eds, *Resistance Through Ritual: Youth Subcultures in Post-war Britain* (London: Hutchinson, 1976), 143; Sebastian Clarke, *Jah Music: The Evolution of the Popular Jamaican Song* (London: Heinemann, 1980), 57–8. Coxsone Dodd, founder of Studio One, got his start as a sound system operator with records he brought back to Jamaica from the U.S.A.

52. Byung Hoo Suh, "An Unexpected Rap Eruption Rocks a Traditional Music Market," *Billboard* vol.104 no.34 (August 22, 1992), S6.

53. Donald Clarke, ed., *The Penguin Encyclopedia of Popular Music* (London: Penguin, 1989), 339–40; Graeme Ewens, *Africa O-Ye!*, 116.

54. Graeme Ewens, *Africa O-Ye!*, 108.

55. John Collins, "Some Anti-Hegemonic Aspects of African Popular Music," in Reebee Garofalo, ed., *Rockin' the Boat*, 188, 189.

56. Robert Hilburn, "Tracing the Caribbean Roots of the New British Pop Invasion," *Los Angeles Times*, calendar section, September 24, 1989, 84. Paul Gilroy's observations about the importance of the U.S.A. and the Caribbean to Black Britain are relevant here. See Paul Gilroy, *"There Ain't No Black in the Union Jack,"* 154.

57. Quoted in Paul Gilroy, "Cultural Studies and Ethnic Absolutism," in Lawrence Grossberg, Cary Nelson, and Paula Treichler, *Cultural Studies* (New York: Routledge, 1992), 191.

58. Chris Stapleton, "African Connections: London's Hidden Music Scene," in Paul Oliver, ed., *Black Music in Britain*, 92.

59. John Collins, "Some Anti-Hegemonic Aspects of African Popular Music," in Reebee Garofalo, ed., *Rockin' the Boat*, 189.

60. John Collins, "Some Anti-Hegemonic Aspects of African Popular Music," 191.

61. "Interview with Manu Dibango," *Unesco Courier* (March 1991), 4.

62. Feroza Jussawalla and Reed Way Dasenbrock, eds, *Interviews with Writers of the Post-Colonial World* (Jackson: University Press of Mississippi, 1992), 41.

63. Feroza Jussawalla and Reed Way Dasenbrock, eds, *Interviews with Writers of the Post-Colonial World*, 93.

64. Frantz Fanon, *The Wretched of the Earth*, 225.

65. Banning Eyre, "Routes: The Parallel Paths of Baaba Maal and Salif Keita," *Option* no.53 (November–December, 1993), 48. Quoted in Neil Lazarus, "Unsystematic Fingers at the Conditions of the Times: 'Afropop' and the Paradoxes of Imperialism," in Jonathan White, ed., *Recasting the World: Writing After Colonialism* (Baltimore, MD and London: Johns Hopkins University Press, 1994), 140.

66. Manu Dibango, "Music in Motion," in Graeme Ewens, *Africa O-Ye!*, 7.

3

"The Shortest Way Through": Strategic Anti-essentialism in Popular Music

MANU DIBANGO

At a dramatic moment in Willa Cather's novel *My Antonia*, her narrator Jim Burden ruminates on the suffocating constraints of growing up in a respectable middle-class midwestern Anglo-Saxon family. "This guarded existence was like living under a tyranny," he explains. "People's speech, their voices, their very glances, became furtive and repressed. Every individual taste, every natural appetite, was bridled by caution."[1]

In order to escape the "tyrannical" repression and caution of his community, Burden begins to attend dances at the local Fireman's Hall. There he finds excitement and danger in the unaffected and uninhibited behavior of the town's "hired girls" – working-class immigrant Bohemian, Norwegian, and Danish young women. When one of them lets Jim kiss her as he walks her home, he feels that he has triumphed over the whole town. Looking "with contempt at the dark, silent little houses" he thinks of the "stupid young men" asleep in them. "I knew where the real women were," Burden boasts, "though I was only a boy and I would not be afraid of them either."[2]

The "hired girls" relieve Jim of his (B)urden. Through his contact with (and imagined conquest of) people whose gender, class, and ethnicity differs from his own, he sees that there is an alternative to the stultifying constraints of middle-class life. He derives erotic stimulation and moral edification from the culture of exploited and aggrieved people. No longer "bridled by caution," he compensates for the diminished sense of self created by his obedience to middle-class mores with an augmented sense of masculinity gained through his boldness with ethnic working-class women.

This use of subordinated populations by disaffected individuals from elite groups is understandable, familiar, and dangerous. Understandable because Jim genuinely admires the "hired girls." His interactions with them free him from some of the prejudices and the parochial concerns of his parents' culture. The enthusiasm for life and openness to others that the "hired girls" display call into question the close-minded judgments and values of middle-class society. Popular prejudice against the working girls and their culture reveals to Jim the ignorance of respectable people, and it makes their disapproval of him easier to bear. But the sense of superiority that Burden derives from his kisses only reinforces and reproduces the hierarchies responsible for his oppression in the first place.

Jim Burden's individuation depends upon an eroticization of difference and an engenderation of conquest. His "triumph" can be secured only within a world where masculine power serves as a key icon of status competition, where hierarchies of class, gender, and ethnicity convey clear connotations of menace, transgression, and contamination. The "prestige from below" that Jim draws from dancing with the "hired girls" depends upon their degraded status in the eyes of polite society and upon his own boldness in flaunting social norms. Jim develops no deep commitment to working-class women, no substantive understanding of their lives, no recognition of what role he might play in helping them achieve *their* ambitions.

Yet before we condemn Cather's narrator too quickly, we need to look at another aspect of Jim Burden's identity. At the beginning of the novel, Cather presents her story as a tale she finds in a manuscript given to her by her old friend Jim Burden, not as her own creation. Since the book is a work of fiction, why would Cather complicate the question of authorship by depicting it as second-hand? If she wanted to portray a masculine perspective, why not just tell the story directly from Jim's point of view?

We cannot know the answer to this question with certainty, but Sharon O'Brien's prize-winning biography of Cather provides some important clues. In *Willa Cather: The Emerging Voice*, O'Brien provides convincing evidence of Cather's lesbianism and of its impact on the author's fiction. In one telling passage, O'Brien writes:

> Cather's fear of the creative process, connected with the opposed yet linked perils of concealment and disclosure, was in part connected with the lesbianism she could not name. If the artist's "secret" included passions the culture deemed unnatural, silence might be the only way to avoid uttering the unspeakable. But if Cather did, in some way, "name" the unnameable or reveal what she knew she must hide, might not punishment follow self-expression?[3]

In the light of O'Brien's description, Cather's depictions of Jim Burden's discoveries take on new meaning. Jim's desire becomes less an eroticization of conquest than a brilliant disguise for Cather's own attraction to ethnic working-class women. These "real women" who do not conform to middle-class standards, provide her with a secret that makes her feel superior to "the stupid young men who were asleep" in her town. Transgressions of class, ethnic, and gender boundaries stand as surrogates for the unnamed crossing of sexual boundaries. For Cather, no less than for Jim Burden, these boundary crossings provide the enabling conditions for a critique of "respectable" society.

O'Brien also notes that Cather's readings in Greek and French literature "introduced her to the 'oriental' world of hedonism and unconventional passions and gave her differing images of the lesbian."[4] While this trajectory hardly makes Cather's references and descriptions any less condescending or offensive to ethnic working-class women or other "orientals" construed as "exotic," it does demonstrate the strategic imperatives that led her to pose Jim Burden's rebellion as she did.

By disguising her own subjectivity, Cather found a way to articulate desires and subject positions that she could not express in her own voice. Confronted with a society whose working vocabulary distorted her true identity into something "unnatural" and which permitted no direct affirmation of lesbian identity, Cather created a subject position that could get away with saying the things she felt. O'Brien portrays Cather as ambivalent about her own sexuality – resisting "the emotionally crippling definition of lesbianism as 'sick' or 'perverse'" and challenging "the equation of female friendship with the unnatural," while at the same time "she could not help accepting it."[5] Yet, by seeming to move away from her identity through the subjectivity of Jim Burden, Cather found a way to express it all the more poignantly. Lacking the social power to struggle openly for the validity of her own definitions and values, she utilized the predisposition within literature for playing with new identities in order to articulate an allegorical critique of bourgeois society and its norms.

This is not to say that once we know that Cather was a lesbian that we can ignore her "orientalism." Her very real oppression as a sexual minority does not make her immune from the tendencies within Euro-American culture encouraging vicarious pleasure from the suffering of others. "White" appropriations of African-American culture, sentimentalized images of "disappearing" Native Americans, condescending caricatures of "inscrutable" Asians or "hot-blooded" Mexicans have a long and disreputable history in the U.S.A. Their consequences are no less poisonous when well-intentioned. Their pervasive presence in U.S. popular culture (and their perpetual re-emergence in every generation) testify to the deep-seated undercurrent of white supremacy that lies beneath surface appearances of assimilation and pluralism.

Recent scholarship on the minstrel show by Eric Lott and David Roediger and on the film *The Jazz Singer* by Michael Rogin emphasize how identification with otherness has become an essential element in the construction of "whiteness" in the United States.[6] The white man in blackface on the minstrel show stage was the first self-consciously "white" stage performer in history; his whiteness could be created only by imitating and then denying blackness. Similarly, Al Jolson's masquerade in blackface in *The Jazz Singer* transformed him from a Russian Jew into a representative American, identifiable as white because he was ostentatiously not black. The fiction of "white" identity created unity among Americans divided by region, religion, and class, but the disguise of blackness also ministered to deeper needs and desires. The minstrel-show "darkie" enacted all the behaviors proscribed by industrial capitalism, especially laziness, lust, and gluttony. As time-work discipline, liberal individualism, and Victorian culture increasingly imposed a regimen of self-regulation on nineteenth-century Americans, minstrel-show caricatures offered an innocuous outlet for suppressed desire: they allowed actors and audiences to identify with transgression while at the same time distancing themselves from it by connecting the violation of cultural norms with the ostensibly "natural" and biologically-driven urges of a despised minority group.

Minstrel-show images served real needs for white Americans, and their performance provoked pleasures that whites sometimes believed expressed genuine affection or admiration for African-American culture. But power and privilege gave whites the luxury to imagine themselves as "others." As Nathan Irvin Huggins observes, for African Americans during the minstrel-show era, it was dangerous to "step out of character" either on or off stage. The enormous rewards available to whites pretending to be Black were never available to Black performers denied control over their own performances and always forbidden to think of themselves as "white." The minstrel show depended upon the premise of whites acting like Blacks, but much of its humor directed ridicule and scorn at the "travesty" of Blacks aspiring to the levels of education, power, or dignity associated with whiteness.

Long after the demise of the minstrel show as a popular form of public entertainment, its premises continue to permeate U.S. popular culture. White Americans have demonstrated many times a pathological need to control, contain, and even take credit for Black culture. Witness the prominence of Euro-Americans in gaining rewards from cultural forms created by Blacks: Paul Whiteman as "the king of jazz," Benny Goodman as "the king of swing," or Elvis Presley as "the king of rock'n'roll." The revival and intensification of white racism in recent years has been reflected in popular films like *Back to the Future* (where a white teenager is credited with the inspiration for Chuck Berry's contributions to rock'n'roll), *Mississippi Burning* (where in direct contrast to the historical record the F.B.I. gets credit for the success of the Civil Rights Movement), and *Bird* (a film so devoid of information about the Black community and the context for the emergence of bop music that it might just as well have been titled "Amadeus and Andy" or "Every Which Way But Black"). All of these films professed an affection for African Americans, but none allowed them to speak in their own voices or serve as anything more than spurs to white creativity and agency.

Yet it is still important to understand how and why the fascination with difference works, to remember that more was going on in *My Antonia* than mere orientalism. The genius of African-American culture in nurturing and sustaining moral and cultural alternatives to dominant values has made it an important source of education and inspiration to alienated and aggrieved individuals cut off from other sources of oppositional practice. The same kind of suffocating "tyranny" that drove Jim Burden to the weekly dances at the Fireman's Hall has also encouraged more principled and productive engagements across cultures. From the abolitionist John Brown in the nineteenth century through civil-rights martyrs Michael Schwerner and Andrew Goodman in the twentieth, recognition of the constraint and corruption of middle-class Euro-American life has provided a powerful impetus for political radicalism. In the sphere of culture, some Euro-American musicians have become part of the cultures they set out to copy, such as Greek American Johnny Otis who has participated so fully in the life of the African-American community that he became "black by persuasion," or the Jewish American Larry Harlow, a salsa musician acclaimed by Latino audiences as "El Judio Maravilloso" (The Marvelous Jew).[7] The alienations of middle-class life helped drive a despairing Bix Beiderbecke to seek succor from the black jazz ensembles of the 1920s, and these alienations play a role today in impelling some young whites to embrace wholeheartedly the moral and political messages of hip hop culture.[8]

For Otis, Harlow, and Beiderbecke, absorption in Black music helped arbitrate the anxieties emerging from their Greek, Jewish, and German ethnic identities. Black music provided them with a powerful critique of mainstream middle-class Anglo-Saxon America as well as with an elaborate vocabulary for airing feelings of marginality and contestation. They engaged in what film critics Douglas Kellner and Michael Ryan call "discursive transcoding" – indirect expression of alienations too threatening to express directly.[9]

Discursive transcoding of ethnic identities has a long history in Euro-American responses to Black music, but other alienations have been expressed in this way as well. The popular Euro-American balladeer Johnnie Ray, for example, told *Ebony* magazine in 1953 that he refused to sing at segregated venues because of "a great big debt which I owe mainly to the kind of people who were forced to walk through Jim Crow entrances in Southern cities."[10] Ray grew up in a white Protestant farm family in Oregon, and became attracted to Black music because of a disability. He suffered from partial deafness that went undiagnosed during his formative years, leading his teachers and classmates to view him as a "dumb bunny." A sad and lonely boy left out of play periods because others grew tired of hollering at him, Ray "needed something to keep me going, to make me feel adjusted to the narrow little world into which I had been shoved." His search led him to "those Negro spirituals which kept the colored people struggling along in the days of yesterday and the Negro blues which gave them some release in the far-from-freedom days they still have to encounter."[11]

Unlike other white singers of his era, Ray could not in conscience appropriate Black music and fail to acknowledge his debts to it. His disability gave him a sense of marginalization that made him think twice about the uninterrogated privileges he enjoyed as a white male. Ray's acknowledgment of his debts did not bring justice to Black musicians or Black communities, but his use of African-American culture can not be dismissed as simple colonialism either.

As Amiri Baraka observed in the course of his discussion of Beiderbecke, "The emergence of the white player meant that Afro-American culture had already become the expression of a particular kind of American experience, and what is most important, that this experience was available intellectually, that it could be learned."[12] Even when ripped out of context by semi-comprehending or non-comprehending outsiders, Black music has played an important role in the lives of Americans of all colors, just as the prophetic tradition in Black religion and politics helped Americans from every ethnic background to learn how to speak truth to power. For Euro-Americans and African Americans, as well as for Native Americans, Asian Americans, and Latinos, "mainstream" culture is not just middle-class Euro-American culture, but rather the creative and often contentious dialogue among all groups that encourages everyone to shift subject positions (however slightly) to be heard by others. What sometimes seems like simple appropriation may take on very different qualities in the context of energetic contestation and conflicts over meaning among individuals and groups.

The key questions come when we try to discern the consequences of cultural collusion and collision: which kinds of cross-cultural identification advance emancipatory ends and which ones reinforce existing structures of power and domination? When does identification with the culture of others serve escapist and irresponsible ends and when does it encourage an enhanced understanding of one's experiences and responsibilities? A comparison between some recent Euro-American appropriations of African and Afro-Caribbean music and some historical examples of inter-ethnic identification among African-American, Native American, Puerto Rican, and Chicano musicians offer some preliminary answers to these important questions.

In 1986, the singer-songwriter Paul Simon recorded *Graceland*, a best-selling and much celebrated album featuring performances by North American, Senegalese, and South African singers and musicians. Simon wrote English-language lyrics which he sang over instrumental tracks by black South African bands including Tao Ea Matsekha and the Boyoyo Boys. He collaborated with a South African vocal ensemble, Ladysmith Black Mambazo, to compose and sing additional songs on *Graceland*, and recruited South African musicians skilled in that nation's kwela, mbube, and mbaqanga styles to back him on other original compositions. Simon also recorded two other songs on the album over the instrumental backing of the Chicano band Los Lobos from Los Angeles and of Rockin' Dopsie and the Cajun Twisters, a Louisiana zydeco band.[13]

Graceland won commercial approval and critical acclaim for its sophisticated blend of superb instrumental work, diverse musical styles, and eloquent postmodern lyrics that stressed the connectedness of cultures exemplified by the album's transnational and trans-cultural musical collaboration. *Graceland* introduced many listeners around the world to the stunning textures and richly inventive styles of South African popular music, led to international tours and major record-label support for Ladysmith Black Mambazo, and provided inter-racial audiences in Africa and America with examples of inter-cultural cooperation in an era of increasing racial hostility and polarization. The singer-songwriter also paid the musicians above scale for their studio work, shared songwriting credits and royalties, and used revenues from the album's promotional tour to support charitable projects in Africa and in African-American communities.

Nonetheless, *Graceland* drew critical commentary for its alleged complicity with dominant power relations in the music industry and in society at large. Simon's supervision of the project, copyright for the finished work, and superimposition of lyrics about cosmopolitan postmodern angst over songs previously situated within the lives and struggles of aggrieved Black communities revealed the superior power he brought to the project and the disproportionate control he exercised over it as a white American artist with ample access to capital, technology, and marketing resources.[14] More important, Simon's recording defied the boycott of the South African music industry called by U.N.E.S.C.O. in an effort to pressure that country's government to abandon its racist policies of apartheid. Individuals and organizations prominent in the liberation struggles in South Africa condemned Simon's project because it provided positive propaganda about alleged black–white cooperation in South Africa. In addition, they charged that *Graceland* de-politicized South African music, and consequently served the interests of that nation's government, Afrikaner white nationalists, and other defenders of apartheid by expressing a sense of shared South African identity without exposing the power imbalances suppressing some parts of the national experience while magnifying others.

Simon and his defenders answered these criticisms with a somewhat contradictory stance, affirming the autonomy of art from politics while at the same time pointing to progressive political results from the album and the world tour that took place in the wake of its massive popularity. Simon properly pointed to the magnitude of his own contributions to the album and its success: his skill in identifying and transforming regional sounds for an international audience, his prowess in writing lyrics, and his hard work producing, performing, and promoting the album. He also argued that his efforts enhanced rather than diluted the commercial and aesthetic qualities of African music. "Did African art suffer because Picasso [was influenced by African art]?" he asked a reporter, adding,

> I don't see that African art suffered. Picasso was enriched, and the Western world was enriched, but African art wasn't depleted. What I think you're finding here are elements of an anti-Western cultural bias or even a racist bias that's not being discussed [openly]. It's easier to say, "David Byrne, Paul Simon, Peter Gabriel, Sting – they all rip off . . . " But what does that mean, "rip off"?[15]

Disavowing any political intentions, Simon explained that he selected South African music for purely aesthetic reasons, and that he considered the only legitimate role for political organizations in response to his album would be that "they should not tell me how I should play or write my music."[16] But as the controversy continued, the singer and his supporters began to stress the positive political consequences of *Graceland*. They argued that the inter-racial character of the album and of its promotional tour implicitly rebuked apartheid, that *Graceland*'s success promoted the popularity of Ladysmith Black Mambazo and other artists on the album, and that the oblique postmodern lyrics of *Graceland* protected the careers and lives of the African artists on the record by not subjecting them to the repression that would certainly have come their way if the album contained more overtly political content.[17]

Thus Simon exempted himself from political criticism, but tried to take credit for the positive political consequences of his recording. He seemed unaware that many people have justifiably claimed that Picasso's appropriations of "primitive" art did do damage to art from Africa, Asia, and Latin America – not because cultural borrowing damages art, but because powerful institutions attach prestige hierarchies to artistic expressions in such a way as to funnel reward and critical attention to Euro-American appropriators, and because ethnocentric presumptions about the universality of Western notions of art obscure the cultural and political contexts that give meaning to many artifacts from traditional cultures that are celebrated as pure form in the West.

Simon credited his understanding of African music for the inspiration of his postmodern lyrics. Claiming that "the African's sense of symmetry is different from Americans' – much fresher because of the role of rhythm in their songs," Simon explained:

Once I understood that musically, I inferred how to approach it lyrically. I began to extract from the choruses key pieces of information and slip them into the verses. And then I began to think that nobody truly remembers songs anyway. I began to write lines that had almost a cliché feel to them. The way the lyric rolled, you didn't have to think about it, and then there would be some image that was really interesting, and then I would move on to another smoothness.[18]

The aesthetic possibilities and combinations that Simon identifies in this discussion display a sophisticated understanding of the categories of Western popular music and Western art, but they are far removed from the motivating practices of South African music. Like his decision to make the South African pennywhistle solo on "You Can Call Me Al" more in tune with Euro-American notions of harmony, Simon's lyrical choices approached African music through the conventions of North America and Europe.

In a persuasive counter to Simon's political claims, the distinguished North American musicologist Charles Hamm points to the promotion and support of *Graceland* by the South African government and by white supremacist groups in that country. Far from challenging apartheid, in Hamm's view, the album strengthened it. Hamm explains that Ladysmith Black Mambazo has served as a pawn in the South African Broadcast Corporation's defense of apartheid for thirty years through appearances on its Radio Bantu. These broadcasts have played a crucial role in the white supremacist strategy of promoting Zulu tribal identity in order to divide the Black majority. Hamm compares the tenor of Simon's postmodern lyrics with the expressly political critiques offered in other collaborations with Black South Africans by white musicians Johnny Clegg and Jake Holmes to refute Simon's claim that anti-apartheid lyrics would have endangered his fellow musicians. Although he expresses approval for the anti-apartheid context of some parts of the *Graceland* world tour, Hamm nonetheless concludes that South African Blacks received very little from the album compared to Simon and his record company.[19] Literary scholar Neil Lazarus notes that the success of *Graceland* made recording executives eager for more music that sounded like it, causing them to encourage musicians to shun innovation and return to styles of music they had abandoned twenty years ago. In Lazarus's view, these pressures by music industry personnel contributed to the "underdevelopment" of Black South African music rather than to its advancement.[20]

Graceland obviously offers a complicated instance of cross-cultural collaboration and inter-ethnic identification. Did Paul Simon colonize African music for his own benefit?

Did he depoliticize and decontextualize the music of oppressed people while celebrating his own openness? Certainly not intentionally. On the contrary, Simon wants his Western audiences to understand and appreciate the diversity of world music, to learn from the differences and the commonalities between U.S. and South African music, and to participate in the creation of a global fusion culture that transcends national, racial, and ethnic lines. But like Jim Burden in *My Antonia*, he remains so preoccupied with what cross-cultural contact means for him, that he neglects addressing what it might mean to others. Consequently, Simon's good intentions do not offset their bad consequences when South African whites portrayed his role as that of a civilizing agent elevating and smoothing off the rough edges of South African Black music, when a liberal South African journalist praised Ladysmith Black Mambazo's singing for emblematizing what it means to be a South African by awakening in white listeners the memory of "a nanny's quiet crooning," and when government and right-wing sources celebrated the success of *Graceland* as proof of South Africa's acceptance and popularity throughout the world.[21]

David Byrne's excursions in the late 1980s into African, Brazilian, and Afro-Caribbean music raise issues similar to those generated by Paul Simon's *Graceland*. On the Talking Heads' Afro-pop-flavored album *Naked* and on his own salsa and samba-oriented *Rei Momo*, Byrne created a fusion between his own new wave/punk music of the early 1980s and styles of music with long histories of interaction with jazz and rock'n'roll. Just as Simon noticed similarities between African music and U.S. doo-wop and soul music (a similarity caused in part by the popularity of American Black music in Africa), Byrne created from his own experience in writing lyrics commenting on cosmopolitan inter-cultural communication to accompany music imitating African, Brazilian, and Afro-Caribbean forms. As he told an interviewer in 1989,

> This is stuff that I have been listening to in New York for eight or nine years. I can literally walk two blocks from where I live and hear musicians like Ray Barretto and Tito Puente. I remember hearing this conga drumming from this little club years ago and it would go on until four in the morning.[22]

Byrne explains that he wrote his song "Loco de Amor" after figuring out in his mind exactly "how Latin songs were constructed." While the form of "Loco de Amor" does follow standard salsa patterns, Byrne's departures from tradition raise questions comparable to those addressed to Paul Simon about *Graceland*. When Byrne sings lyrics that describe love as "like a pizza in the rain" and then calls out to "my little wild thing," he has the great Cuban exile salsa singer Celia Cruz answer him in Yoruba as she sings "yen yere cumbe." In traditional Cuban music, Yoruba lyrics resonate with collective memories of slavery and racism, they reinsert distinctly African identity back into collective national culture. But in Byrne's song, Cruz's Yoruba passage signifies only primitivism, exoticism, orientalism; she is an all-purpose "other" summoned up to symbolize Byrne's delight in musical difference on the west side of Manhattan.[23]

Like *Graceland*, Byrne's album brought much needed and deserved attention to Afro-Caribbean music, and it demonstrated real skill in echoing the music's core figures and devices. In addition, the Brazilian musicians who worked with him voiced both gratitude and admiration for his accomplishment. Brazilian percussionist Cyro Baptista applauded Byrne's openness to free expression from the musicians he hired:

> Most of the time on other people's projects, you have to play the same thing over and over and over again to get exactly the right sound they're looking for, to get this Brazilian déjà vu, but David left a lot of space for us . . . After he had communicated to us his idea of what he wanted from the songs, he really let us loose and allowed us to play in our own way, to make our own contribution to the final project.[24]

Similarly, Reinaldo Fernandes felt that on *Rei Momo* "what we ended up with is something new, something that is not exactly the samba, but something much like the samba – and something that I like very much."[25] Yet, like Simon's album, *Rei Momo* did not effectively illumine the power relations between Western artists and their sources of inspiration from the "Third World." Nor did it accurately represent the aesthetic, political, and social context giving determinate shape to the music in its area of origin.

It is not that Simon or Byrne err in looking to a wider world for inspiration and education. Their enthusiasm and empathy, their creativity and curiosity, lead them to extremely important cultural creations with enormous potential for stimulating crucially important reappraisals of commercial culture and its role in framing understanding of global issues. As Neil Lazarus argues convincingly, for listeners in advanced industrialized nations hearing "world music" can be "a distinctly subversive practice," because "what makes it *world* music is precisely its latent tendency to contribute to the dismantling of the subject of Western popular music, a subject whose identity rests squarely upon the political economy of empire."[26] But these explorations have to be carried out with a self-conscious understanding of unequal power relations, of the privileges available to Anglo-American recording stars because of the economic power of the countries from which they come.

In addition, we need to acknowledge the ways in which market imperatives shape the contours of the music that gets recorded and distributed internationally. Jocelyne

Guilbault identifies the "paradox inherent in the transnational recording industry," that Third World musicians enjoy access to broader audiences only when they conform to the "international sound" which Guilbault correctly identifies as "the use of preponderant Euro-American scales and tunings, harmony, electronic instruments now seen as standards, accessible dance rhythms, and a Euro-American-based intonation."[27]

Popular culture's propensity for serving as a site for experimenting with new identities offers opportunities as well as dangers. To think of identities as interchangeable or infinitely open does violence to the historical and social constraints imposed on us by structures of exploitation and privilege. But to posit innate and immobile identities for ourselves or others confuses history with nature, and denies the possibility of change. Willa Cather's use of Jim Burden as a vehicle for expressing a suppressed lesbian subjectivity and Johnny Ray's resort to Black music as a means of coping with his hearing impairment display processes of de-familiarization and re-familiarization far more profound than Paul Simon and David Byrne's encounters with South African and South American music. When people confront obstacles to direct expression of their aspirations and interests, they sometimes take a detour through fictive identities. These may seem simply escapist. They may involve the appropriation, colonization, or eroticization of difference. But appearances of escape and appropriation can also provide protective cover for explorations of individual and collective identity. Especially when carried on by members of aggrieved communities – sexually or racially marginalized "minorities" – these detours may enable individuals to solve indirectly problems that they could not address directly.

In a characteristically brilliant discussion, Gayatri Spivak explains how under some circumstances individuals and groups may choose to emphasize their common history and interests – to invoke a "strategic essentialism" that overlooks the heterogeneity of the group in order to build unity around common needs and desires.[28] Spivak terms this temporary unity "strategic essentialism." Willa Cather and Johnny Ray did not openly affirm or act on their identities as a lesbian or as a man with a hearing impairment, but they took on disguises in order to express indirectly parts of their identity that might be too threatening to express directly. We might call this "strategic anti-essentialism," because it gives the appearance of celebrating the fluidity of identities, but in reality seeks a particular disguise on the basis of its ability to highlight, underscore, and augment an aspect of one's identity that one can not express directly.

Sometimes, strategic anti-essentialism stems less from fear about expressing oneself directly than from the parts of one's own identity that come into relief more sharply through temporary role playing. Young Maoris and Pacific Islanders in New Zealand started to adopt African-American styles and slang in the late 1980s because "Black Americans provide the strongest image that we can identify with in popular culture."[29] When critics suggested that the prominence of African-American models represented only the success of American cultural imperialism and a defiling of traditional Maoris, one responded that on the contrary, African-American imagery enabled him to realize more fully what the Maoris had already lost in their own country. "With our links to the land broken, our alienation from the mode of production complete, our culture objectified, we have become marginalized and lost," wrote Kerry Buchanan, adding,

> This is not to say beaten. And this is what we have in common with black America. When Maori hip hop activists Upper Hutt Posse visited America recently, these political, social and racial links were brought into perspective. Upper Hutt Posse were welcomed as people involved in a common struggle, linked symbolically through hip hop culture.[30]

In the next chapter, I will discuss the use of strategic anti-essentialism by African-American Mardi Gras Indians in New Orleans, by Puerto Rican musicians playing Black-oriented Latin Bugalu music in New York, and by Chicano punk rockers in Los Angeles. The key to understanding each of these groups is to see how they can become "more themselves" by appearing to be something other than themselves. Like many members of aggrieved populations around the world, these strategic anti-essentialists have become experts in disguise because their survival has often depended on it. Consequently, their escapes differ markedly from what might seem like similar shifts in identity and allegiance on the part of musicians like Paul Simon or David Byrne.

The main problem posed by the inter-cultural collaborations orchestrated by Paul Simon or David Byrne stems from their unwillingness to examine their own relationship to power or to allow for reciprocal subjectivities between and among cultures. By placing themselves at the center, they elide their own historical specificity as well as that of their colleagues and collaborators. They obscure power relations in the present as well as the enduring consequences of past acts of subordination and suppression. Most important, they define delight in difference as a process organized around exotic images from overseas, with no corollary inspection of their own identities. Their escapes into postmodern multi-culturalism, however well-motivated, hide the construction of "whiteness" in America – its privileges, evasions, and contradictions.

Of course, in a world of interconnected evil, there can be no completely pure position. Johnny Ray and Willa Cather used forms of anti-essentialism to address unresolved anxieties about their own oppressions, yet neither provided any significant measure of material help to the class or racial groups that afforded them liberation through de-familiarization and re-familiarization. As author of this text, I know that my own Euro-American identity offers unearned privileges and imposes unpayable debts to aggrieved racial groups whose subjugation has underwritten my own privileges throughout my life. Yet, while it is impossible to speak from a position of purity, strategic anti-essentialism may enable us to understand how our identities have been constructed and at whose expense, as well as offering insights into how we can pay back the debts we incur as examples from others show us the way out of the little tyrannies of our own parochial and prejudiced backgrounds.

Yet, we should also take care not to collapse the complex and plural practices of people's lives into one-dimensional ethnic or racial identifications. For some people, anti-essentialism is a kind of essentialism. They participate in so many communities and cultures all the time that expressing their "essence" means exposing the plurality of their cultural and personal identity. The experiences of musicians Ronnie Bennett, Baldemar Huerta, and the Vegas Brothers, Pat and Lolly, vividly illustrate these dynamics.

Veronica Bennett (later Ronnie Spector) projected an ambiguous ethnic identity as lead singer in the 1960s vocal group, the Ronettes. Fans speculated that she might be Black, white, Puerto Rican, Native American, or even Chinese. In fact, she came from a mixed family – her father was Euro-American, her mother was Native American and Black. But her mother's sister married a Puerto Rican, and Bennett grew up in a Puerto Rican and Italian section of New York's East Harlem filled with Chinese laundries, African-American grocery stores, and Puerto Rican restuarants. When Bennett fell back on her "essential" identity, she had no choice but to be anti-essentialist.[31] (For more about how these identities may have influenced Bennett's music, see chapter 8.)

Baldemar Huerta from San Benito, Texas recorded Mexican, Chicano, Black, and Anglo country music under a variety of names including Eddie Medina, Scotty Wayne, Little Bennie, and most notably, Freddy Fender.[32] Born in 1936, Huerta grew up in a family of farm workers who spoke no English and who listened to Mexican ranchera music on the radio, but he developed an interest in the blues while working in migrant field camps with Black workers. When he joined the Marines he heard Fats Domino and Elvis Presley records for the first time, and incorporated their styles into his own music.[33]

Huerta brought the emotionalism and held notes of Mexican rancheras into country and blues songs. He carried the forms of rhythm and blues into Mexican pop, and illumined the affinities between country music and blues for all of his audiences. Huerta did Spanish-language versions of rhythm and blues hits by Bobby Marchan, Joe

Turner, and Ivory Joe Hunter, and had an English-language success in 1960 with "Wasted Days and Wasted Nights," – a rhythm and blues song based on "Family Rules" by Lonnie Brooks and on "Mathilde" by Cookie and the Cupcakes. He recorded for Falcon Records as "Baldemar Huerta, the Bebop Kid," singing Elvis Presley songs in Spanish, and recorded "Diablo Con Antifaz," a Chicano cover version of a Mexican group's Spanish-language cover of Presley's "Devil in Disguise."

Huerta worked as a mechanic in Texas and as a blues singer in New Orleans, picked cotton in the Rio Grande Valley and served time in a state prison in Louisiana. He enjoyed success as a bilingual country and western singer in the 1970s, and as member of the Texas Tornados, a 1990s rock'n'roll–conjunto collaboration with the great accordionist Flaco Jimenez and Anglo rockers Doug Sahm and Augie Meyer in the 1990s. Many artists have dabbled in different styles, but Huerta did so from his immersion in different communities, from his life experiences as both an insider and an outsider in Chicano, Black, and white working-class communities.[34] His varied repertoire involved changes in identity and identification, but they also all flowed organically from his experiences as a worker in a multi-cultural society.

Pat and Lolly Vegas grew up in a mostly African-American neighborhood in Fresno, California. Although they thought of themselves as "half-Mexican," they picked up the speech and music of their Black classmates, many of whom came from families that had migrated to California from Louisiana during the 1940s. When the Vegas Brothers began to play music they dabbled in "surf" guitar sounds and other pop forms, but showed the strongest affinity for bluesy Louisiana "swamp pop" songs.[35] They wrote "Niki Hokey," a creole-flavored best-selling song in 1967 recorded by James Smith under the pseudonym P.J. Proby.

While playing in a Los Angeles night club, the Vegas Brothers were "discovered" by Peter DePoe, also known as Last Walking Bear. A ceremonial drummer from an Indian reservation in the state of Washington, DePoe liked the music he heard from Pat and Lolly Vegas and decided he wanted to form a band with them. He felt that he had a special affinity for them because "they looked like Indians," but he went home and practiced for two years to be sure he would be good enough to play with them before approaching the Vegas Brothers with the idea of playing in a band together. DePoe convinced the Vegas Brothers that their Mexican ancestry included Indian heritage, and they formed a band together and called it "Redbone" – after a Louisiana creole word they remembered from Fresno that meant "half breed."[36]

Redbone presented themselves as a Native American band to audiences through their stage costumes, references to Native American music, and highly political lyrics.

In "Wovoka" they explained the Ghost Dance religion and struggle for self-defense among Plains Indians in the nineteenth century, while "We Were All Wounded at Wounded Knee" mixed information about the U.S. government's massacre of native peoples at that site in the nineteenth century with evocations of the American Indian Movement's battle with the Bureau of Indian Affairs and the Federal Bureau of Investigation in that South Dakota city in 1973. Their song "Alcatraz" commemorated the A.I.M. takeover of that island in San Francisco Bay in the late 1960s.

Even though Peter DePoe left the group in 1974, Redbone remained immersed in Native American imagery and identity. Many previous performers in popular music claimed Native American ancestry including R.B. Greaves, Marvin Rainwater, and even Jimi Hendrix, but the first fully self-conscious, self-affirming, and visible Native American band came from the efforts of two Mexican American brothers who grew up in a Black neighborhood and became "Indian" largely through a conscious choice based on cultural and political identification with Native American issues.

Toward the end of *My Antonia*, Antonia, and several of the "foreign" girls question Jim about stories they heard that the Spanish explorer Coronado might have journeyed as far north as their section of Nebraska. Jim cannot answer all of their questions: he tells them he only knows that Coronado " 'died in the wilderness of a broken heart.' " This reminds Antonia of her father, his pain in coming to the New World, and his tragic death. She says sadly, "More than him has done that," as the other girls "murmured assent."[37] In that moment, the Anglo-Saxon Jim Burden realizes something about himself and his world by hearing Bohemian and Scandinavian girls draw parallels between themselves and a legendary Spanish explorer.

Yet, Antonia's empathetic connection obscures as much as it reveals. What connects Antonia Shimerda's Bohemian-American farmer-musician father to the greedy and brutal conquistador Coronado? What motivates Antonia, Jim, and the "working girls" to see the subjugation of Native Americans through European eyes? Why do they trace the lineage of their disappointment to a genocidal conqueror seeking cities of gold rather than to the farming people who worked the land before Coronado's arrival?

For the children in Cather's novel, no less than for us, empathy is a way of knowing, of transcending space and time to connect with other people. But empathy also entails understanding and acknowledging the things that keep us divided. It demands that we take responsibility for our social locations and make our choices accordingly. There is no direct path to emancipation, accountability, or justice, but sometimes, the long way around is the shortest way through.

NOTES

1. Willa Cather, *My Antonia* (Boston: Houghton Mifflin Company, 1977), 219.

2. Willa Cather, *My Antonia*, 225.

3. Sharon O'Brien, *Willa Cather: The Emerging Voice* (New York: Oxford, 1987), 205–6.

4. Sharon O'Brien, *Willa Cather*, 136–7.

5. Sharon O'Brien, *Willa Cather*, 137.

6. Eric Lott, *Love and Theft: Blackface Minstrelsy and the American Working Class* (New York: Oxford, 1993); David Roediger, *The Wages of Whiteness* (London and New York: Verso 1991); Michael Rogin, "Blackface, White Noise: The Jewish Jazz Singer Finds His Voice," *Critical Inquiry* vol.18 (Spring) 1992.

7. Johnny Otis, *Listen to the Lambs* (New York: W.W. Norton, 1968); Tony Sabourin, "Latin International" in Billy Bergman, ed., *Hot Sauces: Latin and Caribbean Pop* (New York: Quill, 1985), 118, 121.

8. The rap groups Third Bass and House of Pain exemplify Euro-American contributions to a hip hop community based on culture rather than on color. The engagement with African-American culture in Los Angeles by the Irish photographer and writer Brian Cross presents another example.

9. Douglas Kellner and Michael Ryan, *Camera Politica* (Bloomington: University of Indiana Press, 1988), 1–17.

10. Johnnie Ray, "Negroes Taught Me to Sing," *Ebony* vol.8 (March), 1953, 48.

11. Johnnie Ray, "Negroes Taught Me to Sing," 50.

12. LeRoi Jones, *Blues People* (New York: Morrow Quill, 1963), 154–5.

13. Louise Meintjes, "Paul Simon's Graceland, South Africa, and the Mediation of Musical Meaning," *Ethnomusicology* vol.34 no.1 (Winter 1990), 42–4.

14. Steven Feld points out that while Simon shared songwriting credits and royalties with many African contributors to *Graceland*, he gave no credit to Rockin' Dopsie or Los Lobos. The members of Los Lobos expressed unhappiness with the whole project, citing Simon's lack of interest in their music ("just play something" they claim he told them) and his refusal to share songwriting credit with them for "All Around the World, or the Myth of Fingerprints." See Steven Feld, "Notes on World Beat," *Public Culture Bulletin* vol.1 no.1 (Fall) 1988, 34–5.

15. Keith Moerer, "Paul Simon's Rhythm Nation," *Request* (January) 1991, 31.

16. Louise Meintjes, "Paul Simon's Graceland," 39.

17. Charles Hamm, "Graceland Revisited," *Popular Music* vol.8 no.3 (October) 1989, 299.

18. Jay Cantor, "Paul Simon's Journey, a Return to First Loves," *New York Times*, September 12, 1993, H49.

19. Charles Hamm, "Graceland Revisited," 299–304.

20. Neil Lazarus, "Unsystematic Fingers at the Conditions of the Times: 'Afropop' and the Paradoxes of Imperialism," in Jonathan White, ed., *Recasting the World: Writing After Colonialism* (Baltimore and London: Johns Hopkins University Press, 1994), 142.

21. Louis Meintjies, "Paul Simon's Graceland," 44, 52, 53–4.

22. Robert Hilburn, "Byrning Up the Music World," *Los Angeles Times*, October 8, 1989, calendar section, 5.

23. I thank Greg Landau for pointing out the significance of Cruz's Yoruba vocal to me.

24. David Shirley, "Caribbean Connection: David Byrne's Samba Sidekicks," *Option* no.32 (May–June) 1990, 67.

25. David Shirley, "Caribbean Connection," 68.

26. Neil Lazarus, "Unsystematic Fingers," 157–8.

27. Jocelyne Guilbault, *Zouk: World Music in the West Indies* (Chicago and London: University of Chicago Press, 1993), 150.

28. Spivak qualifies this "strategic essentialism" more carefully than most critics credit. See Gayatri Chakravorty Spivak, *Outside in the Teaching Machine* (New York and London: Routledge, 1993), 3–4.

29. Selina Crosbie, "Doing the Right Thing," *Midwest* no.3 (1993), 22.

30. Kerry Buchanan, "Ain't Nothing But a G Thing," *Midwest* no.3 (1993), 27.

31. Ronnie Spector (with Vince Waldron), *Be My Baby: How I Survived Mascara, Miniskirts, and Madness or My Life as a Fabulous Ronette* (New York: Harper Perennial), 1990, 1–2.

32. Davia Nelson, liner notes, *Canciones de Mi Barrio*, Arhoolie Records, CD 366.

33. John Storm Roberts, *The Latin Tinge* (New York: Oxford, 1979), 180.

34. Davia Nelson, liner notes, *Canciones de Mi Barrio*, John Storm Roberts, *The Latin Tinge*, 180.

35. Janis Schacht, "Redbone and the Top Forty Trap," *Circus* (April) 1972, 60, 61.

36. Donald Clarke, ed., *Penguin Encyclopedia of Popular Music* (London: Penguin, 1990), 968; Janis Schacht, "Redbone and the Top Forty Trap," 61, 62.

37. Willa Cather, *My Antonia*, 244.

4

That's My Blood Down There

GODDESS 13

Because their status as superstars in the culture industry attracts enormous attention, Paul Simon's *Graceland* and David Byrne's *Rei Momo* understandably provoke comment and concern about the nature of inter-cultural communication. But musicians from privileged sectors of advanced industrialized societies are not the only artists who try on new identities through popular culture. Colonized and exploited communities have a long history of cultural expression that uses the protective cover offered by seemingly innocent play with new identities to address and redress their traditional grievances. Masquerades and disguises that may seem postmodern and new to Paul Simon, David Byrne, or their audiences, have been honed and refined over centuries among subordinated populations.

Every year on Mardi Gras Day in New Orleans, working-class Black males don feathered headdresses and elaborate hand-sewn costumes in order to parade through the streets "masked" as Indians.[1] For decades, New Yorkers of Puerto Rican ancestry have immersed themselves in African-American musical idioms, speech, and street styles. In Los Angeles, inner-city Chicano musicians have displayed a special devotion to a punk rock subculture that started among working-class youths and art school students in Britain.

These escapes to other identities may seem similar to the appropriation of South African music by Paul Simon or of Afro-Caribbean music by David Byrne. But Mardi Gras Indians, Puerto Rican devotees of African-American culture, and Chicano punk rockers use temporary disguises to affirm all the more emphatically their collective historical experiences as Blacks, Puerto Ricans, and Chicanos. Their disguises bring to the surface important aspects of who they are by playing at being something they are not. By pretending to be Indians, New Orleans Blacks present themselves as warriors resisting domination. By stressing their affinities to Black culture, Nuyoricans affirm the African aspects of their own culture and distance themselves from the prestige hierarchies of white supremacy. By taking on the flamboyant marginality and anti-establishment anger of punk rock, Chicanos make covert claims about their own status. These forms of "play" are deadly serious; they enable members of aggrieved communities to express indirectly aspects of their identity that might be dangerous to present by more direct means.

As they parade through the streets of New Orleans, the Mardi Gras Indian "tribes" enact vulgar and vicious stereotypes of Native Americans that resonate more with the history of Wild West shows and Hollywood westerns than with the actual historical experiences of Native peoples. Their song lyrics contain lines like "Me big chief, me gottem' tribe, got my squaw right by my side," and phrases like "Big chief, want plenty of fire water." These stereotypical and insulting representations display all of the "orientalism," primitivism, and exoticism that plague so much of popular culture's representations of aggrieved groups.

Yet, there is a strategic logic in the Indians masquerade that gives it a different meaning than might first be evident. In a city that for many years banned Blacks from wearing masks on Mardi Gras day, Indian "war paint" offered an opportunity for African Americans to take to the streets and still hide their identities. On a day reserved for the New Orleans elite to flaunt its social hierarchies and its wealth in big parades on Canal Street, Indian imagery calls attention to the history of conquest and genocide that allowed for the accumulation of European-American wealth in the first place. By becoming "Indians," these African Americans problematize the binary system of racial categorization in the U.S. that historically has defined individuals as either black or white.

In addition, the Mardi Gras Indians call a community into being by parading through Black neighborhoods and drawing people into the streets behind them as "second liners" whose clapping and chanting evokes African forms of ritual and celebration. They also bring to the surface the suppressed and repressed Caribbean presence in New Orleans through Indian costumes that bear a marked similarity to carnival dress in Trinidad, Haiti, Jamaica, and Brazil; through Indian "talk" based on French and Spanish phrases; and through signs, symbols, and songs based on Haitian and African religious rituals.[2] By pretending to be something other than "Black" for a day, the Mardi Gras Indians bring to the surface all the more powerfully their Caribbean and African ancestries.

Mardi Gras Indian imagery contains so many subtleties, nuances, and contradictions that it seems to take on a different meaning each time it is studied. In ethnographic films, Maurice Martinez and Les Blank have presented the Indians both as biological descendants of nineteenth-century runaway slaves who found refuge in Native American tribes and as a dying 1970s subculture clinging desperately to vestiges of tradition in a rapidly changing world.[3] Musicologists David Elliott Draper and Finn Wilhelmsen have depicted the Indians as folk musicians whose social isolation enables them to fashion distinctive melodies and rhythms.[4] Journalists Jason Berry and Jeff Hannusch and American Studies scholar Helen Mayhew have carefully documented the powerful influence that the Indians have exerted on New Orleans rhythm and blues music.[5] Recent scholarly work (including my own, and that of Joan Martin and Rosita Sands) has marveled at the Indians' ability to range across centuries and continents as they preserve in present-day New Orleans remnants of ritual and religion like "rara" and "obeah" from Africa, Haiti and Trinidad.[6]

Each of these accounts focuses on a different aspect of the same phenomenon, and that is as it should be. The Mardi Gras Indian ritual encompasses many stories and many experiences; no single narrative or interpretation could encapsulate all of its complexities. Indian practices range from dance to dress, from speech to sewing, from music to mutual aid. But in addition to its other varied and diverse uses and effects, the Mardi Gras Indian ritual serves as a form of strategic anti-essentialism, as a way of de-familiarizing and re-familiarizing Black people in New Orleans with their shared history and identity.

Contrary to Les Blank's assumption in his film *Always for Pleasure* that he had found the dying remnant of a traditional culture, the past two decades have seen a powerful re-emergence of the Mardi Gras Indians in New Orleans. Blank depicted the Wild Tchoupitoulas tribe as a traditional group threatened with extinction, but the tribe had been formed only five years before. In the 1970s, African Americans in New Orleans revived the Mardi Gras Indian tradition and gave it new meaning. For them, it was an emergent rather than a residual practice, largely because historical and social conditions in the city compelled Blacks to rethink their relationship to the dominant culture.

The transformation of New Orleans in the 1970s from a city with a majority white population to one with a majority black population, the rapid changes in the local economy caused by economic restructuring and de-industrialization, the raised expectations and bitter disillusionment that accompanied Black political mobilization in local politics, all functioned to impose renewed scrutiny on what it means to be poor and Black in the Big Easy. The long-term consequences of urban renewal rendered obsolete old rivalries between Black neighborhoods "uptown" and "downtown," while the fiscal crisis of the state undermined the ability of politics to solve local problems. By 1985, more than a quarter of the city's African-American workers were unemployed. New Orleans had become the third poorest large city in the country. Nearly half of local Black families lived in poverty.[7] Under those conditions, traditions of self-help and mutual aid became more important, while narratives addressing and neutralizing the hegemony of white racism took on more urgency.

In the post-Civil Rights and post-industrial period that began in the 1970s, the Mardi Gras Indian ritual offered a unified identity to the city's restructured Black population, and invoked traditions of self-help at a time when budget cutbacks eviscerated the welfare state. The Indian ritual proved particularly useful because it brought to the surface the long history of struggle against white supremacy that has characterized

Black life in New Orleans. As Joan Martin astutely reminds us, "Rara and the Black Indians of New Orleans came into existence as a reaction to the violence and horror of slavery and its attendant evils. Religion and celebration were the only safe arenas available for these people to voice the anger and grief they felt about their lives."[8]

Caribbean religions, spiritualist churches, and carnival celebrations kept alive social memories and shaped aspirations for the future, for the time when direct political struggle might be possible. New Orleans Black community activist Jerome Smith revealed connections between covert and overt forms of resistance in a discussion of his involvement in the Civil Rights Movement with artist/activist Tom Dent. Smith recalled that his disposition toward social protest started in childhood when his parents told him stories about Black leaders like Mary McLeod Bethune and Paul Robeson, and when his longshoreman grandfather took him to march in Labor Day parades. But then Smith also cited the Mardi Gras Indians as an inspiration for his subsequent activism, explaining that Tuddy Montana, the Chief of the Yellow Pocohontas tribe,

> unconsciously made statements about black power . . . the whole thing about excellence, about uniqueness, about creativity, about protecting your creativity – I learned that in those houses [of the Indians]. Police would try to run the Indians off the street, but we had a thing. You don't bow, you don't run from 'em, not black or white or grizzly grey.[9]

Smith started sewing Indian costumes as a young boy in the 1940s, and he remembered how that experience positioned him in relation to the downtown Mardi Gras festivities: "I never saw Rex on Mardi Gras. We always see Rex as nuthin'. We always felt that, one, they wasn't equal to us, and, two, none of the costumes would be as pretty as what we could do."[10] By itself, this interview does not establish any firm connection between the Mardi Gras Indians and the Civil Rights Movement in New Orleans, but it does remind us that the Civil Rights and Black Power Movements took place in a community with a long heritage of oppositional and alternative cultural practices. Perhaps more important, it reminds us that the rituals and celebrations of the Indians have taken place in the context of oppressive power relations in a city and country where questions of Black and white, savagery and civilization, or America and Africa have a highly charged emotional and ideological meaning. The presence of Indian, Caribbean, and African elements within the Mardi Gras Indian ritual represent more than a "race memory" of actual lines of descent (although they may signify that as well), but also a strategic deployment of memories and images as a shield against the oppressions of the present.

To position themselves as connected to Trinidad, Haiti, and Africa, as the Indians have done, enables them to change their identity from a national minority to a global majority. It invokes religious traditions ranging from African obeah to Haitian rara and African-American voodoo and spiritualism where concrete action in this world can avenge injustice and avert calamities, traditions that share "non-hierarchical resilient faith in the power of oneself and one's community to resist oppressions."[11] In this respect the Indians share the same inspiration for their creativity as do Black New Orleans writers Brenda Marie Osbey, Tom Dent, Kalamu ya Salaam, and Sybil Kein – "the living African-American folk culture of New Orleans."[12] But this is not a static culture immune to historical change; rather it is an evolving dynamic mobilization of images and practices for historically specific purposes. It takes many different forms, but read correctly, all disclose the truth of Salaam's formulation that "living poor and Black in the Big Easy is never as much fun as our music, food, smiles, and laughter make it seem."[13]

The revival of the Mardi Gras Indians demonstrates how pretending to be Indians enables one group of African Americans to understand and emphasize important dimensions of being Black – in other words, how strategic anti-essentialism can be a form of strategic essentialism. But in a further twist, the politics emanating from using Indian imagery to affirm Black nationalism lead logically to a pan-ethnic anti-racism that moves beyond essentialism. Music by the Neville Brothers (Art, Aaron, Charles, and Cyrille), a rhythm and blues band with strong ties to the Mardi Gras Indians, demonstrates the complex dimensions of this strategic switching of identities.

The Neville Brothers' uncle, George Landry, helped start the Wild Tchoupitoulas tribe and ruled as their "Big Chief" under the name Chief Jolly. For a time the Nevilles included costumed Indians in their touring shows, and they have performed many Indian songs. But while firmly grounded in the music and values of their community, the Neville Brothers have also raised broader issues about exploitation and oppression by pointing to families of resemblance that unite diverse aggrieved groups. On their 1989 album, *Yellow Moon*, the Neville Brothers presented a series of songs that projected an extraordinary vision of the connections between group identities and collective struggles for social justice. "A lot of the songs on *Yellow Moon* show how we feel about social issues, which is something we never had a chance to do before," Cyrille Neville explained to a reporter shortly before the album's release. "What people are going to get is a record in which we not only play our music, but bare our souls."[14]

The opening cut on *Yellow Moon* is "My Blood," a song that calls upon "Jah" (the Rastafarian term for God) to come to the "crossroads" and give help to people in need –

Haitians, South Africans, and youths in U.S. ghettos. "That's my blood down there," the lyrics assert, connecting political solidarity to primordial ties of blood and biology. But at a key point in the song other groups emerge as objects of solidarity – people "on the reservations, the first Americans," Nicaraguans, Salvadorans, and people in Northern Ireland – all of whom the Nevilles sing about as "my blood." From the song itself, we have no evidence to tell if these words should be taken literally to signal that the Nevilles have blood ties to these different kinds of people. It is certainly not out of the question. But it is more likely that the group means their words figuratively, that the same "Indian" identity that led them to use imagery from Native Americans, Caribbeans, and Africans, also enables the Neville Brothers to imagine that their "blood" includes all people struggling against oppression.

The rest of the songs on *Yellow Moon* echo "My Blood" in their African-American specificity and global generalizability. They perform Bob Dylan's "With God on Our Side" and their own "Wake Up" to condemn militarism and war. They make musical and lyrical references to the Caribbean in "Yellow Moon" and "Voo Doo," but evoke white working-class experience in the U.S.A. with their renditions of A.P. Carter's "Will the Circle Be Unbroken?" and Dylan's populist "Hollis Brown." They pay homage to the Civil Rights Movement by presenting a new version of Sam Cooke's "A Change is Gonna Come," and "Sister Rosa" – a funk rock rap tribute to the role of Rosa Parks in the 1955 Montgomery Bus Boycott.

Through their songs in *Yellow Moon*, the Neville Brothers venture far from home, commenting on global issues, affirming their commitments to social justice, and combining elements of commercial culture and current events with religious references. But they conclude the album by returning home to New Orleans. In "Wild Injuns," they recite the names of different Mardi Gras Indian tribes and salute them as "the prettiest thing you've ever seen."[15] Over the final four beats of the album's final song, the lyrics celebrate the Nevilles' uncle, "Big Chief Jolly."

In *Yellow Moon* and much of their other work, the Neville Brothers engage in a complex process of strategic anti-essentialism. In an industry that tries to make performers lose their local identities so they will be easier to market around the globe, the Nevilles remain rooted in the history and culture of New Orleans. But part of living in New Orleans means encountering cultures from all over the world. The Mardi Gras Indians owe part of their identity to the Wild West Show that wintered in New Orleans in 1884–5 and part to the carnival traditions brought to the Gulf Coast city from other ports in Cuba, Haiti, Brazil, Jamaica, and Trinidad. In addition to Mardi Gras day, the Indians always parade on St. Joseph's Day, largely because the Italian immigrants to

New Orleans emphasized that saint's day as their own and made it an important local occasion, but also because St. Joseph served as a symbol of social justice who was reputed to have brought bread to the hungry Christ child and miraculously to have provided food for starving peasants in Sicily in the middle ages.[16] When the Neville Brothers look to the wider world, they find much of what they already know from New Orleans. After *Yellow Moon*, their efforts included recording with the Frères Parent (Clarke and Alain Parent, Haitian brothers living in Brooklyn) and pairing their rendition of the gospel hymn "How Great Thou Art" with a chant by Maoris from New Zealand.[17]

The Neville Brothers view their community as aggrieved, and feel compelled to address its problems. As witnesses to the disillusionment that followed in the wake of the Civil Rights Movement and to the devastation wrought on their community by de-industrialization and economic restructuring, they make music that speaks from as well as for their community. "It's desperately important for kids today to have a better outlook on themselves than we had when we were growing up," explains Cyrille Neville.[18] To provide that better outlook, the Neville Brothers combine information about Rosa Parks (in the form of "something they could memorize, like a mini-history lesson," according to Charles Neville) with social protest songs by other singers; they affirm the importance of blood ties within their family, but also draw families of resemblance between themselves and other people resisting oppression and exploitation.[19]

Like the Mardi Gras Indian ritual itself, the music of the Neville Brothers expresses a strategic anti-essentialism – a changing of identities to bring to the surface both the singularity and plurality of experience within the Black community. Latin Bugalu music from New York in the 1960s served many of the same purposes for musicians of Puerto Rican ancestry. Their experiments with Black popular music helped illumine important aspects of what it meant to be Puerto Rican in New York, brought to the surface repressed African elements in Puerto Rican identity, but also laid claim to participating in a broader world through alliances with similar, but not identical, cultures in the U.S.A. and around the world.

In the mid-1960s, Puerto Rican musicians in New York achieved commercial success on the rhythm and blues charts with a music which became known as Latin Bugalu. Inspired by the growing popularity of "soul" music with popular audiences, Ricardo Ray, Johnny Colon, Pete Rodriguez, and Hector Rivera (among others) began releasing records that featured distinctly African-American musical forms including "booga-loo" and "shing-a-ling" dance rhythms, sharply accented beats, Black vocal styles, and

English phrases mixed in with Spanish lyrics. Although the direct commercial popularity of Latin Bugalu was short-lived, it left a lasting impact on rhythm and blues rhythm sections, changing the four-to-the-bar rhythms to a repeated rhythmic pattern for bass or conga drums with rhythmic counterpoint from other percussionists. In 1966, the Joe Cuba sextet released "Bang Bang," the first Latin Bugalu record to sell one million copies and one that reached number 63 on *Billboard*'s Hot One Hundred best-seller charts.[20]

The Latin Bugalu embraced a broad range of musical forms and styles. Joe Cuba played parts generally scored for horns on the vibraphone. Joe Bataan's band included a musician who combined the thumb-picking single-line soloing guitar style of Wes Montgomery with the wah-wah pedals popularized by Jimi Hendrix and other psychedelic rock guitarists. Bataan performed a "cover" version of Curtis Mayfield's 1961 rhythm and blues hit "Gypsy Woman," Jack Constanzo and Gerry Woo recorded a Latin version of "Green Onions" – a song initially performed by Booker T. and the MGs, while both Tito Puente and El Gran Combo offered renditions of South African exile Miriam Makeba's Xhosa-language song "Pata Pata."[21]

At first glance, the Latin Bugalu craze seems like a textbook example of how commercialized mass culture threatens ethnic communities. African-American musicians found some of their core forms gaining financial reward when appropriated by outsiders, while Latino musicians seemed to be abandoning the clave beat, Spanish lyrics, and more complicated rhythms of their culture simply to secure commercial acceptance. Yet, it is also possible to see Latin Bugalu as a rediscovery of African elements in Puerto Rican culture, and as a reconstitution of the dynamic dialogue between Afro-American and Afro-Caribbean musics that had done so much over the years to enrich both cultures.

Juan Flores argues that Puerto Ricans develop a more profound appreciation of the African elements in their culture when they move to New York City than they had while still in Puerto Rico. Crowded into ghettos that invariably border on Black neighborhoods, exposed to the pervasiveness and intensity of anti-Black racism, and profoundly alienated by the injustices that they themselves suffer from North American white supremacy, Puerto Ricans become more aware of the multi-racial composition of their people and more affirmative of their African roots.[22] Popular culture also offers mechanisms enabling Puerto Ricans in New York to think of themselves as African. The "Nuyorican" poet Sandra Maria Esteves writes of a woman who grows up thinking of her "sistas" as an eclectic group of Black and Latino singers – Nina Simone,

Celia Cruz, Billie Holiday, Bessie Smith, Aretha Franklin, La Lupe, Diana Ross, Ronnie Spector, Gladys Knight, and Roberta Flack.[23]

Material conditions as well as cultural affinities encourage Black–Puerto Rican interactions. Migration patterns to the mainland shape Puerto Rican culture in many ways. More than a third of all Puerto Ricans live outside the island in North American cities, and the absolute number of Puerto Ricans in the continental U.S.A. has doubled every decade since the 1950s.[24] The Puerto Rican population of New York City increased tenfold between 1940 and 1970, and by 1980, people with African-American and Latino ancestry made up nearly forty percent of the city's population.[25] Of all U.S. ethnic groups, Puerto Ricans are the most likely to live among Blacks, partially because some Puerto Ricans are dark-skinned, but also because of the affinities between the two cultures.[26] Although conflict between the two groups is constant and recurrent, alliances and fusions have often emerged based upon shared material circumstances and on similar experiences with employers, landlords, welfare officials, teachers, and police officers.

The success of the U.S. Civil Rights Movement in the 1960s in challenging white supremacy made African-American politics and culture an important source of inspiration and information for other aggrieved communities of color. The Black Panthers and other para-military organizations helped inspire the formation of the Young Lords among Puerto Ricans, and the autobiographical descriptions of battles with poverty and racism by Black authors including Claude Brown and Malcolm X helped inspire and shape Puerto Rican author Piri Thomas's *Down These Mean Streets*.[27] As the Civil Rights Movement evolved into a Black Power Movement dedicated to securing resources and self-determination for Black communities rather than merely an end to legal segregation, nationalism emerged as a powerful tool for political and cultural mobilization.

The rise of the Civil Rights Movement in the U.S.A. offered all Americans of color an alternative to feeling like foreigners in their own country or simply seeking assimilation into the mainstream. It provided a language of upward mobility and advancement without deracination, seeking the rewards of inclusion into American society but not the cultural erasure that seemed to presume. In a strategy that Juan Flores calls "branching out," Puerto Ricans found families of resemblance between themselves and Blacks, Chicanos, and Native Americans because they stood in common opposition to white supremacy and racialized exploitation. Alfredo Lopez describes the politicized mood of the 1960s and 1970s among Puerto Ricans as a result of a process whereby:

English-speaking society somehow seemed to fail us. As we grew older, as we began to learn the way things worked, this society became even more distant – seemed unwilling to accept us, and for reasons we did not understand, seemed cold compared to the first authority figures we know: our parents.[28]

In a similar vein, street musician Joe Falcon remembers politics as an important dimension of his choices about music:

In 1969, I was very much influenced by the takeover of City College by a Third World student coalition which was demanding Puerto Rican Studies and other relevant programs geared to their needs. Right then and there and with the direct contact of other musicians such as myself, I realized that for the first time that I wanted to play a music that related to today's realities, not to yesterday's.[29]

The Latin Bugalu grew out of an era of Puerto Rican identification with Black politics and culture, but that led organically to a reconsideration of "Cuban" musical styles (dominant within Puerto Rican popular music) as, in fact, *Afro*-Cuban and for a general reawakening of the African elements within Puerto Rican culture. Condemned by traditionalists as a betrayal of the community, Latin Bugalu instead showed that the community's identity had always been formed in relation to that of other groups in the U.S.A. Like the Mardi Gras Indians in New Orleans, they found that performing an identity that was not entirely their own brought them closer to their roots. But the "essentialist" Puerto Rican identity they discovered as a result of this anti-essentialist strategy revealed the heterogeneity and complexity of their group's identity sufficiently to position them to take part in subsequent national and international fusion musics including salsa, disco, and hip hop – that enabled them to imagine and enact alliances with other groups.

Latin Bugalu musicians brought to the surface a suppressed memory of the ways in which the long history of interaction between African-American and Caribbean cultures in the U.S.A. served as a shaping force within both Puerto Rican music and African-American jazz, bop, and rhythm and blues. For example, Cuban-born Mario Bauzá had played bass clarinet with the Havana Philharmonic before he came to the U.S.A. in 1930. An extremely versatile artist, Bauzá joined black bandleader Noble Sissle's aggregation as a saxophonist, and then went to play lead trumpet with the great Chick Webb orchestra. After stints with Don Redman and Fletcher Henderson, he became a part of Cab Calloway's orchestra, where he persuaded his boss to hear a young trumpet player named Dizzy Gillespie.

Although Bauzá soon left that band to help found Machito's Afro-Cubans with his brother-in-law Frank "Machito" Grillo, he made a big impression on Gillespie, who later recalled, "My roommate and best friend in [the] band . . . was a Cuban, Mario Bauzá . . . Mario helped me a lot, not just by giving me an opportunity to be heard and land a good job, but by broadening my scope in music."[30] One reason for Gillespie's receptivity to Latin music came from his own earlier apprenticeship with Cuban flautist Alberto Socarras's band, as well as from his admiration for Duke Ellington's Puerto Rican trombonist Juan Tizol.[31] Bauzá convinced Gillespie to hire Chano Pozo, who further refined the trumpeter's knowledge of Afro-Cuban forms, eventually appearing in compositions like "Manteca," "Cubop," and "A Night in Tunisia."[32]

The sounds that Chano Pozo brought to jazz soon worked their way into rhythm and blues as well. Johnny Otis encountered Afro-Cuban bands at the Cavalcade of Jazz concerts at Wrigley Field in Los Angeles in the 1940s and recorded with conga drummers that he borrowed from Machito's Afro-Cubans. In 1951, Otis recorded "Mambo Boogie" featuring the conga drumming of Gaucho Vahrandes, an Afro-Jukla Indian from Brazil.[33] Laverne Baker's 1955 hit "Tweedle Dee" employed a pattern based on the clave in Afro-Cuban music. Bo Diddley used maracas and mambo rhythms on many of his songs and Clyde McPhatter's 1957 "Long Lonely Nights" featured a marimba and a shuffle rhythm influenced by the triple-meter Spanish bolero.[34]

Bauzá's influence on Gillespie helped secure a place within African-American music for Afro-Cuban sounds, but African-American forms and artists also played an important role in the development of Latin music as well. Blacks flocked to New York's Palladium Ballroom at Broadway and 53rd to dance to the polyrhythms of Tito Puente, Tito Rodriguez, and other Puerto Rican bandleaders. Initially, the Palladium's owners tried to bar Blacks from their venue, but Puerto Rican promoter Federico Pagani dissuaded them by pointing to the commercial importance of Black audiences and dancers, explaining, "If you want the green, you gotta have the Black."[35]

New York-born Puerto Rican conga player Ray Barretto took up his instrument while stationed in Germany with the U.S. army. Growing up in New York he listened to albums by Machito that his mother owned and he liked the jazz music he heard on the radio. But his commitment to a life in music really began the first time that he heard Chano Pozo and Dizzy Gillespie. "When I heard Pozo," he later recalled, "I picked up a banjo that was lying around and tore off the arm. The back of the head was calfskin. I put it between my legs and that was the beginning."[36] Barretto started playing jazz at the Orlando Club in Munich and introduced musicians from all over the world to

Puerto Rican Afro-Cuban conga drumming. But he learned about other music there as well. "In the Orlando," he told an interviewer, "no one cared if you were Black, white, French, or German. The only important thing was making music."[37] After returning to the U.S.A. from military service, Barretto played on many rhythm and blues recording sessions, and worked as a sideman for jazz musicians including Red Garland, Gene Ammons, Lou Donaldson, and Kenny Burrell. Barretto's recording of "El Watusi" reached *Billboard*'s Top Twenty in 1963, exposing rhythm and blues as well as pop audiences to more Latin sounds.[38] Barretto also recorded songs written by Hector Rivera, who would later record one of the biggest Latin Bugalu hits in 1967, "At the Party."

The dynamic fusions that Ray Barretto enjoyed at the Orlando Club have long been a staple of Puerto Rican culture. The biographies of the community's prominent musicians offer ample demonstration of an ability to learn from contact with others without losing one's own identity. Charlie and Eddie Palmieri grew up in a Jewish neighborhood in the South Bronx; Eddie took music lessons from Margaret Bonds, an African-American pianist who specialized in classical music.[39] Salsa star Larry Harlow recorded "Yo Soy Latino" ("I am Latino"), and bills himself as "El Judio Maravilloso" ("The Marvelous Jew") in reference to his origins as Lawrence Ira Kahn, a Jewish American who discovered Afro-Cuban music on a trip to Havana in the 1960s. Most bugalu, salsa, and hip hop fans think of Joe Bataan as Puerto Rican, but he is actually Afro-Filipino. Nuyorican disc jockey and hip hop entrepreneur Charley Chase established a strong presence within African-American hip hop, in part because: "I always grew up with Black people; my best friends were always Black people."[40]

Just as African-American jazz contained strong elements of Afro-Caribbean music, so did rhythm and blues. Two Puerto Ricans, Herman Santiago and Joe Negroni, sang backup for Frankie Lymon in the Teenagers in the 1950s and contended years later that they had written the group's big hit "Why Do Fools Fall in Love?". In the early 1960s, Anglo songwriters Jerry Leiber, Mike Stoller, and Doc Pomus patterned many of their compositions after Puerto Rican and Brazilian dance music, including "Save the Last Dance for Me," "Sweets for My Sweet," and "There Goes My Baby" recorded by the Drifters, an African-American vocal group. Mike Stoller remembers composing Top Forty hits with his partner Jerry Leiber by immersing themselves in the possibilities created by Afro-Cuban music. "We had a fascination with different sounds. In fact, we rented a lot of instruments from Carroll's Music on Broadway – various congas, large tom-toms, triangles, marimbas, and something we called the African hairy drum."[41] When Stoller and Leiber wrote "There Goes My Baby" for the Drifters, they used the baion rhythm from South America.

Similarly, Mort Shuman credits the Puerto Rican presence in New York as a great inspiration for his efforts as a songwriter:

> The Puerto Rican influence was very strong in New York. You had terrific bands like Tito Puente, Tito Rodriguez, and Machito. There was a great ballroom, the Palladium at 53rd and Broadway and every Wednesday night was mambo night. You'd get two or three bands on the same bill. The place was jam packed with people who worked in factories. Cleaning ladies. It was a great melting pot and the catalytic agent was Latin music. I was there every night it was open.[42]

Yet, for all of their influence, Puerto Rican musicians received very little reward. Anglo- and African-American composers and performers reaped most of the benefits of their popularizations of Afro-Cuban sounds, and very little came back into the community that created them in the first place. This lack of remuneration provided an important impetus for the creation of Latin Bugalu – above and beyond its political and cultural imperatives. By turning to Black music, Puerto Rican musicians also moved to where they thought the money was. With the popularity of rock'n'roll and rhythm and blues, old-time salsa bands provided too few opportunities for employment for young Nuyorican musicians in the 1960s. To get work they had to play the kinds of rock'n'roll they heard in school with their Anglo, Black, and Asian friends. Economic pressures also made it necessary to abandon the big sounds provided by horn sections in traditional Afro-Cuban music. Instead, Latin Bugalu musicians used raucous group shouting and keyboard instruments to replicate the rhythmic interpellations previously made by full sections of trombones and trumpets.

By the early 1970s, many of the conditions that encouraged the rise of Latin Bugalu changed radically. De-industrialization and economic restructuring worked particular hardships on Black and Puerto Rican communities, undermining their power as citizens and their purchasing power as consumers. The monopolistic structure of the music industry worked to marginalize Latin Bugalu as a regional phenomenon and limit its exposure nationally and internationally. The rise of "salsa" music pulled Latin Bugalu musicians back to Spanish-language lyrics and song forms suited to the styles of Caribbean dancing. Changes in immigration law made it easier for Spanish-speaking migrants from the Western Hemisphere to enter the U.S.A., giving Puerto Rican artists in New York an enormous new audience. Yet, the musicians could not simply return to traditional Puerto Rican forms to entertain the large numbers of Dominicans, Mexicans, Central Americans, and Colombians whose aggregate numbers exceeded the population of Puerto Ricans in New York by 1985.[43] The turn away from Latin Bugalu music did not entail re-entry into a discrete and homogeneous Nuyorican identity, but rather to an embrace with new fusions that entailed strategic anti-essentialisms of their own. Latin Bugalu and salsa musicians played an important part in the disco craze of the 1970s, and late in the decade began to play a crucial part as well in the rise of hip hop in New York.

Very real historical oppression and exploitation lies behind the complicated history of Nuyorican music. "Puerto Rico is like a stray dog," complains visual artist Jaime Carrero, adding: "we've been pushed around for 500 years."[44] Colonized by Spain and the U.S.A., stained by genocide and the slave trade, and segregated into segments of the U.S. economy that pay the least, Puerto Ricans have had to struggle constantly to maintain their cultural and political integrity. The dynamic creativity and change-ability displayed by Puerto Rican musicians has enabled their music to survive and thrive, but reward for it has too often gone to someone else. These problems continue today as the eight Anglo-owned corporations that control more than half of Spanish-language radio stations continue to marginalize salsa and merengue while promoting variants of "Latin pop" favored by advertisers in search of upscale crossover audiences.[45]

Yet, without dismissing the terrible price that Puerto Ricans have paid for their place in global and national politics, economics, and culture, their history also gives them advantages in dealing with the interconnected world of the present and future. The dynamic cultural fusions, interactions, and alliances fashioned by Puerto Ricans offer an impressive model for other groups who realize that they can be neither essentialist believers in a homogeneous unified original and authentic group identity nor anti-essentialists who think that the power to cast off and take on identities is infinitely open. Instead, like all people struggling with power, they teach us that strategic decisions about essentialism and anti-essentialism enable aggrieved populations to fight for new identities without forgetting the very real circumstances that continue to unite them in common destinies.

Like the Mardi Gras Indians and Latin Bugalu musicians, young Chicanos in Los Angeles embraced their own kind of strategic anti-essentialism in the late 1970s and early 1980s when they turned to playing punk rock in bands including Los Illegals, Odd Squad, the Bags, and the Brat. Hailed by some critics as the most important expression of East L.A.'s participation in popular music since the 1950s when Ritchie

Valens (Richard Valenzuela) had best-selling records on the charts (before his tragic death in a plane crash at the age of eighteen), this "Eastside Revival" seemed remarkable mostly for its distance from Mexican-American culture. Chicano punk rockers adopted the simple chord structures, driving rhythms, energetic amateurism, and "pogo" dancing first made popular by working-class dropouts and art school bohemians in England and appropriated by alienated suburban youth in the U.S.A. They sounded much more like the Sex Pistols or the Ramones than they did like previous Chicano artists who secured commercial success in popular music – Ritchie Valens, Cannibal and the Headhunters, and El Chicano, among others.

In fact, claims could be made connecting punk rock to early Chicano rock'n'roll. Rock critic Lester Bangs once called Valens's "La Bamba" the first punk record, and he also pointed to the similarity between the Ramones' "Blitzkrieg Bop" and Valens's "Come On, Let's Go."[46] But even more than its musical influences from Chicano rock, punk music projected a disdain for mainstream society that young Chicanos found useful as a vehicle for airing their own grievances. The power of mass media and the culture industry made British punk rock more visible and more accessible to the general public in Los Angeles than Chicano rock'n'roll. By appropriating punk, young Chicanos could gain visibility for their own views by emphasizing their families of resemblance to the alienations aired by punk. As Ruben Guevara, a veteran Chicano musician, explained to a reporter in 1980:

> Most of these kids playing locally aren't punks. That's a joke. If you want to talk about punks, you've got to talk about East L.A. Because the real, true punks . . . the real outcasts, the people with something to bitch about aren't middle-class white kids. They're the *cholos* man. You want to talk about injustice? Hey, it's been going on here for the last 50 years – not in Hollywood. And if rock'n'roll is supposed to be the real social reflector then I'm putting the mirror right here in East L.A.[47]

The appropriation of punk music by young Chicanos as a means of making visible aspects of their lives and culture that would otherwise be ignored reveals much about what it means to be Mexican American in Los Angeles. In a city with more than three million Spanish-speaking residents, the Chicano presence has been consistently obscured, stereotyped, and marginalized by journalists, the entertainment industry, and political leaders. As exploited workers, as second-class citizens, and as artists and intellectuals with few commercial outlets for their work, Mexican Americans in Los Angeles have struggled to define themselves and their interests against great odds.

The rich cultural life of the *barrio* has been virtually invisible to the rest of Los Angeles, even when it has exerted enormous influence on important aspects of "mainstream" Anglo-American culture. Comedian, film actor, and director Cheech Marin has argued that all of the subcultural practices celebrated within James Dean's *Rebel without a Cause* originated in Chicano communities, even though that film depicted a Los Angeles with no Mexicans in it. Los Angeles jazz, rhythm and blues, and rock music owes extensive unacknowledged debts to Chicano artists including Gil Bernal, Bobby Rey, Chico Sesma, the Don Tosti band, Lalo Guerrero, and Sonny Chavez as well as to all the *cholos*, car customizers, and dancers whose dress, dance, speech, and style provided much of the core vocabulary of 1950s rock'n'roll.[48]

For more than two centuries, the continuing migrations that have made Chicanos both the oldest and newest residents of Los Angeles have generated an extraordinarily rich body of cultural expression in the visual arts, music, theater, and literature. Many of them have displayed what Gloria Anzaldua describes as a *mestizaje* sensibility – a delight in difference and an ability to accommodate many different identities at the same time.[49] Anzaldua views tensions in Chicano life between English and Spanish, between being Mexican and being American or between being Chicano and being Indian as productive forces generating a richer cultural vision. By acknowledging Chicano identity as a crossroads of many different identities, she celebrates its dynamic, flexible, and composite qualities.

Chicano punk rock emerged from the *mestizaje* consciousness in its community of origin. During most of the 1970s, Willie Herron thought of himself primarily as a visual artist – he produced some of East Los Angeles's most aesthetically sophisticated and most politically aware murals in the early 1970s. But by the end of that decade he found himself working as a musician, drawing upon his experiences playing in bands oriented toward playing British rock'n'roll. With mischievous inter-lingual provocation, Herron's band named itself "Los Illegals" – a name designed to challenge Anglo anti-immigrant and anti-Mexican sentiments by invoking the term "illegals" as an emblem of pride.

While grounded in distinctly Chicano realities, Los Illegals also aimed their messages at a punk rock audience that included Anglos and Blacks and Asians as well as Chicanos. In their song "We Don't Need a Tan (We're Already Copper)" Los Illegals lampooned all of southern California's bourgeois culture, not just its racism against Mexican Americans. In "The Mall" they surveyed the city of Los Angeles and declared, "I hate the mall, I hate the(m)all." Los Illegals sang in English and in Spanish, drawing parallels between the historical oppression of Mexican Americans and the expressions of alienation by punk rockers. They sought allies among the disaffected outside their own community, and attempted to create a community within the discursive space of popular music that did not exist anywhere else in Los Angeles.

Group member Jesse Velo once described Los Illegals as what would happen if Tito Puente took LSD and hung out with the Clash.[50] But he was not saying that their identity made them any less Chicano – quite the contrary. "Santana isn't the only thing you hear in the *barrio*, you know," Velo argued. "You can be walking down the street at night and hear the Buzzcocks through an open window too, or Kraftwerk."[51] Los Illegals mixed these diverse influences as a way of expressing their identity rather than as a means of distancing themselves from it. As Willie Herron told a Texas newspaper reporter, ". . . what we're trying to do is feel for ourselves and bolster the bilingualness of our lifestyle. It all goes back to the way we were brought up . . . our culture. Our parents spoke sentences in both English and Spanish. It's important to hold on to that."[52]

Herron remembers being attracted to rhythm and blues because of the music of James Brown, whose uncanny ability to scream on key reminded Herron of Mexican music. He recalls,

> For me, [it] was James Brown. I mean, he, to me had the urgency, he had the passion . . . I heard just in his voice. I mean, and the *gritos*, I mean I really related to that, that *grito* he had . . . he just made it; I mean, personally, that's how I really started and got into the R&B was when I was first exposed or around the James Brown sound.[53]

Jesse Velo also cherishes the mixed influences in his youth, " 'Las Mananitas' on one side, and who knows what on the other side, you know – 'Peppermint Twist.' " He described the band's music as "nothing that was totally, completely popular within the community, but it was for, by, and about the people in our community."[54]

For Therese Covarrubias of the Chicano punk band the Brat, Chicano identity contained many conflicts. The Brat's song lyrics denouncing U.S. intervention in Central America on the one hand, and ridiculing the social pressures in a Catholic high school on the other hand, certainly seemed grounded in an East L.A. sensibility. In "The Wolf," Covarrubias sang about "a star-spangled wolf " that "says that this land was made for all." In a verse that seems securely rooted in experiences with racial discrimination, her lyrics challenged listeners with "you say this democracy, believes in our equality, you lie!"[55] Yet, Covarrubias grew up speaking English at home, learning Spanish only in her high school language classes. Her father liked listening to the big-band sounds of the Benny Goodman orchestra, while her older brothers and sisters introduced her to Bob Dylan, the Rolling Stones, and the Who. Covarrubias listed British pop and rock performers David Bowie and Bryan Ferry as her own favorites; nowhere in her genealogy of musical influences did she recall any Chicano artists.[56] In fact, she told an interviewer that the major significance to her of having the Brat described as a Chicano band, was that it got their name in the paper. "I think the whole idea of an East L.A. renaissance, whatever, is something that a newspaper made up," she explained.

> There's all these bands out there, by coincidence, coming out of the same area. If anything, I find that a lot of bands want to jump off that bandwagon, because they think that it's going to pigeonhole them in some way, and it kind of does sometimes . . . because we can start this whole little network here, like everyone knows we put out these records together. But you're kind of separating yourself from a whole other thing that's happening. And really, if you want to get your music out there, you want to get the word out, whatever you're writing about or singing about, you've got to get on the radio. You've got to get mainstream radio airplay.[57]

In her denial of Chicano roots and her zeal to become successful on mainstream radio, Covarrubias might seem representative of a generation for whom ethnicity no longer matters. It appears as if her identity as a consumer of British popular culture has a more powerful hold on her than her experiences as a Chicana. Yet, if one reads her words carefully, it seems clear that she had no interest in being *marketed* as part of a Chicano band, because that might close off opportunities to be heard on mainstream radio. Her identity remains quite well grounded in her ethnic group, but in its complexities and contradictions as well as in its enduring identities and traditions. To be Mexican-American in Los Angeles also involves listening to popular music from all over the world, music by David Bowie, Bryan Ferry, the Ramones, and the Sex Pistols as well as Lydia Mendoza, Los Lobos, and Poncho Sanchez.

Covarrubias remains active in music as a member of Goddess 13, a group that she formed along with another alumna of Chicano punk – Alicia Armendariz, who played with the Bags. They play an eclectic blend of musical styles, mixing elements of folk, rock, country, and jazz in powerful songs built around memorable melodies and intricate vocal harmonies. Their sophisticated English and Spanish lyrics touch on an extraordinary range of stories and issues, ranging from romantic love to domestic violence, from multi-culturalism to misogyny. Goddess 13 grew out of Las Tres, a band that Covarrubias and Armendariz formed after a chance meeting motivated them to get together with Angela Vogel (who had been in the Chicano punk band, the Odd

Squad) to play some music. "We took out guitars and started singing," Armendariz remembers, "and one person started singing lead and then someone else dropped in a harmony, and then someone else did the third, and it just felt real natural."[58]

In addition to their compatibility as musicians, Covarrubias and Armendariz found that they enjoyed the opportunity to work with other women. "Women are more cooperative, maybe we're just raised that way," Armendariz claims. "I feel there's a lot more cooperation than there's been in other bands I've been in. And there's lots of encouragement. Even if you come in with a song that's not quite finished, we always take the time to nurture the song."[59] The gender consciousness that underlies their musical collaboration also helps explain the emphasis in the lyrics of Las Tres and now Goddess 13 on women's experiences and perspectives. "'I don't think when we started off doing Las Tres that we really thought, 'Let's write about women's issues.' It just sort of evolved. We've all noticed that women in the audience just seem to pick up on that.'"[60] Armendariz adds,

> When you're trying to write from your personal experiences, the fact that you grow up in a misogynist, racist society – it's just bound to pop up. And when you start writing about it and people react to it, then you realize it's something that has to be said – and it inspires you to focus on it.[61]

Listeners who remember Covarrubias and Armendariz from the Brat and the Bags are sometimes surprised to realize that they are feminist folk-rock-jazz singers. But they insist that they carry the legacy of Chicano punk with them in important ways. For them, punk elevated enthusiasm over artistry, breaking down barriers between artists and audiences by encouraging an aesthetic of amateurism and emotion above all. Fiercely democratic, punk culture asserted that everyone was an artist. "I feel like the essence of what we're doing now still has a punk attitude," confides Covarrubias.

> We're not exceptional guitar players, but we're still playing guitars. I think the whole thing with punk back then was you don't have to be a maestro, you don't have to be an excellent player or singer. You just get up there and you do it, and that truth and that heart is what gets your point across.[62]

Armendariz and Covarrubias proudly present themselves as post-punk feminists, but they remain rooted in their ethnic identity as well. "Everything I write has some Chicano consciousness because that's what I am," insisted Covarrubias to an interviewer in 1983, but she complains about people's expectations that "you have to represent your ethnic background, and sometimes I think you don't really have to."[63] Armendariz adds, "You do [represent your ethnic group], but you represent it in your own way. You don't have to represent it the way they want you to represent it."[64]

In their insistence on being Chicanas in their own way, Armendariz and Covarrubias grapple with the historical invisibility of their community in the mass media as well as with their determination to avoid being reduced to their race to the point of erasing their experiences as women, as workers, and as citizens. Chicano artists have long grappled with these problems, and they have often found solutions by taking on unexpected identities in order to make visible the hybridity and heterogeneity of their own community.[65] An East Los Angeles Chicano Band, Los Lobos, follows a similar pattern, mixing surrealism, jazz, and Japanese instruments with rock'n'roll on their album *Kiko* – not as a way of denying their Mexican heritage, but rather as a way of claiming citizenship in a larger artistic and political world as *part* of the Chicano experience.[66] Like all strategic anti-essentialists, they temporarily become who they are not to affirm all the more powerfully who they are so they can then move on to become something new. They pay a price for their disguises, but they also use them to make advances blocked by other means. As Chicano rapper Kid Frost (Arturo Molina) explains in relation to his own use of African-American forms to dramatize Mexican-American realities, ". . . if people don't see us – what we're about and where we came from – then nothing will be attributed to the Aztec people."[67]

NOTES

1. Generally tribes march only on St. Joseph's Day and Mardi Gras Day, but in recent years they have been willing to march on other days for neighborhood celebrations or municipal events like the Jazz and Heritage Festival.

2. See David Draper, "The Mardi Gras Indians: The Ethnology of Black Associations in New Orleans," Ph.D. Dissertation, Tulane University, LA 1973; Jason Berry, Jonathan Foose, and Tad Jones, *Up from the Cradle of Jazz* (Athens: University of Georgia Press, 1986); George Lipsitz, *Time Passages: Collective Memory and American Popular Culture* (Minneapolis: University of Minnesota Press, 1990); Joan Martin, "Rara Reborn," unpublished paper delivered at the Social Science History Association meetings, 1991.

3. Maurice M. Martinez and James E. Hinton, *The Black Indians of New Orleans* and Les Blank, *Always for Pleasure* (Flower Films, 1978).

4. David Draper, "The Mardi Gras Indians"; Finn Wilhelmsen, "Creativity in the Songs of the Mardi Gras Indians of New Orleans, Louisiana," *Louisiana Folklore Miscellany* vol. 3, 1973.

5. Jeff Hannusch, *I Hear You Knockin'* (Ville Plat LA: Swallow Publications, 1985); Jason Berry, Jonathan Foose, and Tad Jones, *Up from the Cradle of Jazz*; Helen Joy Mayhew, "New Orleans Black Musical Culture: Tradition and the Individual Talent," (M.A. Thesis, University of Exeter, U.K., 1986).

6. George Lipsitz, "Mardi Gras Indians: Carnival and Counter-Narrative in Black New Orleans," *Cultural Critique* no. 10 (1988); Joan M. Martin, "Rara Reborn: The Black Indians of Mardi Gras," unpublished paper (1990); Rosita Sands, "Carnival Celebrations in Africa and the New World: Junkanoo and the Black Indians of Mardi Gras," *Black Music Research Journal* vol.11 no.1 (1991).

7. Huey L. Perry and Alfred Stokes, "Politics and Power in the Sunbelt: Mayor Morial of New Orleans," in Michael B. Preston, Lanneal J. Henderson, Jr., and Paul L. Puryear, eds, *The New Black Politics: The Search for Political Power* (New York: Oxford University Press, 1987); and Allen Katz, "Bleak Picture," *New Orleans Times-Picayune*, May 4, 1986, 27.

8. Joan M. Martin, "Rara Reborn," 19.

9. Jerome Smith interview with Tom Dent, September 23, 1983, quoted in Kim Lacy Rogers, *Righteous Lives* (New York: New York University Press, 1993), 111–12.

10. Jerome Smith interview with Tom Dent. See also Jerome Smith interview with Kim Lacy Rogers, July 8, 1988, ibid.

11. Caroline Senter, "Beware of Premature Autopsies," (M.A. Thesis, University of California, San Diego, 1991), 6.

12. Caroline Senter, "Beware of Premature Autopsies," 37.

13. Kalamu ya Salaam, "Notes from a Banana Republic," *Dialogue* (1986), quoted in Caroline Senter, "Beware of Premature Autopsies."

14. Stephen Holden, "The Pop Life," *New York Times*, February 15, 1989, C18.

15. Neville Brothers, *Yellow Moon*, compact disc 5240, A&M Records, 1989.

16. No author, "St. Joseph's Day in the Big Easy," *New Orleans* (March) 1986, 41.

17. Philip Sweeney, *The Virgin Directory of World Music* (New York: Henry Holt, 1991), 215; Neville Brothers, *Family Groove*, compact disc 75021 5384 2, A&M Records, 1992.

18. Stephen Holden, "The Pop Life," C18.

19. Sevilla Finley, "Neville Brothers Put Musical Touch to Civil Rights Fight," *New Orleans Times-Picayune*, February 19, 1989, F2.

20. See Isabelle Leymaire, "Salsa and Latin Jazz," in Billy Bergman, ed., *Hot Sauces: Latin and Caribbean Pop* (New York: Quill, 1985), 105; Donald Clarke, ed., *The Penguin Encyclopedia of Popular Music* (London: Penguin Books, 1989), 136, 306.

21. Donald Clarke, ed. *The Penguin Encyclopedia of Popular Music*, 757; Various Artists, *The Latin Vogue*, compact disc Charly 229; Various Artists, *We Got Latin Soul*, compact disc Charly 91; El Gran Combo, *El Gran Boogaloo*, Blues Interactions PCD-2366.

22. Juan Flores, "Que Assimilated, Brother, Yo Soy Asimilao: The Structure of Puerto Rican Identity in the U.S.," *Journal of Ethnic Studies* vol.13 no.3, 10. Of course, this does not mean that anti-Black racism is

non-existent among Puerto Ricans, only that powerful forces exist encouraging identification with African Americans.

23.   Sandra Maria Esteves, "Sistas," *Bluestown Mockingbird Mambo* (Houston TX: Arte Publico, 1990), 19.

24.   Jorge Duany, "Popular Music in Puerto Rico: Toward an Anthropology of *Salsa*," *Revista de Musica Latino Americana* vol.5 no.2 (Fall/Winter) 1985, 195.

25.   Roy Rosenzweig and Elizabeth Blackmar, *The People and the Park* (Ithaca NY: Cornell University Press, 1992), 470.

26.   Douglas S. Massey and Brooks Bitterman, "Explaining the Paradox of Puerto Rican Segregation," *Social Forces* vol.64 no.2 (December) 1985, 306.

27.   See the forthcoming work by Marta Sanchez for a detailed analysis of this inter-cultural communication between Blacks and Puerto Ricans.

28.   Quoted in Felix Padilla, "Salsa: Puerto Rican and Latino Music," *Journal of Popular Culture* vol.24 no.1 (Summer) 1990, 87–104.

29.   Felix Cortes, Angel Falcon, and Juan Flores, "The Cultural Expression of Puerto Ricans in New York: A Theoretical Perspective and Critical Review," *Latin American Perspectives* vol.3 no.3 (Summer) 1976, 117.

30.   Quoted from Dizzy Gillespie, *To Be or Not . . . to Bop* (Garden City, Long Island: Doubleday, 1979) by Vernon W. Boggs in "Founding Fathers and Changes in Cuban Music Called Salsa," in Vernon W. Boggs, ed., *Salsiology: Afro-Cuban Music and the Evolution of Salsa in New York City* (New York: Excelsior Music Publishing, 1992), 98.

31.   Isabelle Leymaire, "Salsa and Latin Jazz," 98.

32.   Vernon W. Boggs, "Founding Fathers and Changes in Cuban Music Called Salsa," 99–100.

33.   Vernon Boggs, "Johnny Otis: R&B/Mambo Pioneer," *Latin Beat Magazine* vol.3 no.9 (November) 1993, 30, 31.

34.   John Storm Roberts, *The Latin Tinge* (New York: Oxford, 1979), 137.

35.   Isabelle Leymaire, "Salsa and Latin Jazz," 102.

36.   Brooke Sheffield Comer, "Ray Barretto's Latin Jazz," *Modern Percussionist* vol.1 no.3 (June–August) 1985, 23.

37.   Brooke Sheffield Comer, "Ray Barretto's Latin Jazz," 23.

38.   Donald Clarke, ed., *The Penguin Encyclopedia of Popular Music*, 73–74.

39.   John Storm Roberts, "Salsa's Prodigal Sun: Eddie Palmieri," *Downbeat* vol.43 no.8 (April 22, 1976), 21. Isabelle Lemaire, "Salsa and Latin Jazz," 105.

40.   Donald Clarke, ed., *The Penguin Encyclopedia of Popular Music*, 81, 514; Juan Flores, " 'It's a Street Thing!' An Interview with Charlie Chase," *Callalloo* vol.15 no.4 (1992), 999–1000. In this interview, Chase reveals that his real name is Mandes, and that his ancestors were French and Jewish.

41.   Colin Escott, liner notes for *The Drifters 1959–1965* compact disc, Atlantic Records 81931-2.

42. Colin Escott, liner notes for *The Drifters 1959–1965*.

43. Peter Manuel, "Latin Music in the United States: Salsa and the Mass Media," *Journal of Communication* vol.41 no.1 (Winter) 1991, 104–16.

44. Joanne Silver, "9 Artists Explore Their Own Puerto Rico," *Boston Sunday Herald*, May 19, 1991, 51.

45. Peter Manuel, "Latin Music in the United States: Salsa and the Mass Media," 108, 114–16.

46. George Lipsitz, *Time Passages*, 133–60.

47. *Los Angeles Times* October 12, 1980, calendar section, 7.

48. David Reyes and Tom Waldman, "That Barrio Sound," *Pulse* (June) 1992, 49–50.

49. Gloria Anzaldua, *Borderlands/La Frontera* (San Francisco: Spinster: Aunt Lutte Press, 1988).

50. Steven Loza, *Barrio Rhythm: Mexican American Music in Los Angeles* (Urbana and Chicago: University of Illinois Press, 1993), 221. Puente is the great Puerto Rican "salsa" musician and the Clash were among the best and the most political British "new wave" and punk bands of the 1970s.

51. John Mendelssohn, "Los Illegals Ain't Smiling," *Record* (August, 1983). Santana was the Afro-Cuban-styled band fronted by the Mexican-born San Francisco blues-oriented guitarist and singer Carlos Santana. The Buzzcocks were a British new wave/punk band formed in 1975, while Kraftwerk was a techno-art-rock band from Dusseldorf, Germany.

52. Steve Harmon, "Getting Message Out Important for Illegals," *Laredo Morning Times*, July 29, 1983, 2B.

53. Steven Loza, *Barrio Rhythm*, 269.

54. Steven Loza, *Barrio Rhythm*, 217.

55. Steven Loza, *Barrio Rhythm*, 191.

56. Steven Loza, *Barrio Rhythm*, 186–7.

57. Steven Loza, *Barrio Rhythm*, 188–9.

58. Interview with Alicia Armendariz, August 12, 1993, Los Angeles, California.

59. Interview with Alicia Armendariz.

60. Interview with Therese Covarrubias, August 12, 1993, Los Angeles, California.

61. Interview with Alicia Armendariz.

62. Interview with Therese Covarrubias.

63. Dave Zimmer, "East L.A. Bands," *Bam* (July) 1983, 24; Interview with Theresa Covarrubias.

64. Interview with Alicia Armendariz.

65. I am indebted to the excellent scholarship by Lisa Lowe on changes in Asian-American identities for the very useful concepts of hybridity, heterogeneity, and multiplicity.

66. Elena Oumano, "The Making of a Great American Band," *San Francisco Examiner* (Sunday Magazine), October 25, 1992, 12–13.

67. Lorraine Ali, "Latin Class: Kid Frost and the Chicano Rap School," *Option* no.53 (November–December) 1993, 68.

5

London Calling: Pop Reggae and the Atlantic World

MUSICAL YOUTH

During the winter months of 1982–3, eleven-year-old Kelvin Grant attracted the attention of television viewers throughout the world. Staring directly into the camera, the Black Jamaican youth raised in England announced that "this generation rules the nation" to begin the energetic music video version of the song "Pass the Dutchie" by Grant's reggae band, Musical Youth. The engaging singing and dancing by Grant and the other four teenagers in Musical Youth helped "Pass the Dutchie" sell more than two million copies worldwide within two weeks of its release, and their video brought reggae music to new audiences. Industry insiders credited the "freshness of the video" for the song's surprising commercial success, noting that it became one of the rare videos by Black musicians to secure regular rotation on U.S. cable television's MTV network.[1] The president of MCA Records International Division told a trade journal that his company's marketing strategy for "Pass the Dutchie" focused on aggressive promotion of the video on local and national television in the U.S.A., and most reviews of Musical Youth's recorded and live performances made reference to the popularity of their memorable video.[2]

As one of the first hit songs whose popularity in the U.S. market rested on the appeal of its music video, "Pass the Dutchie" called attention to the strengths and weaknesses of the emergent video medium. On the one hand, their video enabled Musical Youth to achieve a degree of commercial success in North America that eluded previous reggae musicians. In this respect, music video enabled a historically grounded oppositional subculture to reach a mass audience in new and effective ways. On the other hand, the content of the video seemed to direct attention away from the historically and socially grounded traditions of reggae, substituting instead a narrative story line shaped to the contours of conventional mass-media messages. In that respect, music video smoothed off the rough edges of an oppositional subculture, delivering it to a mass audience only by bending its discourse toward the pre-existing expectations of viewers and listeners. Thus the music video of "Pass the Dutchie" illumines both positive and negative characteristics of the video medium, and it provides an appropriate focus for an examination of the generation and circulation of cultural messages through the machinery of today's electronic commercial mass media.

COMMERCIAL SUCCESS AND CULTURAL QUESTIONS

Despite the genre's commercial viability in the Caribbean, Europe, and Africa, relatively few reggae songs have reached the U.S. Top Forty best-selling singles charts. Yet if

"Pass the Dutchie" was one of the most successful reggae songs of all time in the U.S. market, it was also one of the tamest – a quality that disturbed many American critics. A *Los Angeles Times* reviewer categorized Musical Youth's music as "prepubescent pop" suggesting that "Reggae purists might be pulling out their dreadlocks over the fact that these kids – ages 11 to 16 – are now taking the Jamaican pop sound into areas of the U.S. charts that major figures like Bob Marley and Toots and the Maytals have yet to enter."[3] A *Rolling Stone* reviewer wondered if "Pass the Dutchie" represented a new genre – "reggae bubblegum," and claimed that "The five Musical Youth have reduced reggae's musical vocabulary to a dependable bag of licks, removing many of the stylisms that prevent the music from being accessible to a mass audience."[4] In a similar vein, the popular-music critic for *High Fidelity* contended that Musical Youth had succeeded only by purging from their act "whatever people find threatening about reggae – the dreadlocks, the simmering radical anger and religious imagery, the reference to ganja . . . the dub techniques that stretch songs out hypnotically."[5] The most serious critical complaints about the song arose from the ways that Musical Youth changed lyrics to make their record acceptable to a mass (and presumably white) audience, and from the way that the music video superimposed a new visual narrative on the song, altering its original message and meaning.

Musical Youth took "Pass the Dutchie" from the reggae group the Mighty Diamonds, who had used the melody of an older song, "Full Up," as the basis for their hit record "Pass the Kouchie." In their version, the Mighty Diamonds celebrate the ritual passing of a kouchie, a pipe used for smoking marijuana by the Rastafarian cult in Jamaica. Smoking ganja (marijuana) has religious significance for the Rastafarians because the ritual employs the natural herbs made by Jah (God) to help blot out the oppressions of colonialism and poverty. "Pass the Kouchie" contains lyrics asking "How does it feel when you've got no food?" and the answer comes in the sound of a smoker inhaling on a kouchie to the rhythms and chord progressions of the song.[6] Connected to an illegal act (drug use) by an oppositional subculture (Rastafarianism), and rooted in a rejection of colonialism and racism, "Pass the Kouchie" remains embedded in "the fabric of tradition," and remains tied to "the location of its original use value" as an icon of resistance for Jamaican black nationalists.[7] In their song, Musical Youth substitute a "dutchie" (a pot used for cooking) for the Mighty Diamonds' kouchie. With this change, the refrain's question "How does it feel when you've got no food?" becomes one-dimensional and literal, while the song's answer now presents eating rather than rebellion as the proper response to deprivation.

In Musical Youth's video, Rastafarian themes fade far into the background, and a seemingly contextless universal playfulness takes its place. We see Musical Youth setting up their guitars and drums to play music in a park, where they are confronted by a truant officer determined to send them back to school. While trying to apprehend them, the officer trips over their amplifiers and guitar cords. Consequently, he brings them to court on charges of assaulting him. Led by Kelvin Grant, the Youth "defend" themselves by singing and dancing in the courtroom. A delighted judge and jury feel the spirit of their music and set them free – to the consternation of the defeated truant officer.

On the surface the compromises incorporated into "Pass the Dutchie" seem to reveal the corruption of organic folk music by the apparatuses of commercial popular culture. A song with origins in a historically specific subculture becomes "mainstreamed" by muting the oppositional character of its lyrics, and by adding a visual narrative that converts profoundly social alienations into slapstick comedy.[8] By wrenching reggae music out of its anti-colonial and anti-racist contexts, "Pass the Dutchie" appears to trivialize the rich textures of Jamaican resistance into little more than eccentric local color, into a novelty offering only diversion and escape for an uncomprehending mass audience. By substituting innocent youthful rebellion for Rastafarianism, by making the "enemy" an individual state functionary rather than systemic oppression, and by seeking ideological and narrative closure through the approval of the judge and jury, the "Pass the Dutchie" video transposes divisive issues of class and race into a universally accessible scenario about a harmless form of rebellion. It forges a false unity between the reggae subculture that spawned it and the mass audience receiving it, masking the real exercises of power and authority against aggrieved populations.

Yet underneath the very real cooptation and misappropriation basic to "Pass the Dutchie" lay a sedimented consistency. Even while being mainstreamed for commercial success, the content of Musical Youth's song retained overt and covert references to Rastafarianism, disseminating them to a wider audience than ever before. Both the revised lyrics and the video contained retentions of Rastafarian imagery as well as signs and symbols from other oppositional cultures. The anti-authoritarian sentiments and class resentments of "Pass the Dutchie" lay beneath the surface, but they nonetheless spoke directly to the circumstances of audiences facing the severe economic crisis that coincided with the song's popularity. Far from representing the elimination of oppositional content from popular culture, the success of "Pass the Dutchie" displays the creative plurality, plasticity, and persistence of oppositional traditions and symbols.

Commercial pressures and political self-censorship altered the content of "Pass the Dutchie," but the ingenuity of the Musical Youth and the resiliency of the culture they drew upon combined to leave significant historical, semiotic, and social oppositional content within their hit song. Specifically, it retained elements of the collective history of the Rastafarian movement, icons and images encoding oppositional meanings within the song, and a message of immediate relevance to its American audience.

RASTAFARIAN HISTORY AND "PASS THE DUTCHIE"

In fairness, Musical Youth can not be accused of diluting the organic purity of folk music and folk religion, because no such purity ever existed. The imperatives of capital that transform religious and cultural traditions into commodities like phonograph records created the very fissures and dislocations that brought Rastafarianism into existence in the first place. Musical Youth stand on traditional ground when they adapt an old song to new realities. Indeed, the camouflaging of subversive messages within appealing and seemingly harmless images constitutes an essential part of the Rastafarian heritage. Born out of the dislocations of international capitalism and nurtured in nations around the globe, Rastafarianism always involved complicated negotiations among diverse cultural symbols. Thus, the adaptation to commercial pressures fashioned by Musical Youth in England in 1982 marks them more as legitimate heirs to the reggae/Rastafarian tradition than as apostates from it.

Although a long tradition of "Ethiopianism" influenced Jamaican religion and Black nationalism, the core doctrines of Rastafarianism emerged from the cultural creations of Jamaicans dispersed around the globe. Work in the mines of South Africa, on the construction and maintenance of the Panama Canal, and in the factories of the United States drew Jamaican laborers overseas in the first part of the twentieth century. Under these circumstances, the oppressions of race and nation took on new meaning, while biblical accounts of exile and return provided powerful metaphors for describing current conditions. The precursors of Rastafarianism emerged among these exiled Jamaicans in dialogue with the politics and cultures of other countries. David Athlyi Rogers enunciated the core doctrines of Rastafarianism in *The Holy Piby*, sometimes referred to as "The Black Man's Bible," which he wrote and published in Newark, New Jersey in 1924. Rogers's followers included Jamaicans working in the factories of northern New Jersey, but his Afro-Athlican Constructive Gaathly Church had its headquarters in Kimberley, South Africa. Grace Jenkins Garrison and Reverend

Charles F. Goodbridge discovered *The Holy Piby* among Jamaican workers in Colon, Panama, and upon their return to Jamaica founded the "Hamatic Church," – the Jamaican branch of Rogers's Afro-Athlican Constructive Gaathly. *The Holy Piby* declared Marcus Garvey an apostle of a new religion that looked to the crowning of a Black King in Africa and an eventual return home to that continent for oppressed Jamaicans.[9]

In the 1930s, Jamaican Ethiopianist sects began to stress their claims of divinity for the Ethiopian Emperor Haile Selassie, whom they called Ras Tafari. Leonard Percival Howell played an important role in popularizing the idea of Selassie's divinity and Garvey's status as his prophet during that decade. Howell had worked as a porter and construction worker in New York in the years immediately after World War I, where he dabbled in radical politics and mystical faith healing. Howell corresponded with the West Indian George Padmore, at one time a leading intellectual in the Communist Party (U.S.A.), and sought (without success) Marcus Garvey's approval for his Black nationalist activities.[10] Other Jamaicans with histories of religious and political activism overseas also spread the word about Ras Tafari, including David and Annie Harvey who had lived in Costa Rica, Panama, the U.S.A., and Ethiopia before establishing a religious sect, "The Israelites," in Jamaica in 1930. These activists drew upon biblical psalms as justification for prophecies of divine punishment against evil, which they envisioned coming in the form of Ras Tafari's reign which would "scorn" the nation. Coupled with indigenous folk traditions and elements of Hindu and East Indian mysticism, the Rastafarian cults provided important ideological legitimation for the 1938 labor uprisings in Jamaica as well as for rural millenial movements.[11]

Initially, the Rastafarians had no distinctive music of their own, but they gradually absorbed a variety of folk music styles from other cults. In the slums of Jamaican cities, Rastafarians encountered members of the Burru cult who celebrated the return to their community of discharged prisoners with a ceremonial dance accompanied by three drums.[12] The bass, funde, and repeater drums of Burru music became the basis for subsequent Rastafarian musics, including reggae. Important Rasta musicians like Count Ossie of St. Thomas Parish also drew upon the drumming styles of the Kumina cult. But all available musics, both religious and popular, found their way into Rastafarian celebrations. Instruments ranged from native thumb pianos to imported trumpets and saxophones played by jazz musicians, while popular melodies and revival-meeting-style hand-clapping provided determinate features for the music. Just as their religion blended African and Christian images and beliefs, just as their politics blended class, racial, and national themes, Rastafarians' music drew upon an eclectic mixture of styles and forms.[13]

Jamaican popular music borrowed freely from the diverse repertoires of Rastafarian musicians who provided the basic components for "ska," "rock steady," and reggae musics. Reggae guitar patterns evolved out of Burru funde styles, while the reggae bass line emanated from the Burru bass and repeater drums.[14] But reggae artists also borrowed from Anglo-American popular music, especially from the instrumentation and arrangements popularized by artists from Detroit's Motown label in the 1960s. Fusing the folk musics of Jamaica with the international commercial musics they heard on the radio (and which they encountered on their travels to England and the U.S.A. as workers and as musicians), reggae artists created in the field of music the same kind of international/national fusion that Rastafarians forged in the realms of religion and politics. Although not all reggae artists considered themselves Rastafarians, nearly all employed some Rasta forms and ideas in creating their multi-cultural fusions. Born in Jamaica, attuned to the popular cultures of England and North America, and ideologically focused on Africa for inspiration and identity, reggae musicians quickly grasped the possibilities for cultural mixing latent in all commercial popular culture. At the same time, their fusions always remained rooted in specific historical and social concerns. They wished to participate in the making of a global popular culture by bringing the particular traits and tendencies of their own culture in dialogue with those from other nations. Economic and cultural imperialism extended the reach of global media monopolies into Jamaican folk culture, but the same conduit that brought North American and British popular styles into Jamaican music, also carried the moral concerns, self-respect, and revolutionary nationalism of Rastafarians in Jamaica out to the rest of the world.

In both form and content, Musical Youth carried on the eclectic traditions of the reggae past in their approach to "Pass the Dutchie." Their adaptation of a previous hit record reflects a folk consciousness that privileges clever modification of collective forms over the invention of "new" and "original" ones. In the reggae tradition, "toasters" prove their mettle by creating "version" or "dub" renditions of existing songs. On the streets, this can take the form of turntable and sound system operators creating new music by distorting or combining existing records recorded by others. In the recording studios, it takes the form of "version" adaptations of already familiar songs like "Pass the Kouchie." Musical Youth's reformulation of that song by the Mighty Diamonds was less a watering down of a traditional song than an improvisation on it – an ingenious application of a work written under one set of circumstances to a similar, but not identical set of circumstances. The lyrical changes made by Musical Youth in actuality extended rather than limited the radical social content of the Mighty Diamonds' record by encoding multiple meanings in the new version.

Critics derided Musical Youth for changing "Pass the Kouchie" to "Pass the Dutchie," but their true relationship to the song is quite complicated. "Pass the Kouchie" did not originate with the Mighty Diamonds, but rather with the 1968 instrumental by Sound Dimension titled "Full Up," written by Jamaican musician Leroy Sibbles (later with the Heptones). As was their custom, Fitzroy Simpson and L. Ferguson of the Mighty Diamonds used "Full Up" as a base "riddim" or instrumental track for lyrics which became "Pass the Kouchie." Musical Youth learned the song from reggae artist Jackie Mittoo, the keyboardist for Sound Dimension, whom they incorrectly credited with authorship of the original tune when they changed the lyrics to "Pass the Dutchie." Musical Youth's Michael Grant told *Billboard* that "Jackie Mittoo did the original version, so the song has been passed around a bit, you see."[15]

Although misidentifying the song's exact lineage, Grant's comment shows that Musical Youth recognized the song as part of a collective tradition. They did not break with that tradition in supplying an old song with new effects or lyrics – Mittoo, Ferguson, and Simpson had already borrowed Sibbles's melody toward that end. But the nature of Musical Youth's changes, especially their apparent sanitizing of the lyrics did seem like a break with the past to some critics, a difference in kind not just in degree.

By substituting "dutchie" for "kouchie" Musical Youth's lyrics talked about eating rather than marijuana smoking. Indeed, censorship influenced this change – producer Peter Collins demanded new lyrics in order to make the adolescent group's record more marketable. By excising references to Rastafarianism, and by stressing youthful innocence in the video, the record company encouraged Musical Youth to hide their true identity and seek a more neutral public image in order to avoid offending potential customers. But such pressures are routine in commercialized mass media, and aggrieved populations often find their artists forced to disguise their identity in order to please those in charge of marketing mass culture. Musical Youth drew upon sedimented currents of opposition within the reggae past to devise a form of camouflage enabling them to satisfy those in power while subtly conveying oppositional messages at the same time. Their new lyrics and video extended some of the original messages of "Pass the Kouchie" even while tampering with its content.

By declaring that "this generation rules the nation – with version," at the beginning of "Pass the Dutchie" Kelvin Grant announces that the song involves "version" – a rendition of an existing song rather than a new composition. But this "version" involves more of a transformation of social consciousness than an obliteration of it. "We write songs about what's happening," boasted fourteen-year-old bass player Patrick Waite as he explained the song to a reporter. Conceding that the group enjoyed the song's rhythm and "happy" sound, Waite nonetheless insisted that "it's also about things today – the words are true."[16] Those words include a "toast" in which Kelvin Grant claims that "music happen to be the food of love," as he promises listeners some "sounds to really make you rub and scrub." Thus music, food, and love become interchangeable. Passing the dutchie involves related acts of pleasure and passion. For audiences familiar with Rastafarian language this connection contains logical and political significance as well. In the Rasta lexicon, "dub" not only means "to mix" in the sense of putting together different sounds and musics into "version," but it also refers to cooking. "Sip" can mean "to eat or drink," but it also connotes drawing on a pipe. Thus the word substitutions that appear to reflect a capitulation to censorship in standard usage, actually undermine censorship in the Rasta vernacular by encoding multiple meanings in the substitute phrases.[17]

The lyrics of "Pass the Dutchie" resonate throughout the song with ambiguous multiple meanings. Passing the dutchie results in music that "make me jump and prance," blending the "dub" practices of cooking with those of music making. Background voices caution "it a gonna burn," although it is not clear whether they mean the music or the food or both. As in "Pass the Kouchie" the narrator encounters a "ring of dreads" (a circle of Rastafarians with their hair matted into dreadlocks) who provide the answer to the question "How does it feel when you've got no food?" The dreadlocks answer "pass the dutchie," – sharing their food and their love, their music and their spirituality. To complete the message, the lyrics celebrate the pervasive presence of this music – "the food of love" – on the radio, on the stereo, and at the disco.

Although listeners equipped with special competence in Rastafarian terminology can easily decode "Pass the Dutchie," the song's complicated subversions of language offer a challenge to those who do not understand its exact meanings. The Rasta argot relies upon a radical undermining of univocal narratives and linear descriptions, replacing them with ambiguous and layered multivocal meanings. As Dick Hebdige notes, Rasta speech succeeds by threatening "to undermine language itself with syncopated creole scansion and an eye for the inexpressible."[18] In his view, this comes from the origins of reggae music in a "culture which had been forced, in its very inception, to cultivate secrecy and to elaborate defenses against the intrusions of the master class."[19] Consequently, part of the meaning of any reggae song lies in creative wordplay designed to both disguise and gradually disclose that meaning, to nurture an oppositional vocabulary incapable of control by outside authorities.

It is not unusual for oppositional subcultures to cultivate artistic ambiguity as a means of resisting unambiguously undesirable power relations. The Armenian painter Arshile Gorky counselled other artists that "what the enemy would destroy, he must first see," adding that "to confuse and paralyze his vision is the role of camouflage."[20] Subsurface Rastafarian elements in "Pass the Dutchie" retain their own kind of camouflage in order to enter mainstream discourse without fully internalizing mainstream values. Whether by replicating in speech the musical practices of "dub" and "version" with their creative adaptations and seemingly inappropriate juxtapositions, or by direct references to "dreadlocks" and "the spirit of Jah," the lyrics of "Pass the Dutchie" set limits on outside appropriation. This is not to assert that every listener receives the intended message of the song. (The final section of this chapter will take on the question of audience response and its complicated ambiguities in greater detail.) But the existence of tropological subversions and multiple meanings in the lyrics of "Pass the Dutchie" reveals a link to historical traditions and a capacity for employing multiple meanings as a form of protective coloration.

Just as Rastafarianism itself represents a religious form of "version," – taking the Judeo-Christian bible and "flinging it back rude,"[21] reggae musicians like Musical Youth play upon commonly accepted pop music forms and idioms in order to subvert them. Musical Youth accepted one form of censorship by allowing direct references to marijuana to be excised from their song, and they adapted their music to standardized pop music conventions. Yet these changes disguised rather than compromised the ethical core of their culture; traditional meanings remained encoded in the song, waiting to be discovered by listeners. In the same fashion, the video reached a mass audience by adding another story line to the song and by transposing Rastafarian resistance into schoolboy slapstick. At the same time, however, subordinated oppositional elements permeated the video as well, providing a visual subtext appropriate to the complexity of the already multi-layered musical messages encoded in the song "Pass the Dutchie."

SEMIOTICS AND "PASS THE DUTCHIE" – THE SPECULAR TEXT

MCA Records' successful strategy of using the video to "break" "Pass the Dutchie" in the U.S. market raised questions among critics about whether audiences responded to the music itself or to the video. Some reviewers saw the group as a television novelty act rather than as a rock'n'roll band, dismissing them as "Reggae Chipmunks" and "Rasta Smurfs."[22] A record store clerk in Chicago complained that "People don't buy that record because they like the music; they buy it because they saw those kids on TV."[23] A pre-teen in Houston disclosed that he bought the record "because I like the way that kid [Kelvin Grant] jumps around."[24] These reactions seem to confirm critical fears that the video of "Pass the Dutchie" decontextualized the song – severing its links to reggae and Rastafarian traditions and foregrounding it as an atomized media artifact. Yet the video emerged from the same forms of negotiation between commercial pressures and cultural traditions that gave determinate shape to the song itself, and a careful examination of the video reveals an abundance of sedimented historical and cultural referents.

Initially Musical Youth and their video director Don Letts collaborated on a video of the song "Youth of Today," that showed them being chased by a policeman. But their record company ordered them to come up with a different video, one with a less insurrectionary theme. In response, they did "Pass the Dutchie," substituting a truant officer for the policeman.[25] Yet both Letts and the band refused suggestions that they totally drain their work of oppositional content. As one of the few commercially successful Black video directors, Letts felt an obligation to inject social commentary into his work, and he proudly wore his hair in Rastafarian dreadlocks to proclaim his anti-establishment views. Letts had been an important figure in the development of punk rock music in England when he worked as a disc jockey in London night clubs in the 1970s, and his skillful work directing a motion picture documentary on punk bands had led him to assignments making videos for rock groups including the Clash and the Pretenders. Years after completing his work with Musical Youth in the 1980s, Letts went on to make videos for the Punjabi "bhangramuffin" rapper Apache Indian in the 1990s. "I'll only work with a band or a song that I like," Letts vowed, "and that means they or the song have to be saying something, doing something honest and with quality."[26] In "Pass the Dutchie" he found a means of fulfilling those commitments.

The video opens with a full-frame shot of Kelvin Grant's face as he announces "This generation rules the nation – with version." The camera pans back as he "toasts" music as the food of love, revealing him to be standing on the banks of the Thames in front of the Parliament buildings in London. Along with the other members of Musical Youth, Grant starts setting up equipment, evidently to play their music for tourists. The opening connection between "this generation" ruling "the nation" and images of the Parliament immediately introduces a provocative tone to the video. It connects music and politics, and underscores the incongruity of five Black teenagers from Birmingham laying claim to ruling the nation. This claim raises the issue of what it means to be Black in Britain and how that identity relates to concepts of the nation at large. Reggae musician and poet Linton Kwesi Johnson has eloquently discussed the core tensions involved in those questions in a description of his own identity, asking

> What does it mean to be black in Britain? It means that you have to wage a tremendous amount of struggle over things that other sections of society take for granted, like housing, education, trade union rights and so on. It means that even though you were born in England, you're forever being referred to as an immigrant. It means that you are at the very bottom of this society, forever trying to break out of the colonial mode.[27]

The oppositions endemic to being Black in the U.K. form the opening visual contrast in the "Pass the Dutchie" video, juxtaposing five Black teenagers to the majestic government buildings behind them. In conjunction with the song's lyrics, the video draws a clear distinction between the state as embodied in Parliament, and the nation as represented by a young generation practicing "version" in the streets.[28] It constitutes the streets as a site of cultural contestation and challenges national iconography with an oppositional prestige from below. The next scene underscores that contrast by cutting to a judge's gavel striking a desk, then panning back to a courtroom in which Musical Youth appear as defendants before a jury – on trial by the state. The first three shots are not really a narrative, rather they introduce questions to be answered by the narrative to follow. What is the connection between Kelvin Grant's claim about ruling the nation, the band setting up their instruments, and the courtroom scene?

As he does throughout the video, Kelvin Grant provides the dramatic action that pushes the story to its next stage. He jumps up in court, singing the first verse – and his action magically transports the camera back to the park where we see close-ups of the band members playing their instruments. Grant is "testifying" in this scene in the literal sense of giving testimony in court, but he is also "testifying" in the way that Black religion and music define the term – speaking from the heart about true feelings. A crowd of appreciative white adults gather around the band, delighted by the singing and dancing of sixteen-year-old lead singer Dennis Seaton and the other youths. At this point, a quick cut introduces the truant officer arriving on the scene, followed by a cut back to the courtroom where we see the judge and jury.

On the witness stand, Kelvin resumes his testimony. Springing out of his chair and singing with enthusiasm, his words seem to push the prosecuting attorney right off the screen. The jury watches sympathetically as the youths "testify" – the camera pans each of them individually as they sing at the defense table. Then quick cuts show us the five defendants and their persecutors – the prosecutor, the judge, and the truant officer. The next scene unravels the narrative. In the park we see the truant officer running toward the band, intent on ending their fun. He trips over their guitar cords and amplifiers, giving himself a black eye. Immediately we see a Black man with dreadlocks on the jury, nodding and smiling knowingly. The earlier reference in the song to "the ring of dreads" takes on new meaning with this shot – in retrospect it reveals a subordinated Rastafarian current in the entire video.

In his role as narrator, guide, and mischievous trickster, Kelvin Grant takes on the role of Anansi the Spider, a stock character in West Indian folklore. Like other tricksters in the Afro-Caribbean tradition, Anansi uses guile and pluck to conquer more powerful opponents.[29] Grant's boast about ruling the nation seems incongruous in the first scene with his tiny frame dwarfed by the government buildings behind him. But his simple and direct affirmations about love and music incite the truant officer to rage. That rage provides the force that defeats the officer in the end. His zeal to capture the youths propels him into their equipment, leaving him with injuries. Musical Youth direct no violence at the officer, it is his own anger that (literally) trips him up. That scenario plays out a basic theme of Rastafarianism as moral ju-jitsu – as a withdrawal from the negativity of Babylon as a means of letting the system destroy itself. The role played by the musical instruments in the "Pass the Dutchie" video bears special relevance to this theme. Bob Marley once explained that "destruction come outta material things," illustrating his point by saying that an electric guitar can make joyful music, but it can also kill if there is a short circuit. But Marley's point resonates with broader Rastafarian themes, identified by Hebdige as an ideology whereby "technology capitulates to belief; belief succumbs to knowledge, and thought is really felt."[30]

As the video concludes, the camera takes us back inside the courtroom where Kelvin demonstrates the power of "material objects correctly used." He joyfully describes the ubiquitous presence of music – on the radio, stereo, and at the disco – introducing as "evidence" an assortment of "boom box" radios and "walkman" cassette players. Another leap by Kelvin launches the band into performing their song in court, followed by a quick cut showing the truant officer telling his story to the jury. They laugh at his account and declare the defendants not guilty. The five Musical Youth jump up and dance in the courtroom, and despite the judge's call for order their enthusiasm provokes pandemonium. Musical Youth's dancing in this segment displays the high kicks and leaps off the ground that Marjorie Whylie, head of the Division of Folk Music

Research at the Jamaica School of Music, has identified as characteristic of traditional Rastafarian dance.[31]

What is important here is not Rastafarianism as doctrine, but Rastafarianism as a symbol of resistance. As Linton Kwesi Johnson explains:

> I'm not a religious person myself, but Rastafarianism is the most important positive cultural movement that we have experienced in Jamaica and whose impact has been much wider than Jamaica in fact. What the Rasta have succeeded in doing is to correct the imbalance of colonial brain-whitening – as some people would call it – brainwashing. Rasta made Jamaicans proud of their history, their culture, their African heritage and their roots. As a spiritual force, it has brought a tremendous amount of creativity into reggae music. And it has contributed to the popular language of the people. A lot of people who are not even Rastas use Rasta words.[32]

The claims that Johnson makes for the influence of Rastafarianism on black Jamaicans can be extended to a mass audience as well. Even when the particular vocabulary does not resonate with immediate experience, the resistance to authority and the affirmation of moral force central to Rastafarianism offer an appealing voice to audiences with similar if not identical grievances.

"PASS THE DUTCHIE" AND AUDIENCE RESPONSE

The existence of sedimented Rastafarian signs and symbols in "Pass the Dutchie" hardly guarantees their reception by a comprehending audience. People watched and listened to "Pass the Dutchie" in a variety of contexts and they brought diverse frames of interpretation to the song. As a second-order sign system, mass communications represent ideas and experiences imperfectly – through allusion rather than exact representation. Mass mediated myths take on some of their powerful influence precisely because they are open to interpretation, capable of being related to personal values and experiences. Yet the very "openness" that allows artists like Don Letts and Musical Youth to inject a sedimented layer of politics into mass-marketed cultural commodities, also allows audiences to interpret those artifacts in the contexts of their own experiences and aspirations.

For more than a decade, Dick Hebdige's superb book, *Subculture*, has served as the definitive scholarly work on the meaning of reggae and Rastafarianism as cultural practice. Hebdige demonstrates that in the context of the disappearance of familiar symbols of British working-class culture, some segments of white working-class youth turned to reggae music and Rastafarian imagery as a means of restoring a lost sense of community. Quoting John Clarke, Hebdige sees the white youth as attracted by the "defensively organized collective" in West Indian communities which no longer existed in their own neighborhoods. Yet for Hebdige one of the most important aspects of white working-class interest in reggae was the subculture's ultimate failure to arbitrate enduring tensions of class identity. In his view, reggae music's association with Black nationalism posed insurmountable barriers to lasting acceptance among white youths who, logically enough, saw themselves excluded from a collective past that included the experiences of slavery and anti-colonial rebellion. As allegiance to race superseded points of class unity, Rasta imagery failed to serve as the basis for a classwide counter-hegemony. Reggae continued to influence the subsequent punk subculture, but even in that context, the centrality of commodity form to subcultural revolt reduced its potential for rebellion into trivial questions of fashion and style, according to Hebdige.[33]

As a model for social analysis, Hebdige's work opened up new possibilities for cultural criticism. Yet some of the contradictions in his argument now disguise more than they disclose. Hebdige's grasp of semiotics enables him to see the ways in which dominant ideology can be encoded within ordinary objects of everyday life, as well as the ways in which dress, grooming, and music can serve as signs of latent opposition. Yet his overview of social relations, his insistence on viewing subcultural practices largely as blocked class politics, compels him to view cultural discourse as less dialogic than it actually is. Why should the encoding of dominant ideology be treated as more powerful than the encoding of oppositional messages? If dominant powers require cultural legitimation as a precondition of continued rule, why wouldn't challenges to that legitimacy be of great significance, even if they disguise themselves in the form of commodities? Hebdige's grounding in a class analysis enables him to see the white working-class youth appropriation of reggae as a manifestation of "blocked" class politics, But he sees no autonomous identity for that appropriation other than a substitution of race for class. Why should the "defensively organized collective" aspects of Rastafarian culture necessarily form the sole basis of its appeal to white working-class youths?

As Stuart Hall explains, the loss of empire, de-industrialization, and the growing Afro-Asian and Afro-Caribbean populations in England have all combined to create a crisis of legitimation for traditional symbols of British cultural identity. In an age of

de-colonization worldwide, the white youth appropriation of reggae can be an identification with the culture of the colonized rather than with the culture of the colonizers.
In the face of late capitalism's legitimation crisis it calls attention to the original plunder
endemic to the capitalist system. For a population bombarded with messages explaining how to fit into society and conform with its imperatives, Rastafarian imagery offers
an experience of detachment through drugs, avoidance of authority, and celebrations
of sensuality and solidarity. In a society whose univocal cultural narratives are being
undermined by profound social change, the multi-vocality and multi-culturalism of
"Pass the Dutchie" offer a significant alternative, a competing set of signs and symbols
proclaiming prestige from below. Most important, in an age of unparalleled emphasis
on commercial mass media, the internal ideological tensions of any one center of
cultural production become available to alienated groups in other societies; real and
invented memories of colonial societies help shape the contours of popular culture in
contemporary England, while the unresolved racial and cultural conflicts of Great
Britain play a role in racial and class consciousness in the U.S.A.

Hebdige is so concerned with the white "appropriation" of reggae that he under-
plays the creativity within the reggae community that sucessfully fashions signs and
symbols capable of appealing to members of the dominant community. Entrepreneurs
and "skinheads" may both "appropriate" Rastafarian symbols, but their appropriation
is limited and constrained by the internal authority of the signs themselves. Of course,
all icons and images can be misappropriated and ripped out of context, but all have an
internal logic providing guidelines for preferred readings that can be defended as
"correct." Rastafarian imagery is not just some bizarre "otherness" to be appropriated
by white youth and capitalist record companies. It is a historically sanctioned language
that skillfully unmasks the internal contradictions and historical sins of Western
colonialism and racism. As a heavily coded subculture it is not easily translated into
direct political action, but for precisely that reason, it retains a freedom of action that
enables it to insinuate its message in the discourse of its enemies.

Don Letts felt that the pressures he received from Musical Youth's record company
to make them more acceptable to a mass audience displayed the racism of the
recording industry. "That's the kind of politics you have to deal with," he complained
in reference to their request to drop "The Youth of Today" and make a new video for
"Pass the Dutchie."[34] It angered Letts that his track record of success as a film-maker
meant little to white businessmen who assumed that Black artists had to look and sound
more like white artists in order to be commercially successful. As he saw it, record
company executives tried to eliminate all content that might offend the imagined

consciousness that they attached to the mainstream white record-buying audience. But Letts felt obligated to fight that kind of censorship and get as much oppositional content into his videos as possible. Letts describes his battles with record company executives over music video content as essentially racial, explaining,

> First of all, me being Black and over six feet and wearing dreadlocks like a Rastafarian, and usually wearing shades and combat fatigues – when I walk into a record company, they just bug out, man. I'm there trying to explain a concept to them and they can't believe I can speak English. In a way, that sort of attitude carries over to the way they do Black artists' videos, even to the way they do all videos.[35]

In order to make "Pass the Dutchie," Letts and Musical Youth did make compromises. No doubt their record penetrated into markets that had resisted Bob Marley and Peter Tosh in part because of their safe image. But they did not compromise completely. Musical Youth presented their song in the context of a battle with authority (the truant officer and the courts), they presented their own faces and performed their own songs with a dignity and legitimacy that undermined any expectations of deference, and they showed themselves as beating the system by drawing upon their internal resources. In the final analysis, the amount of Black nationalism, class-consciousness, and self-affirmation that remains in the video is far more significant than what has been purged from it. They dealt with their Blackness by acting as if it didn't need to be explained, and by building upon it to fashion universal values open to all regardless of race. But they also spoke to frames of reception other than race, especially youth.

Nearly every account of Musical Youth's concerts in the U.S.A. in April 1983 mentioned the youthfulness of their audience. Their crowds might have a preponderance of white or black faces, but they always had a majority of young faces. A writer for the *Village Voice* described their audience as pre-teens, teens, and their parents, while the reviewer for *Billboard* spoke about "a biracial crowd largely of youngsters under 16."[36] Yet the reviewers also stressed that the band's appeal made them more than a youth phenomenon. *Variety's* "New Acts" column noted that "there is nothing cloying or precocious about Musical Youth's presentation," adding that they displayed "an engaging sense of understatement that's diametrically opposite to the show-offishness indulged in by other kid groups."[37] In a similar vein, the *Village Voice* reviewer argued that "Musical Youth is less a novelty or child labor routine than a good working reggae band that happens to be a bunch of kids."[38] But they obviously served as role models for other kids too – this reviewer related that a friend of his working in a Harlem Day

Care Center told him that many of the four-year-olds in her play group knew each member of the band by name.

Published reviews of "Pass the Dutchie" indicate that Musical Youth came across as both legitimate reggae musicians and as social critics. The *Rolling Stone* reviewer who worried that the group might be the harbinger of a new "reggae bubblegum" genre, nonetheless conceded that their reggae retained "much of the form's original feeling."[39] Michael Shore reviewed Musical Youth in *The Rolling Stone Book of Rock Videos* as "both adorable and potentially unlawful," and described their persona as in keeping with the song "Pass the Dutchie" which "itself disguises hard-bitten social protest ('How does it feel when you got no food?') with lilting pop-reggae."[40]

Within the U.S. market, the popularity of "Pass the Dutchie" came from a serendipitous confluence of circumstances – the emergence of music video as a new vehicle for reaching audiences, the economic crisis of de-industrialization, the ascendancy of Black artists mastering the forms and styles of pop music as exemplified by Michael Jackson and Prince, the popularity of British groups with traces of reggae in their music like the Clash and the Police, and the desire by young audiences to escape the demographic tyranny of the 1960s and have pop heroes of their own. "Pass the Dutchie" arbitrated tensions of class, youth, race, and culture in the short run, and its success helped create space for the subsequent successes of Eddy Grant and UB40 on the U.S. pop charts with politically trenchant reggae songs of their own.[41] Musical Youth's historical codes enabled them to speak powerfully to crucial issues in the lives of their listeners and viewers, to insert the experiences of young Jamaicans living in England into the consciousness of rock music fans in the U.S.A. The vocabulary and imagery of reggae enabled them to "trip up" a system that intended to deny them a future as legitimate citizens and artists, and it provided the vehicle for liberation by transmitting their message to sympathetic audiences around the globe. Audiences around the world might not have caught every nuance of Musical Youth's complicated codes in "Pass the Dutchie," they might easily have reincorporated their oppositional tendencies back into dominant narratives. But the contents of the group's performance and the circumstances under which it was consumed allowed for unexpected oppositional possibilities. In the U.S.A., audiences may have known little about the inverted symbols of British democracy or the tropes of Rastafarian language in the video, but when Kelvin Grant looked them in the eye and proclaimed that his generation ruled the nation, they did not blink. Instead, they accepted a video and a song that encouraged them to sympathize with Grant and to see the world through his eyes. In the process, they acknowledged the shifting sands of authoritative discourse in the modern world, and joined in the creation of families of resemblance and prestige from below that have characterized the Rastafarian project from the start.

NOTES

1. Richard Gold, "Juvenile Music Acts Blossom Worldwide: U.K., Latin Groups Head Invasion of U.S. Market," *Variety*, January 12, 1983, 199.

2. Richard Gold, "Juvenile Music Acts Blossom Worldwide," 199.

3. Richard Cromelin, "Reggae by the Younger Generation," *Los Angeles Times*, January 22, 1983, calendar section, 1.

4. J.D. Considine, "Youth of Today," *Rolling Stone*, March 3, 1983, 51.

5. Mitchell Cohen, "Youth of Today," *High Fidelity*, April 1983, 182–3.

6. Stephen Davis, *Reggae Bloodlines* (New York: Anchor Books, 1977), 10, 131; *Variety*, January 26, 1983, 67; Dick Hebdige, "Reggae, Rastas, and Rudies," in Stuart Hall and Tony Jefferson, eds, *Resistance Through Rituals* (London: Hutchinson, 1976), 138–9.

7. The quotes are from Walter Benjamin's essay "The Work of Art in the Age of Mechanical Reproduction," in James Curran, Michael Gurevitch, and Janet Woollacott, eds, *Mass Communication and Society* (Beverly Hills CA and London: Sage Publications, 1979), 389–90.

8. This is not to assert that slapstick humor lacks political content. It adheres to the notions of "uncrowning power" as humor advanced by Mikhail Bakhtin among others.

9. Robert A. Hill, "Dread History: Leonard P. Howell and Millenarian Visions in Early Rastafari Religions in Jamaica," *Epoche: Journal of the History of Religions at UCLA* vol.9 (1981), 32–4.

10. Robert A. Hill, "Dread History", 37

11. Robert A. Hill, "Dread History", 41–5.

12. Wendell Logan, "Conversation with Marjorie Whylie," *The Black Perspective in Music* vol.10 no.1, 86, 92; Dick Hebdige, "Reggae, Rastas, and Rudies," 142–3.

13. Wendell Logan, "Conversation with Marjorie Whylie," 89.

14. Wendell Logan, "Conversation with Marjorie Whylie," 82, 86, 88.

15. Stephen Davis, *Reggae Bloodlines*, 131; *Billboard*, December 18, 1982; *Variety*, January 26, 1983, 67. According to Chris I-Tone in the liner notes for Heartbeat Records' *Best of Studio 1*, producer Clement Dodd remembers Robert Lyn as the keyboardist for Sound Dimension the day they recorded "Full Up." See *Best of Studio 1*, Heartbeat Records, HB-14.

16. *Musician* no.52 (February) 1983, 44–5.

17. Stephen Davis, *Reggae Bloodlines*, 69.

18. Dick Hebdige, "Reggae, Rastas, and Rudies," 147.

19. Dick Hebdige, "Reggae, Rastas, and Rudies," 147.

20. Quoted by Michael M.J. Fischer, "Ethnicity and the Postmodern Arts of Memory," in George Marcus and James Clifford, *Writing Culture* (Berkeley: University of California Press, 1986), 307.

21. Dick Hebdige, "Reggae, Rastas, and Rudies," 138.

22. See *Trouser Press* no.10 (June) 1983, 12–14; *Musician* no.52 (February) 1983, 44–5.

23. Personal conversation with the author, January 8, 1983, Chicago, Illinois.

24. Personal conversation with the author, January 15, 1983, Houston, Texas.

25. Michael Shore, *The Rolling Stone Book of Rock Videos* (New York: Quill, 1984), 125.

26. Michael Shore, *The Rolling Stone Book of Rock Videos*, 125.

27. "Interview: Linton Kwesi Johnson," *Los Angeles Weekly*, July 13–19, 1984, 42.

28. I am grateful to Ronnie Serr of the Theater Arts Department of the University of California, Los Angeles, for pointing out this connection to me.

29. Stephen Davis, *Reggae Bloodlines*, 10; George P. Rawick, *From Sundown to Sunup* (Westport CT: Greenwood Press, 1972), 98–100.

30. Dick Hebdige, "Reggae, Rastas, and Rudies," 140.

31. Wendell Logan, "Conversation with Marjorie Whylie," 90–1.

32. "Interview: Linton Kwesi Johnson," 42; Stuart Hall, "Culture, the Media, and the Ideological Effect," in James Curran, Michael Gurevitch, and Janet Woollacott, eds, *Mass Communication and Society* (Beverly Hills: Sage, 1979) 315–48.

33. Dick Hebdige, *Subculture: The Meaning of Style* (London and New York: Methuen, 1985), 92–4.

34. Michael Shore, *The Rolling Stone Book of Rock Videos*, 125.

35. Michael Shore, *The Rolling Stone Book of Rock Videos*, 45.

36. Leo Sacks, "Talent in Action," *Billboard*, April 23, 1983, 38; John Piccariella, "Little Big Youths," *Village Voice*, April 26, 1983, 66.

37. "New Acts," *Variety* April 20, 1983, 184.

38. John Piccariella, "Little Big Youths," 66.

39. J.D. Considine, "Youth of Today," 51.

40. Michael Shore, *The Rolling Stone Book of Rock Videos*, 296. For material about Musical Youth's collaboration with Donna Summer see Richard Harrington, "Summer and Ross: Women at Work," *Washington Post*, August 25, 1983, E9.

41. Joel Whitburn, *Top Pop Singles, 1955–1986* (Menomonee Falls, Wisconsin: Record Research, 1987), 216, 519.

6

Immigration and Assimilation: Rai, Reggae, and Bhangramuffin

APACHE INDIAN

During the 1980s, popular-music listeners and enthusiasts throughout Europe began to notice new musical forms that captured their fancy. In London, the band Alaap blended bhangra music from the Indian state of Punjab with Greek, Middle Eastern, Spanish, and Anglo-American pop styles. At the same time, Joi Bangla, made up of immigrants from Bangla Desh, mixed African-American funk sounds with traditional Bengali folk songs.[1] For their part, listeners in Paris expressed enthusiasm for a techno-pop album displaying "a faintly Moorish" sound underneath English, French, and Arabic lyrics by a Mauritanian singer recording under the name Tahra.[2]

Soaring to popularity at the same time that immigrant populations in London and Paris faced increasing hostility and even attacks from anti-foreign thugs, these recordings demonstrate the complicated connections and contradictions that characterize the links between popular music and social life. Audiences and artists in these cities carried the cultural collisions of everyday life into music, at one and the same time calling attention to ethnic differences and demonstrating how they might be transcended. Sophisticated fusions of seemingly incompatible cultures in music made sense to artists and audiences in part because these fusions reflected their lived experiences in an inter-cultural society.

Of course, inter-cultural communication and creativity does not preclude political or even physical confrontations between members of groups fighting for a share of increasingly scarce resources. But the very existence of music demonstrating the interconnectedness between the culture of immigrants and the culture of their host country helps us understand how the actual lived experiences of immigrants are much more dynamic and complex than most existing models of immigration and assimilation admit.

Ugly incidents of anti-immigrant violence have occurred in countries all over the globe with ever increasing frequency in recent years. In times of uncertainty and instability, people cling to what they perceive to be foundational truths about their identities and about the identities of others. The collapse of communism in the East has destroyed one type of totalitarian rule, but it has also opened the door to resurgent racisms and undiluted ethnic antagonisms. De-industrialization, economic restructuring, and the evisceration of the welfare state in the West undermines attachments to places and communities that have given meaning to people's lives for more than a hundred years. The mass migrations taking place in the wake of these upheavals make our time one of acute anxiety about cultural identity and about the boundaries between cultures.

Immigration almost always raises anxieties about assimilation. In the popular press, political debates, and scholarly studies, immigration often appears as simply a social problem rather than as a social process. Immigrants are assailed for their failure to assimilate, sometimes by the very people blocking the path to assimilation. Poverty, crime, and inter-generational tensions among immigrants rarely appear in public debate as consequences of the dislocations wrought by the transnational economy. Instead, immigrants themselves receive the blame for the conditions they endure, largely because of the perception that the cultures they bring with them from their home countries differ so sharply from the cultures they confront in their new places of residence. These discussions invariably assume that immigrants should want to become more like the people who are native-born, and they assume as well that the interests of nations and individuals are always best served by creating an undifferentiated "common culture" for all inhabitants.

To be sure, the prospect of assimilation promises real rewards for immigrants. Excluded from opportunities and amenities in their new lands, why wouldn't immigrants want to secure the fruits and benefits of full citizenship and cultural enfranchisement? Just and decent societies would allow and encourage all people to participate fully in their national political, economic, and cultural life. But models of immigration and assimilation that posit the existence of a discrete, homogeneous, and thoroughly unified center in any society fail to describe the dynamism and complexity of contemporary culture. On the other hand, models of immigration and assimilation that presume an absolute incommensurability between different cultures elide the very rich histories of syncretism that characterize most countries with extensive experiences with immigration. Both of these models leave us with unrealistic and unsatisfactory choices – between a static mono-culturalism that destroys all forms of cultural difference in the name of some greater unity or a static multi-culturalism that acknowledges diversity and differences only by rendering them permanent, necessary, absolute, and inevitable.

Throughout the world today, immigrants reject binary oppositions that force them either to give up their cultural identities completely or that force them to cling to them eternally, with no opportunity for transformation or change. As Lisa Lowe demonstrates in her original and generative scholarship on migration to North America from Asia, many immigrants pursue cultural and political strategies that emphasize the heterogeneity of their group, the hybridity of their culture, and the multiplicity of identities available to people who are not only immigrant or ethnic subjects, but also people with gendered identities, class positions, sexual preferences, and political beliefs.[3] Through self-active struggles for recognition and power, they often recognize that the act of immigration itself changes both the immigrants and their host countries, that ethnic and national identities are floating equilibria that are constantly being constructed, negotiated, and changed. The practices of popular music as they are carried out among immigrants and their descendants in several contemporary European cities illumine important issues about assimilation in an age where the principles of contemporary capital accumulation, the enduring legacies and consequences of centuries of colonial rule and anti-colonial struggle, and emergent inter-cultural relations meet at a dangerous crossroads.

In an erudite rumination on anti-foreign violence and national identity in Europe, Julia Kristeva argues for a "cosmopolitan" position built on the necessity of both recognizing and refusing "the cult of origins." Kristeva describes herself as someone who has chosen "a transnational or international position situated at the crossing of boundaries."[4] Sincere and forthright in its opposition to racism and balanced in its efforts to reconcile universal aspirations with national conditions, Kristeva's "cosmopolitanism" nonetheless rests upon largely uninterrogated racial and class privileges, as well as upon an evasion of the relationship between national identities and trans-national capital.

Nowhere is the weakness of Kristeva's argument more apparent than in her open letter to French anti-racist activist Harlem Desir. In it, Kristeva proclaims that it is time "to ask immigrant people what motivated them (beyond economic opportunities and approximate knowledge of the language propagated by colonialism) to choose the French community with its historical memory and traditions as the welcoming lands. The respect for immigrants should not erase the gratitude due the welcoming host."[5]

This formulation is reasonable enough as an abstract proposition about the rights and responsibilities of citizens, and it is clearly a question that Kristeva has asked herself as an intellectual who moved from Bulgaria to France. But it is completely out of touch with the realities that most immigrants face. It refuses to acknowledge how colonialism, imperialism, and the transnational circulation of capital have devastated Third World nations and left their inhabitants struggling for survival. Was there ever an opportunity to invert the question – for residents of Haiti, Senegal, or Indochina to ask French colonialists what motivated them (beyond economic opportunities) to choose the Haitian, Senegalese, or Indochinese communities, to show their respect for "the welcoming host"? Do most immigrants make deliberate choices on the basis of political theory or do they flee to the opportunities open to them? As the contributors to a volume about immigration to Great Britain explained, "We're over here, because you were over there."

Moreover, Kristeva's question is really a command; it orders immigrants to explain and justify themselves, to account for their foreignness and to affirm their intention to assimilate into the France that existed the day before they arrived. Kristeva seems to have no sense that immigrants from the former French empire might already be French in their own way, that immigrants might want to assimilate into the French society created everyday among Arabs, Africans, Asians, or Antilleans in the country's cities and suburbs as much as they want to assimilate into the traditions of French language and culture as they are explained at the nation's elite universities. She asks immigrants to explain themselves, but the form of her question makes it clear that she is already not listening.

Most immigrants to Europe from Third World countries experience the crossing of boundaries and borders in a manner very different from Kristeva's "cosmopolitanism." Their cognitive mapping of the world's culture and economy disrupts her paradigm of citizenship. The persecution and subordination they suffer as workers, citizens, and subjects force them into identities that are both more local and parochial than Kristeva's sense of what it means to be a French citizen and more mobile and global than her sense of what it means to be cosmopolitan.

For example, consider the cognitive mapping of Paris offered by Simon Njami, a French author and editor whose parents came from Cameroon but who was born in Switzerland. "It's an African town in some ways," he explained to literary scholar Wendy Walters.

> If somebody wants to meet some Africans, eat some African food everywhere, and hear some African music, or whatever, he just has to go to Paris. In Paris you have much more of Africa than in Africa. Because in Africa you have the different countries and from one country to another people wouldn't know what's going on in the other country. But if they're in Paris they will know what's going on all over Africa. They will listen to music coming from here and there, that they couldn't do in Africa. And even for Africans Paris is a meeting place, because you know, you don't have any flights so every flight goes from Paris to this country or this other one.[6]

Just as New York and London have become important Caribbean cities, Paris is an African as well as a European city. Njami's writings make it clear that this Paris is no paradise; his characters are often overcome with nostalgic desire to return home. But the Paris they inhabit is both familiar and unfamiliar, a place of exile as well as a home, a site for escape from Africa as well as for return to it.

Many popular musicians in France display the complicated cognitive mapping encoded in Njami's comments about Paris. Jazz saxophone and vibraphone player Manu Dibango emphasizes the conflict of cultures that has characterized his artistic career:

> At first people in Africa said that I made Western music, that I was black-white. I carried that around for a long time. In France, people often told me that I made American music. And when I went to the United States, the Americans thought that I made African music. It's impossible to be more of a traitor than that![7]

Dibango's dilemma illustrates the inadequacy of binary models of assimilation. He never had the luxury of being completely inside or completely outside of African, European, or American culture, but instead experienced them together at all times. Baaba Maal from Senegal also sees his multiply-situated perspective as an advantage. "I feel myself to be a universal musician singing in Pulaar, coming from Africa, not trying to calculate, but letting it come," he explains. "I can sing what is happening around me in Senegal, and when I travel I sing with Pulaar eyes who see France – or Miami."[8]

Government control over the production and distribution of popular music and the peculiarities of French culture have left French citizens with far less connection to international rock'n'roll than their neighbors in Germany, Spain, or the Netherlands. In fact, the cultural fit over the years between rock'n'roll and French culture has been so bad that it gave rise to a saying that *"le rock français, c'est comme la cuisine anglaise."* ("French rock is to rock as English cooking is to cooking"). But with the rise of rap, French musicians of African descent have become more involved with the currents of international popular music. Members of the rap group I.A.M. come from North African neighborhoods in the southern city of Marseilles. They titled their album *From the Planet Mars*, as a pun about Marseilles, but also as a statement about how different their experiences are from those of cosmopolitan and metropolitan French citizens. I.A.M. stands for "Imperial Asiatic Men," but their music and lyrics deal mostly with Egypt, Algeria, and America.[9] The African-born Parisian rapper M.C. Solaar has immersed himself in the French hip hop subculture which he describes as "the cult of the sneaker," and "pretty much a U.S. branch office."[10]

The complicated culture mixing that has given rise to new forms of inter-cultural communication within French popular music has also had important political implications. Salif Keita of Mali recorded a powerful and popular French-language song,

"Nous Pas Bouger," which championed the cause of immigrants resisting depor-tation.[11] Similarly, the men and women in the anti-racist folk/punk/new wave band Les Négresses Vertes base their music on French multi-culturalism. Their name means green black women, and the band's members are male and female, European and African, white and black. "It's music from the street today," explains Mathias, who plays accordion. "We all grew up with a large variety of different people who might have different roots but who are, nevertheless, French. Our musical hybrid wasn't a deliberate policy, it's the way we are. It mirrors the reality of France today."[12]

Clearly the most important and most complicated expression of musical multi-culturalism in France comes from the popularity of Algerian "rai" music. During the 1980s, political and cultural mobilizations by young people of North African origin competed with intense anti-Arab and anti-foreign organizing by French right wingers for the power to define "French" culture and citizenship.[13] Rai music took on extra-musical importance as a visible weapon in that struggle.

Referenced by many artists including Les Négresses Vertes and I.A.M., rai music blends Arabic lyrics and instruments with synthesizers, disco arrangements, blues chord progressions, and Jamaican reggae and Moroccan gnawa rhythms. Rai origin-ated as women's music in the Algerian port city of Oran where *meddahas* sang to other women at weddings and other private occasions and by *chiekhas* who sang for men in taverns and brothels. In a city where French, Spanish, and Arabic are all spoken, the music known as "Oran Modern" emerged from interactions among Spanish, French, and North African musicians.[14] Now sung by both female Chebas and male Chebs, the term "rai" comes from the Arabic phrase "Ya Rai" ("It's my opinion").[15] Reed flutes and terracotta drums provided the original instrumentation for rai, but over the years musicians added violin, accordion, saxophone, and trumpet. Bellemou Messaoud played a particularly important role in the emergence of modern rai when he added guitars, trumpets, and synthesizers to rai ensembles.[16] Disco-influenced arrangements and blues chord progressions came later to bring rai closer to the Anglo-American international style.

A product of cultural collision between Europe and North Africa, rai music has its defenders and its detractors in both places. Some factions in Algeria see rai as too French, too Western, too modern, too obscene. At the same time, there are those in France who dismiss rai as too foreign, too primitive, too exotic, too strange. It is not easy to tell if a North African immigrant to France is being assimilationist or separatist by listening to rai music. Cheb Khaled spends more time in Marseilles than in Algiers, and uses rai music to comment on "racism in France, about what's happening in

Algeria, and of course, I always sing about love."[17] Cheba Fadela created a sensation as a mini-skirted seventeen-year-old on French television in the late 1970s and helped start modern "pop rai" with her 1983 song "N'sel fik" ("You are Mine").[18] Cheb Sid Ahmed is openly homosexual and performs with a troupe of traditional female wedding singers.[19] At the other extreme, Cheba Zahouania performs mainly at women's events, does not allow herself to be photographed, and does not appear on television, reportedly because her husband threatened to take her children from her if she sang in public for men.[20]

Not surprisingly, rai has been embroiled in repeated political controversies. "The history of rai is like the history of rock and roll," explains Cheb Khaled, one of the genre's premier performers.

> Fundamentalists don't want our concerts to happen. They come and break things up. They say rai is street music and that it's debauched. But that's not true. I don't sing pornography. I sing about love and social life. We say what we think, just like singers all over the world.[21]

The Algerian government has sporadically looked with favor on rai as a source of revenue and as a cultural voice capable of competing with Islamic fundamentalism. Its popularity in France persuaded the authorities in Algiers to sponsor international youth festivals featuring rai performers in Algiers and Oran in 1985.[22] In France, racist attacks on Arabs led to the formation of SOS-Racisme, a massive anti-racist organization affiliated with the Socialist Party. It embraced rai as an expression of faith in France's inter-cultural future.[23] They helped persuade the French government to sponsor a rai festival in a Paris suburb in 1986, which seemed to mark the emergence of rai as a permanent force in French popular music.[24] In fact, rai may have become more secure in France than it is in Algeria. When anti-government rioters in Algiers adopted Cheb Khaled's "El Harba Wine" ("Where to Flee?") as their unofficial anthem in what become known as the "rai rebellion," many rai artists hastened to disassociate themselves from the violence.[25]

Yet, the popularity of rai music among French and "world beat" audiences may mean little for children of immigrants facing massive unemployment and racist attacks. In Lyons, for example, seventy percent of the children of immigrants between the ages of 16 and 25 have no jobs and no vocational training. Even the success of an assimilationist group like France-Plus which has managed to elect close to 400 people of North African lineage to municipal offices throughout France may increase rather than decrease the pressures on those immigrants and their children who seem less assimilated.[26]

Traditional arguments about immigration, assimilation, and acculturation assume that immigrants choose between two equally accessible cultures that are clearly differentiated and distinct from one another. But what if immigrants leave a country that has been shaped by its colonizers and enter one that has been shaped by those it colonized? What if immigrants leave a modernizing country that turns anti-modern and fundamentalist while they are gone? What happens if the host country becomes deeply divided between anti-foreign nativists and anti-racist pluralists? Which culture do the immigrants carry with them? Into which culture do they assimilate? Rai music might be defended as either Algerian or French music, but a more exact interpretation would establish it as a register for the changing dimensions and boundaries of Algerian, French, and Beur (a popular term for Arab mostly used in Paris) identities.

Afro-Caribbean and Southwest Asian immigrants to Britain experience many of the same dynamic changes facing North African immigrants to France. Here again, musical syncretisms disclose the dynamics of cultural syncretisms basic to the processes of immigration, assimilation, and acculturation in contemporary societies. Immigrants leaving the Caribbean and Asia took on new identities in Britain. If nothing else, they became "West Indian" or "East Indian" in England instead of Jamaican or Bahamian, Bengali, or Hindi as they had been at home. But they also became "Black" in Britain, an identity that they generally do not have in their home countries, but which becomes salient to them in England as a consequence of racism directed at them from outside their communities as well as from its utility to them as a device for building unity within and across aggrieved populations. Of course, the influx of immigrants changes England too. Once immigrants from the Indian subcontinent or the Caribbean arrive in the U.K., they transform the nature of British society and culture in many ways, changing the nature of the "inside" into which newer immigrants are expected to assimilate.

Popular music in Britain plays an important role in building solidarity within and across immigrant communities, while at the same time serving as a site for negotiation and contestation between groups. Music is a powerful but easily recognizable marker of cultural identity. It can be created by many people at many different sites because of the strength of diverse grass-roots musical traditions and because it requires relatively little access to capital. Although popular music can never be a "pure" or "authentic" expression of an undifferentiated group identity, as a highly visible (and audible) commodity, it comes to stand for the specificity of social experience in identifiable communities when it captures the attention, engagement, and even allegiance of people from many different social locations.

Abner Cohen's investigation into carnival celebrations by West Indians in London illustrates the power of music as a social force. He shows that music not only shapes and reflects dominant and subordinate social and cultural relations, but that music making and other forms of popular culture serve as a specific site for the creation of collective identity. Carnival breaks down barriers between island groups, bringing together immigrants from different islands to express a "unified" West Indian identity that exists largely in England. Of course, West Indian identity held important meaning in the West Indies as well, most notably through the West Indian Board of Control for cricket formed in 1927 and in the establishment of the University of the West Indies. But these identities became augmented by experiences in England that lessened allegiances to individual islands and emphasized a pan-West Indian identity. By offering an opportunity for large numbers of Black Britons to take to the streets, carnival reveals to revelers the reach and scope of racism in their daily lives – how police surveillance and popular suspicion make it dangerous for them to use those streets during the rest of the year. Through the aggressive festivity of carnival, West Indians dramatize the gap between the lives they lead every day and their desires for pleasure, power, and participation in British society.

For Blacks in Britain according to Cohen's account, reggae music and its Rastafarian ideology have become "articulating principles for the formation of primary neighborhood groups" whose connections to one do not depend upon formal organization, but rather on "communal relationships and cultural forms supported by cultural imperatives."[27] Reggae's role in bringing different groups together stems in part from its formal properties and historical uses and effects (see chapter 5), but it also originates in the historically specific circumstances and needs of Afro-Caribbean and even Afro-Asian immigrants.

Mass migration from the West Indies to Britain began shortly after World War II. The expanding English economy offered jobs to immigrants, but the nation's cultural institutions rarely acknowledged their presence. According to Anthony Marks, as late as 1963, when some 15,000 records from Jamaica entered England every month, the British Broadcasting Corporation studiously ignored West Indian music and record shops rarely carried products from the Caribbean.[28] Denied the dignity of representation in the mainstream media, Afro-Caribbeans in England created spaces for themselves with neighborhood sound systems and record collections that enabled them to express their own culture and share it with others. At the heart of these new spaces was music from Jamaica.

While immigration flows included residents of all Caribbean islands, Jamaicans accounted for more than sixty percent of England's Caribbean population by the 1960s. Because of the size of the Jamaican-British community and because of the ways in which the politically-charged doctrines of Rastafarianism helped all diasporic Blacks in Britain understand and endure their treatment, Jamaican culture became the crucial unifying component in the composite Caribbean culture created in England. Differences between island identities that might be deeply felt in the West Indies, and even in England, receded in importance because of the unifying force of Jamaican music, but even more because of the uniformity of British racism against *all* West Indians. "When you're in school you all get harassed together," explained one immigrant.[29] Another adds, "I think most of my friends feel Jamaican, the English helped us do it."[30]

Popular music affirms the positive qualities of the unity forged in part by negative experiences with British racism. Through shared experiences with music, carnival celebrations, and the political activism that sometimes grows out of them, primary groups dispersed over a broad territory find themselves united by elements of a Jamaican culture that many of them had never known first hand.[31] Jazzie B of the British group Soul II Soul remembers the prominence of Jamaican "sound systems" – record players and amplified speakers – in his neighborhood as he grew up, and what they meant to him as the British-born son of immigrants from Antigua. "By the time I was 15 or 16, there was a sound system on every single street in the community. I'd guess that eight out of every 10 black kids would be involved in one way or another in a sound system."[32] These devices offered a focal point for social gatherings, allowed disc jockeys opportunities to display their skills, and provided a soundtrack to mark the experiences and aspirations of inner-city life. But they also served as one of those sites where people made new identities for themselves as West Indians and as Black Britons.

Just as the Paris described by Simon Njami functions as an African city offering opportunities found nowhere in Africa, London and other British cities became important centers of West Indian and Jamaican cultural forms found nowhere in the Caribbean. But these forms have important uses and implications for Southwest Asians in Britain as well. The pervasive practices of British racism and occasional self-defense strategies by immigrants lead West Indians and East Indians to a shared identity as "Black" in England. Interactions between Afro-Caribbeans and Southwest Asians have a long if not completely comfortable history in the Caribbean, especially in Trinidad, but in Britain the antagonisms can be even sharper. For members of both groups, the things that divide them often seem more salient than those bringing them together. One survey showed that more than eighty percent of West Indians and more than forty percent of East Indians felt they had more in common with British whites than with each other. Almost a third of Indians and Pakistanis stated that they had nothing in common with either white Britons or West Indian Blacks. Only eight percent of West Indians and twenty percent of Pakistanis and Indians felt that they had more in common with each other than they had in common with the English.[33] In a few extremely significant cases, Afro-Asians and Afro-Caribbeans have successfully repressed their differences to defend themselves and each other from white racist attacks or judicial frame-ups, but sustained political and cultural alliances have been elusive.[34]

Yet, alliances between Southwest Asians and other groups that might appear unlikely in political life already exist within popular culture. Bhangra musicians fuse folk songs from the Indian state of Punjab with disco, pop, hip hop, and house music for appreciative audiences made up of people from many different groups. Like Algerian rai, bhangra originated in a part of the world characterized by extensive intercultural communication, but remained largely a music played for private parties, weddings, and harvest festivals before its emergence as a syncretic popular form. Bhangra brings together Punjabis of many religions (Hindu, Sikh, Muslim, Jain, and Christian) and from many countries (India, Pakistan, and Bangla Desh), but in the past decade has started to speak powerfully to new audiences and interests.[35]

Like West Indians, East Indians came to England in the years after World War II, and like West Indians they found that their labor was more welcome than their culture in their new nation. As Sabita Banerji notes in an apt phrase, "South Asian communities in Britain have remained invisible, and their music inaudible, for a surprisingly long time."[36] In the early 1980s, South Asian youths following the Jamaican example set up sound systems to play reggae, soul, jazz, and funk records during "daytimer" discos in dance halls and community centers. At first the disc jockeys and sound systems took Caribbean-sounding names, but when they started to mix bhangra with the other musical styles they used Punjabi names like "Gidian de Shingar" and "Pa Giddha Pa."[37] Almost a decade after Jamaican reggae established itself as a popular form capable of attracting audiences from every ethnic background, bhangra broke on the British scene as a viable commercial force. Alaap's 1984 album, *Teri chunni di sitare* drew an enthusiastic response from listeners for its blend of disco, pop, and Caribbean styles with bhangra. Holle Holle and Heera drew large crowds to mainstream venues including the Hammersmith Palais by adding digital sampling to the mix in their music, while bhangra groups in the Midlands blended bhangra with house music.[38] But the ultimate fusion awaited – the mixture of Jamaican "raggamuffin" and African-American hip hop with "bhangra" to create the "bhangramuffin" sound of Apache Indian (see chapter 1).

Steve Kapur took the name Apache Indian as a reference to his Punjabi ancestry and as a tribute to the Jamaican raggamuffin star "Super Cat," sometimes known as "the wild Apache."[39] But he took his art from the cultural crossroads he negotiated every day. He told a reporter,

> As a young Asian in Britain, you constantly lead a double life. At home, everything is as it was – very traditional, very strict. But when you close the front door and move onto the streets everything changes. I've had so many relatives disown my family because of my love for reggae. Now, after hearing my music, and hearing the Indian influences in it, it appeals to them. But my music is first and foremost street music.[40]

For Apache Indian, the "street" is a place where Afro-Caribbean and South Asian youths learn from each other. As a teenager he wore his hair in dreadlocks, danced to the blues, and spent hours shopping for reggae records.[41] His first recording, "Move Over India," paid tribute to the India that he had only visited once but knew well from the Indian films that his parents watched "every time I went home."[42] Apache Indian knew that his music was a success when his West Indian neighbors began saying hello to him in Punjabi. His song "Come Follow Me" offers a hip hop history and travelogue of India for the edification of a West Indian friend who closes the number by telling Apache Indian that his country sounds "lovely, and next time you go send a ticket for me."[43]

Standing at the crossroads of Punjabi and Jamaican cultures, Apache Indian shows that Afro-Asian and Afro-Caribbean Britons share more than a common designation as Black people, that they share a common history of using culture to strengthen their communities from the inside and to attract support from the outside. Punjabis and Jamaicans both come from regions that contain diverse cultures and beliefs, and they both belong to populations that transnational capital has dispersed all over the globe. From their historical experiences at home no less from what they have learned in order to survive abroad, Punjabis and Jamaicans draw upon longstanding and rich traditions when they create cultural coalitions that transcend ethnic and political differences.

The music made by Apache Indian uses performance to call into being a community composed of Punjabis and Jamaicans, South Asians and West Indians, reggae fans and bhangra enthusiasts. But it also demonstrates the potential for all of Britain to learn a lesson from the extraordinary adaptability and creativity of its immigrant cultures. Apache Indian reads "British" culture selectively, by venerating Mahatma Gandhi and Bob Marley rather than Winston Churchill or George Frederick Handel. He assimilates into the culture of the country where he was born by proudly displaying the diverse identities that he has learned in its schools and streets. He creates problems for nation states with their narratives of discrete, homogeneous, and autonomous culture, but he solves problems for people who want cultural expressions as complex as the lives they live every day.

Yet, we should not let the brilliance and skill of Jamaican or Punjabi musicians in securing space for themselves within popular culture blind us to the harsh realities facing immigrants all over the world. Despised and degraded, they face unremitting racism and exploitation with few opportunities to communicate their condition to others. People making popular music for communities like these must address immediate issues of survival and self-respect within their group before they can think about reaching a larger audience.

For example, on the west coast of North America Los Tigres del Norte (the Tigers of the North) sing for and about migrant communities shuttling back and forth between the U.S.A. and Mexico. The five musicians in the band grew up poor in a rural family with eleven children and a disabled father. They have lived the lives they sing about in their songs, and constantly receive suggestions for new stories from farm workers who tell them about their troubles. With expressly political lyrics, they turn their listeners' lives into poignant and powerful songs. "We talk a lot about immigration," explained group leader Jorge Hernandez to a reporter, "because it has given problems to a lot of people. We talk about families who come from different countries to learn a different language and lose where they came from. We tell them it's important not to lose where you are from."[44]

Los Tigres del Norte have appeared in ten Mexican films, sold millions of albums, and regularly draw huge crowds to their live performances. Yet they have secured almost no "mainstream" commercial recognition in the U.S.A., perhaps because they sing in Spanish in a country dominated by Anglophone markets, but also perhaps because their lyrics contain values that threaten vested interests too much. In "La Jaula de Oro" ("The Gilded Cage"), an undocumented worker laments his decade of labor in the U.S.A., claiming that "even if the cage is made of gold it does not cease being a prison."[45]

The mechanisms of commercial culture that deprive Los Tigres del Norte of exposure to a broader audience also deprive Anglo listeners of needed knowledge about their country. As Jose Cuellar, Chairman of San Francisco State's La Raza Studies Department observes, "Those of us who are English-dominant would learn a great deal of the needs and aspirations of our immigrant population, of their frustrated hopes, their frustrated dreams. In these songs, it's all there."[46]

Anti-immigrant and anti-foreign sentiment plagues de-industrialized nations in the West as well as de-Stalinized countries in the East. During times of economic decline and social disintegration, it is tempting for people to blame their problems on others, and to seek succor and certainty from racist and nationalist myths. But the desire to seek certainty and stability by depicting the world solely as one story told from one point of view is more dangerous than ever before. As technology and trade inevitably provide diverse populations with common (although not egalitarian) experiences, the ability to adapt, to switch codes, and to see things from more than one perspective becomes more valuable. In the last analysis, nation states may be best served by those who refuse to believe in their unified narratives, and who insist instead on cultural and political practices that delight in difference, diversity, and dialogue. These do not need to be conjured up by political theorists, or wished into existence by mystics and visionaries. They already exist (albeit in embryonic form) in the communities called into existence by rai, raggamuffin, bhangra, and many other unauthorized and unexpected forms that people have for understanding and changing the world in which they live.

NOTES

1. Sabita Banerji, "Ghazals to Bhangra in Great Britain," *Popular Music* vol.7 no.2 (May) 1988, 208, 213.

2. Philip Sweeney, *The Virgin Directory of World Music* (New York: Henry Holt, 1991), 17.

3. Lisa Lowe, "Heterogeneity, Hybridity, Multiplicity: Marking Asian American Differences," *Diaspora* vol.1 no.1 (1991), 28.

4. Julia Kristeva, *Nations without Nationalism* (New York: Columbia University Press, 1993), 16.

5. Julia Kristeva, *Nations without Nationalism*, 60.

6. Wendy Walters, "Interview with Simon Njami," La Jolla, California, April 21, 1993, unpublished, 1.

7. Manu Dibango, "Interview," *Unesco Courier* (March) 1991, 6.

8. Banning Eyre, "Routes: The Parallel Paths of Baaba Maal and Salif Keita," *Option* no.53 (November–December, 1993), 45.

9. John Rockwell, "Felicitous Rhymes and Local Roots," *New York Times*, August 23, 1992, section 2, 23.

10. Jay Cocks, "Rap Around the Globe," *Time* (October 19, 1992), 70.

11. Banning Eyre, "Routes," 46.

12. Jo Shinner, "Zzzzzobie!," *Folk Roots* vol.74 (August) 1989, 35.

13. Azouz Begag, "The 'Beurs,' Children of North-African Immigrants in France: The Issue of Integration," *Journal of Ethnic Studies* vol.18 no.1, 2–4.

14. Philip Sweeney, *The Virgin Directory of World Music*, 9.

15. Miriam Rosen, "On Rai," *Artforum* vol.29 no.1 (September) 1990, 22; David McMurray and Ted Swedenburg, "Rai Tide Rising," *Middle East Report* (March–April) 1991, 39.

16. Miriam Rosen, "On Rai," 22; Philip Sweeney, *The Virgin Directory of World Music*, 9.

17. Banning Eyre, "A King in Exile: The Royal Rai of Cheb Khaled," *Option* vol.39 (July–August) 1991, 45.

18. Miriam Rosen, "On Rai," 23.

19. Philip Sweeney, *The Virgin Directory of World Music*, 12.

20. Miriam Rosen, "On Rai," 23.

21. Banning Eyre, "A King in Exile," 45.

22. Miriam Rosen, "On Rai," 23; Philip Sweeney, *The Virgin Directory of World Music*, 10.

23. David McMurray and Ted Swedenburg, "Rai Tide Rising," *Middle East Report* (March–April) 1991, 42.

24. Philip Sweeney, *The Virgin Directory of World Music*, 10.

25. David McMurray and Ted Swedenburg, "Rai Tide Rising," 42; Miriam Rosen, "On Rai," 23.

26. Azouz Begag, "The 'Beurs,' " 9.

27. Abner Cohen, *Masquerade Politics* (Berkeley: University of California Press, 1993), 36, 83.

28. Anthony Marks, "Young, Gifted and Black: Afro-American and Afro-Caribbean Music in Britain 1963–88," in Paul Oliver, ed., *Black Music in Britain: Essays on the Afro-Asian Contribution to Popular Music* (Milton Keynes and Philadelphia: Open University Press, 1990), 106.

29. Winston James, "Migration, Racism, and Identity: The Caribbean Experience in Britain," *New Left Review* no.193 (May–June) 1992, 32.

30. Winston James, "Migration, Racism, and Identity," 28.

31. Abner Cohen, *Masquerade Politics*, 36.

32. Robert Hilburn, "Tracing the Caribbean Roots of the New British Pop Invasion," *Los Angeles Times*, September 24, 1989, Calendar section, 6.

33. Winston James, "Migration, Racism, and Identity," 45.

34. Winston James, "Migration, Racism, and Identity," 34, 46.

35. Sabita Banerji and Gerd Bauman, "Bhangra 1984–8: Fusion and Professionalization in a Genre of South Asian Dance Music," in Paul Oliver, ed., *Black Music in Britain*, 137–8.

36. Sabita Banerji and Gerd Bauman, "Bhangra 1984–8," 138.

37. Sabita Banerji and Gerd Bauman, "Bhangra 1984–8," 146.

38. Sabita Banerji and Gerd Bauman, "Bhangra 1984–8," 142.

39. Thom Duffy, "Apache Indian's Asian-Indian Pop Scores U.K. Hit," *Billboard*, February 20, 1993, 82.

40. Brooke Wentz, "Apache Indian," *Vibe* (November) 1993, 9.

41. Paul Bradshaw, "Handsworth Revolutionary," *Straight No Chaser* no.23 (Autumn) 1993, 13, 26.

42. Paul Bradshaw, "Handsworth Revolutionary," 29.

43. Brooke Wentz, "Apache Indian," 86; Apache Indian, *No Reservations*, Mango 162-539 932-2.

44. Carolyn Jung, "S.J. Band's Rhythms Transcend Borders," *San Jose Mercury News*, March 5, 1994, 10.

45. Carolyn Jung, "S.J. Band's Rhythms Transcend Borders," 10.

46. Carolyn Jung, "S.J. Band's Rhythms Transcend Borders," 10.

7

But Is It Political? Self-activity and the State

FELA KUTI

In a series of lectures presented in 1960 under the auspices of the adult education program at the Public Library in Port-of-Spain, Trinidad, the great scholar and activist C.L.R. James urged his audience to prepare themselves to participate in the political struggles that were then transforming the world in which they lived. Aware that he was addressing an audience of ordinary citizens from a small country in an often over-looked part of the world, James nonetheless insisted that his listeners think of themselves as people whose political choices would make a difference in the years ahead. He told them: " . . . we must not be afraid, we must not think because we are small and insignificant that we are not able to take part in all that is taking place."[1]

To the uninitiated or uninformed, the scholar's advice must have seemed quite mad. To suggest that night-school students with no apparent economic, political, or military resources should think of themselves as people whose own actions could help deter-mine their future must have appeared dangerously demagogic. But James based his advice on empirical analysis and ideological understanding, on the role that ordinary people have actually played in history. His studies of the Haitian Revolution, the Paris Commune, the Russian Revolution, and of the infinitely plural and diverse struggles for democracy waged around the world in every era convinced James that the self-activity of ordinary citizens and workers held the key to social change. His plea for popular mobilization proved prophetic in the 1960s when massive anti-colonial and anti-racist struggles helped instigate an era of grass-roots participatory democracy that transformed social relations in substantive and lasting ways.

Political reaction and repression, technological change, and economic restructuring have eroded many of the gains made by the popular movements of the 1960s and 1970s, but the resolve by ordinary people to stand and be counted – to see themselves as entitled to participation in decisions that shape their own destinies – remains a crucial resource for social change. At a time when transnational capital and repressive state apparatuses hold the upper hand everywhere, cultural production plays a vital role in nurturing and sustaining self-activity on the part of aggrieved peoples. Culture enables people to rehearse identities, stances, and social relations not yet permissible in politics. But it also serves as a concrete social site, a place where social relations are constructed and enacted as well as envisioned. Popular culture does not just reflect reality, it helps constitute it.

It is no accident that the state so often involves itself in questions of culture. Governments sustain or suppress artistic expression out of self-interest, out of recog-nition of the complex connections linking "the nation" with the imagi-nation. In his subtle and knowing discussion of carnival celebrations among West Indians in London,

Abner Cohen comments that "cultural symbols and the communal relationships they express and sustain are so powerful in their hold on people that political formations everywhere, including the state, always manipulate them in their own interests."[2] But if artists and musicians are manipulated, they also manipulate; they use their license as performers and their standing as celebrities to advance their interests as citizens and subjects.

Popular music can play a complicated role in politics. It helps to construct the nation state while at the same time being constructed by it. As a commercial enterprise established essentially to secure profitable returns on investments, it rarely respects the limits of national boundaries and rarely runs the risk of being too closely identified with divisive political positions. At the same time, because popular music functions as a node in a network of international capital, it sometimes offers subordinate populations opportunities to escape the limits of their own societies, to find new audiences and allies by appealing to an international market and embarrassing local authorities by exposing them to international censure and ridicule.

Different national circumstances inflect the politics of popular music in different ways. Groups seeking to build nation states often do not have the same interests as indigenous peoples resisting conquest, who, in turn, often do not have the same interests as national or ethnic minorities seeking parity with other groups or a state of their own. In Africa, for example, musicians have been able to participate directly in politics through nationalism – through music that calls for anti-colonial liberation, that rebukes corrupt authorities, or that serves as a focus for reformers and revolutionaries in their countries. But indigenous peoples around the globe produce distinctly different kinds of political music, largely because they have very different relationships to narratives of national identity. As the people whose displacement and erasure provides the preconditions for the modern nation state, native people often have to assert their allegiance to entities both smaller and larger than the nation state. Consequently, their music often aims to circumvent the nation by asserting their own autonomy or by affirming alliances with other aggrieved groups. For their part, ethnic or national minorities often create music that both affirms and denies their connections to the nation states that they sometimes seek to join more fully and sometimes seek secession from.

When Patrice Lumumba led a delegation to Brussels in 1959 to negotiate for the independence of what was then the Belgian Congo, he brought with him experts on international law, military officials, economic development specialists, and a seven-piece Congolese rhumba-jazz band directed by Joseph Kabaselle, "le Grand Kalle" of

African jazz. Some European and American observers ridiculed the inclusion of a jazz band at such a solemn event of statecraft, but Lumumba knew that "Grand Kalle et l'African Jazz" provided a potentially powerful source of unity for a new nation the size of Europe populated by some 240 tribal groups.

Kalle's acoustic ensemble had soared to popularity during the revolutionary decade of the 1950s by fusing rhumbas and sambas with African-American jazz instead of the previously pervasive European music heard in the Congo. Kabaselle celebrated Lumumba's diplomatic triumph by composing and recording "Independence Cha-cha," and hailed Louis Armstrong's visit to the newly-independent nation in 1960 with his composition "Okuka Lokole."[3] Because their music played an important role in shaping a non-colonial identity in Zaire, Grand Kalle et l'African Jazz became important to the state, while at the same time their association with the state enhanced their cultural prestige and influence.

Thomas Mapfumo's chimurenga (music of struggle) creations played an even more important role in the liberation struggle that created the nation of Zimbabwe out of colonial and neo-colonial Rhodesia. Like many African musicians, Mapfumo had learned to play successfully in the "international" Anglo-American style, but he began to feel uncomfortable with his music as political conflict in the country intensified. "I kept saying to myself, 'Why am I chasing after these foreign sounds? Haven't I got something of my own that can be called Zimbabwean?'" he recalled years later.[4] Mapfumo decided to sing in his native Shona language and to base his music on the sound of a traditional local instrument, the mbira, albeit modernized through simulation on electronic instruments.

Mapfumo explains:

> People started to face the reality that there was war between the masses and the exploiters and everybody came to realize what we were fighting for. Then even the music started changing and I thought I could do my country a favor – to sing chimurenga songs, so as to encourage those boys who were fighting in the bush. Sure, I could have just kept on playing rock'n'roll, but to our own country that was nothing.[5]

In 1976 the neo-colonial authorities in the Ian Smith government banned his album *Hokyo* and detained Mapfumo for three months without charges. The government tried many forms of repression and deception to neutralize, contain, and coopt Mapfumo, but to no avail. His lyrics ridiculed the authorities but in coded and covert language that proved hard to censor, but easy for the masses to understand. "They wanted to be themselves and be called Zimbabweans, so they were rallying behind my music," he recalls.[6]

Just as music by Joseph Kabaselle and Thomas Mapfumo helped build national independence for Zaire and Zimbabwe, music by Fela Kuti in Nigeria, Alpha Blondy in Côte d'Ivoire, and Johnny Clegg and Mzwakhe Mbuli in South Africa have played a role in popular pressure against corrupt regimes in their countries. Fela Kuti came from a political family; his mother helped win women the right to vote in Nigeria as one of the founders of the Nigerian Women's Union, and she later served as an emissary from her nation to China.[7] Kuti used the attention he attracted as a celebrity playing music to crusade for radical reform. He condemned corruption, poverty, and police brutality in Nigeria, and predicted that he would one day be the President of the country because "artists are the real leaders of society."[8] In 1977, the Nigerian government sent troops to burn and loot Kuti's "Kalakuta Republic" compound and arrest him for his seditious activities. But international and national pressure secured his freedom, and he continued to play a dual role as entertainer and activist. "I see music as a weapon," Kuti explains. "Musicians should be using music to find out what is wrong in the establishment."[9]

Reggae singer Alpha Blondy has played a prominent role in blending African, Caribbean, and European cultures through music that has become popular in many countries (see chapter 2). But he made an important intervention in the politics of his home country with "Brigadier Sabari," a song protesting a raid in Abidjan (conducted under the name "Operation Fist") by police officers who drove citizens from their homes and beat them.[10] Johnny Clegg, a white South African born in Britain but raised in Zimbabwe and South Africa, used his training as an anthropologist and his talents as a musician to assemble inter-racial groups to perform Zulu dances and sing mbaqanga rock songs with political themes.[11] Similarly, Mzwakhe Mbuli, a cultural activist within the African National Congress, helped popularize the anti-apartheid cause by recording his own poems backed up by a music group he founded, the Equals.[12]

Unlike the African nationalists, reformers, and revolutionaries, musicians producing popular music from the perspective of indigenous peoples need to neutralize the nation state as the primary object of their audience's affiliation and identification. They have been particularly adept at using the fusions made possible by contemporary inter-cultural communication to illumine the historic grievances and pressing problems of native peoples around the globe. Indigenous artists from Australia have been particularly creative and influential in winning visibility for themselves and their concerns by deploying a fascinating mixture of old and new musical forms in recordings that have strengthened the solidarity of their own people while securing impressive attention and alliances from other groups. Mastering a dazzling range of indigenous and imported musical styles, Australian indigenous artists have fashioned songs with powerful politically-charged lyrics. Their extraordinary capacity to make music that is both firmly rooted in its place of origin and broadly accessible and appealing, stands as an exemplary model for musicians from other aggrieved communities all around the globe.

Perhaps the most remarkable aspect of Australian indigenous popular music is that it exists at all. Few communities in advanced industrial nations have been more oppressed or more isolated geographically and culturally from cultural and economic power than the native inhabitants of the Australian continent. Scattered about on remote tribal lands, in cattle station communities, on government and church missions, and increasingly in the slums of towns and cities, indigenous people account for less than two percent of the Australian population, but in some areas they make up more than forty percent of the prison population.[13] Despite some modest reforms initiated by a Labor government during the 1970s, centuries of economic exploitation, political suppression, and grotesque social welfare policies have forced indigenous peoples to struggle simply for their own survival.

In an oft-quoted remark, a Black South African intellectual commented during a lecture tour of Australia in 1980: "My own people in South Africa are incredibly degraded and humiliated, but I have never seen a people so psychologically battered as the Aborigines."[14] Material deprivation and cultural oppression rarely help people's self-esteem, and tribal communities show many signs of demoralization and disintegration. Yet, these same communities have also been sites for the creation of a powerful protest music. Indigenous artists have appropriated the apparatuses of commercial culture to tell the truth about local resistance to racism, conquest, and oppression. "This Land" by Coloured Stone and "Thou Shalt Not Steal" by Kev Carmody rewrite Australian history by insisting on indigenous ownership of the nation's territory. Archie Roach's "Took the Children Away" recalls how social welfare authorities took thousands of indigenous children away from their parents and "relocated" them with white families. "Bran Nue Dae" by Kuckles ridicules government promises of a better life for indigenous Australians, while Yothu Yindi's "Treaty" calls on the Australian government to negotiate with indigenous peoples, such as their own Yolngu tribal group, as members of sovereign nations. In Yothu Yindi's "My Kind of Life," Coloured Stone's "I'm Going Back to Alice Springs," and the Tjapukai Dancers' wonderful

"Proud to Be (Aborigine)," indigenous groups affirm their attachment to the places where they grew up and to the traditions and values they learned there.[15]

For tens of thousands of years before Europeans arrived in Australia, songs had served as sources of strength and knowledge in indigenous culture. Through music, indigenous Australians practiced medicine, passed along their histories, and communicated with spiritual forces. Leila Rankine, a Ngarrindjri poet and musician, helps explain how musical expression emerged as a site of cultural resistance. She remembers that the authorities discouraged indigenous children from speaking out, but encouraged them to sing. Evidently, many of them developed a way of doing the former by means of the latter.[16] But the particular political perspective permeating indigenous popular music draws as much from political mobilization as it adds to it. Explicitly political lyrics emerged in this music only after mass mobilizations succeeded in winning concessions that created spaces for them to grow and develop.

In 1975 indigenous activists joined with environmentalists to demonstrate against government policies that permitted mining on sacred tribal sites. At one of those protests, indigenous musician Jimmy Chi wrote "Bran Nue Dae," which later became the signature song of his band Kuckles.[17] Broad-based political mobilization led to new sensitivity to cultural differences, which in turn helped give rise to centers for the study, preservation, and development of indigenous music in Adelaide and in Alice Springs.[18] Many of the leading indigenous popular-music performers including No Fixed Address, Us Mob, Kuckles, and Sunburn used the resources of these centers. But perhaps the greatest spur to indigenous musical and political activism came from the 1979 tour of Australia and New Zealand by the Jamaican reggae singer, Bob Marley.

When Marley appeared in Adelaide early in 1979, he provoked a tumultuous response from indigenous Australians for his claim that all Black men are brothers. He inspired the members of No Fixed Address and other indigenous bands to embrace reggae as "the Black music of the future."[19] By taking on Marley's pan-African vision, indigenous Australians transformed themselves from a tiny national minority into part of the global majority of "non-white" people. Like the Maoris in neighboring New Zealand who starting favoring green, red, and yellow attire (the colors of pan-Africanism) after Marley's visit to their country later that year, indigenous people in Australia found that the Jamaican's genius for situating "Blackness" in Caribbean, African, European, and North American contexts helped them understand what it meant to be "Black" in former British colonies in the South Pacific.[20]

The combination of successful centers for indigenous music and the momentum of Marley's visit inserted an enduring political purpose within indigenous popular music that endures to this day. Jimmy Chi of Kuckles drew upon his experiences at the Centre for Aboriginal Studies in Music when he returned to Broome and started the Broome Musicians' Aboriginal Corporation in the mid-1980s. "We started that up to get something happening up here, to make musicians more aware of what they can do . . . music keeps people together in the community framework," he recalls.[21] Similarly, No Fixed Address took pride in the ways that their performances created desegregated spaces that rebuked traditional Australian racism. As a member of the group explained to musicologist Chester Schultz, "I think our biggest feeling when we're up on stage is seeing mixed people together. Like with half the crowd white and half black, getting along together with no trouble. Most of the black fellows who come to see us really feel proud. We're just trying to get respected."[22]

Although they often employ indigenous languages, instruments (didjeridu, clapsticks), choral singing, and variable rhythms, the popular songs recorded by indigenous Australians also access a broad range of commercial popular music including country and western, calypso, gospel, reggae, and rock'n'roll. Before the 1970s, the indigenous presence in Australian popular music amounted to little more than ballads by Jimmy Little, novelty records by prize fighter Lionel Rose, and occasional cover versions of country songs. A significant exception came in the country music recorded by Dougie Young from rural southeastern Australia, whose songs directly addressed racial discrimination, poverty, and police surveillance of the indigenous population.[23] "To many aboriginal people, country and western was traditional aboriginal music," recalls one veteran of the Australian music scene cognizant of the influence of Jimmie Rodgers, Elvis Presley, and Kris Kristofferson among indigenous singers.[24] This was a matter of resources as well as of taste; Euro-Australian dominance of the music industry left little room for indigenous compositions. As Jimmy Little once explained, "the very fact that an Aboriginal performer gets on stage and sings is a political act."[25]

Since the political and cultural transformations of the 1970s, however, indigenous popular music has embraced the styles of a wider world – not only reggae and calypso, but contemporary rock music has been influential as well. Rick Lovegrove Maher, the lead singer of Uluru and later a member of No Fixed Address, lists Bob Dylan, Pink Floyd, and Bad Company among the major influences on his music.[26] Yet, their music is more dialogic than derivative; the ability of indigenous musicians to insert their own culture and experiences into popular music has been astounding. Yothu Yindi's dance mix version of "Treaty" sung in the Gumatj language made the Australian best-seller charts in 1992.[27] Of course, some audiences and much of the music industry may treat indigenous music as a simply exotic element in an otherwise undifferentiated pop scene, but the success of a band like Yothu Yindi nonetheless opens up new and important space for airing indigenous Australian issues within the public culture of Australia and the rest of the world.[28]

Connections to a broader world pose problems for any group of musicians playing local music, but even more so for indigenous Australians. Their attachment to place is sacred as well as secular; their songs evoke specific local sites, not just abstract or idealized landscapes. Scrap Metal and Jimmy Chi insist on remaining in Broome, far removed from the public relations and musical production centers of Australia.[29] In addition, the presence of clapsticks and didjeridu in popular music call attention to indigenous issues in important ways. As Karl Neuenfeldt argues in an insightful discussion of traditional instruments in indigenous rock songs, "although the musics and instruments of indigenous peoples . . . may become incorporated within an all-pervading 'universal pop aesthetic' . . ., they still resonate most fully and profoundly in the local context."[30] Like the mbira among the Shona in Zimbabwe, a traditional sound can serve non-traditional purposes when redeployed in the present.

Australian indigenous musicians have also proven themselves particularly adept at using musical performances to articulate their concerns to outsiders and particularly skilled at appropriating musical forms from other places to express attachment to their own spaces and sites. Success overseas can win respect at home, as Yothu Yindi discovered when the North American edition of *Time* did a story about them in 1991.[31] In addition, indigenous peoples have discovered that the global economy affects them in immediate and concrete ways in every area of life from the exploitation of the environment by mining interests to the spread of disease. In 1989, a number of indigenous bands including the Areyonga Desert Tigers, the Amunda Band, and the Tableland Drifters collaborated on an album titled *AIDS: How Could I Know* designed to educate their audience about the dangers of AIDS and the need for safe sex practices.

Just as global issues effect indigenous life in Australia, the international nature of the entertainment business brings Australian indigenous bands in direct contact with other aggrieved populations around the world. In 1981, a Californian impressed by the Australian film *Walkabout* brought a troupe of indigenous singers and dancers to the U.S.A. for a series of concert performances. They drew favorable reviews and sympathetic press coverage, even when they made it a point to make contacts and open discussions with Native Americans in Los Angeles and African Americans in Harlem about issues of cultural survival and social justice.[32] When Yothu Yindi traveled from their home in Yirrkala in eastern Arnhem Land to perform in New York City, they expressed their solidarity with African Americans by doing an interview with a reporter from a Black radio station at Marcus Garvey Park in Harlem.[33]

Connections between indigenous Australians and African Americans became even clearer in January 1990 when Circuit Court Judge Lawrence Johnston in Rockledge, Florida sentenced indigenous Australian James Hudson Savage to death in the electric chair for the murder, rape, and robbery of a fifty-seven-year-old Melbourne, Florida woman in 1988. The twenty-six-year-old Savage had been taken from his teenaged indigenous Australian mother shortly after he was born and sent to live with a white missionary couple. He never adjusted to white society and wound up living a criminal life in the United States. His attorney asked for a life sentence rather than the death penalty on the grounds that Savage's life of crime stemmed, in part, from Australia's racist paternalism. But Judge Johnston ruled that "drugs, alcohol, and violence are personal choices, not family excuses."[34] Savage's story became the basis for "Munjana," a popular protest song by indigenous Australian singer Archie Roach. In his song, Roach details the pain of those children taken from their families and thrust into an alien environment by the state, concluding that no matter what Savage had done himself, "another crime committed here was genocide."[35]

As Roach's "Munjana" demonstrates, the accumulated legacy of centuries of oppression leaves indigenous peoples facing enormous problems. Commercial success by a few bands is no substitute for true justice and equal opportunity. Moreover, high visibility in the music industry by individual artists and bands hardly means an end to anti-indigenous racism. As Kev Carmody notes,

> You know, even if you do get a gig, say it's in one of the clubs somewhere or something, you immediately wind up with four times the bouncers on the door. That's the whole fear mentality. And I think there's an underlying subliminal thing there. There's fear that what's being said in the music is undermining the concept of their imported culture. So there's a thousand things happening there. They use things like dress sense to keep the black fellas out, door prices to keep the black fellas out. There's a million things that are used to sort of stereotype us. And they're just preconceived colonial ideas.[36]

Yet the extraordinary ability of indigenous Australian musicians to fuse local concerns with global issues and exposure positions them effectively to participate in inter-ethnic ecological and anti-racist coalitions in Australia. Euro-Australian artist Paul Kelly performs with and produces records by Archie Roach, while Peter Garrett's band Midnight Oil plays up indigenous concerns in their democratic-socialist songs, including the international hit "Beds Are Burning." Yothu Yindi's Mandawuy Yunupingu wrote "Treaty" in collaboration with Kelly and Garrett as a way of underscoring the philosophy expressed in his lyrics that Yolngu (his tribal affiliation) and Balanda (European identity) equal "Australia."[37] This collaboration amounts to more than a marriage of convenience within the logic of the recording industry, but rather expresses the Yolngu concept of *ganma* – the place where the water from the sea and the water from the land meet, mingle, and become inseparable.[38]

Indigenous Australian bands themselves frequently feature mixed membership; Scrap Metal's musicians claim French, Filipino, Scottish, Japanese, and Indonesian ancestry in addition to their Yawru tribal lineage. The members of Kuckles have Chinese, Filipino, and Malaysian names. Neither Yothu Yindi nor the Warumpi Band have all-indigenous line-ups. Like so many other contemporary cultural and political formations emanating from aggrieved racial groups, indigenous Australians in popular music have fashioned a coalition based on culture rather than color, on shared politics rather than on the skin color of people's parents. In so doing, they show how one of the world's oldest traditional communities stands ready to engage in the newest and most innovative forms of politics and culture.[39]

In similar fashion, American Indian musicians in North America have used their unique perspectives to create musical and political spaces built upon inter-ethnic anti-racism. *Reservation of Education*, recorded in the mountains of New Mexico in 1993 by Robby Bee and the Boyz from the Rez deploys the musical forms and moral framework of African-American hip hop to articulate the needs and interests of Native Americans. But it also reflects and reinforces emerging social relations among Native Americans, Blacks, Chicanos, Asians, and anti-racist whites. Through what the group calls "pow wow hip hop," Robby Bee and the Boyz from the Rez draw upon the historical grievances and triumphs of Native Americans to accent the critique of American racism and inequality offered through rap music. In their song "Ebony Warrior" they celebrate the historical alliances and inter-marriages that have united Blacks and Native Americans, lauding "Frederick D" (Douglass) as "an ebony warrior who fought for you and me." At the same time, they point to wrongly imprisoned American Indian Movement leader, "Leonard P" (Peltier), as our own Nelson Mandela.[40]

In "Stand and Be Counted," Robby Bee and the Boyz from the Rez exhort young people with a message similar to the one offered by C.L.R. James in Trinidad thirty-five years ago, telling their listeners that "young people have the power to do something great, the chance to change the world, before it's too late."[41] Their samples of Indian music, rhythm and blues, and rock'n'roll undergird selections from speeches by Martin Luther King, Jr. and John F. Kennedy as well as lyrics teaching lessons about Native

American history and affirming pride in Indian culture. Like indigenous Australian musicians, they use national and international forms of commercial culture to locate their local and culturally-specific grievances within new social relations emerging from new patterns of work, leisure, and consumption. Once again, fundamentally new forms of politics and culture seem to emerge from one of the oldest communities on earth.

Québécois nationalists – the French speakers in the Canadian province of Quebec fighting to preserve their culture and advance their interests as a nation – confront fundamentally different challenges from those facing the nationalists and reformers in Africa or indigenous activists in Australia and the U.S.A. As Canadians, they reap the benefits of citizenship in an independent nation, enjoy a standard of living and social welfare benefits superior to most of the rest of the world, and exercise control over powerful political and economic institutions. Indeed, they have reaped extensive benefits from French, British, Canadian, and U.S. exploitation around the world and conquest of Native peoples in North America.

Yet, they are also only six million people surrounded by more than two hundred million English speakers. To determine their own destiny they have to overcome the legacies of French domination over Quebec, British and U.S. domination over Canada, and federal Canadian domination over Quebec and other provinces with significant numbers of Francophone citizens. Even within their own ranks, there have been deep divisions between those who seek greater power and influence for French speakers within the Canadian confederation and those committed to establishing their own nation, between those who see Québécois nationalism largely as a way of maximizing the power of French speakers in the existing social, economic, and political system, and those who view it as an opportunity to establish radically different kinds of institutions and relations. At various times, Québécois nationalists have secured significant concessions from the Canadian government, especially on cultural issues, and on occasion they have secured electoral majorities that have given them control over the provincial government in Quebec. But like all nationalisms, Quebec nationalism is an ever-changing construct, a dynamic entity that gets articulated, modified, and transformed daily on a dozen fronts, including the field of popular music.

Not all of Canada's French speakers live in Quebec, but the demographics in the province and its political history make it the center of Francophone nationalism. Consequently, when artists from other provinces sing in French (like Edith Butler from Paquetville, New Brunswick or Daniel Lavoie from Dunrea, Manitoba), they are considered "Québécois" artists. For many years, music from France, English-speaking

Canada, or the U.S.A. dominated the commercial field in Quebec. For their part, Québécois artists often sought success in France, performed French-language versions of U.S. pop songs, or recorded music in English to tap the Canadian and U.S. markets. But in the 1960s, a group of singer-songwriters led by Gilles Vigneault and the great writer Félix Leclerc drew upon folk traditions to fashion music that served as a focal point for the creation of a new Québécois identity. The enthusiasm and energy unleashed by the fusion of popular culture and politics in Quebec generated the production of an extraordinarily diverse range of creative and compelling music that transformed Québécois culture and secured extraordinary commercial success for over a decade. From the wild antics and counter-cultural appeal of Robert Charlebois to the European-flavored pop of Diane Dufresne to the blues-tinged rock'n'roll of Claude Dubois, Francophone music from Quebec in the 1960s and 1970s served nationalist ends by creating sites where the commonalities of Québécois culture become the basis for new social relations and aspirations.

In the mid-1960s, Gilles Vigneault wrote and recorded "Mon Pays" ("My Country"), a song that combines images of winter and the singer's memories of his father to the national destiny of Quebec. Its opening lyrics assert that "my country is not a country, it is the winter," as a way of tapping the shared experiences of Quebeckers with their landscape and way of life while reminding them of the ways in which not having their own nation frustrates their aspirations for self-determination. In the last verse, Vigneault appeals to his listeners to recognize the connection between art and social life with a line that states "my song is not my song, it is my life." By tapping traditional styles of Québécois folk music and mobilizing memories of ancestors and obligations to them as a spur for political action in the present, Vigneault's "Mon Pays" and songs like it played a powerful role in making the abstract principles of nationalism immediate, tangible, emotional, and sensual for millions of Quebeckers.

Vigneault, Leclerc, and Charlebois provided important role models for young Quebeckers. During the mid-1960s, François Guy had been involved in music primarily as a rock singer in English-language bands including the Silver Spiders and the Sinners. But when the nineteen-year-old became acquainted with Charlebois in 1968, he realized that he could sing in French. He formed a trio with Richard Tate and Angelo Finaldi calling themselves La Révolution Française. They stayed together only six months, but in that time they wrote and recorded the anthemic song "Québécois." Young audiences embraced "Québécois" as an expression of their hopes for nationhood at the annual June 24 festivities celebrating the saint's day of St. Jean-Baptiste, the patron saint of Quebec.[42]

At the same time, counter-cultural musicians interpreting international youth and "hippie" concerns from a Québécois perspective played an important role in fusing music and politics. Lucien Francouer, who helped form the group Aut'Chose, expressed admiration for the abilities of Gilles Vigneault and Félix Leclerc, but denied that they influenced his music in any significant way. "I was marked by the counter-culture," he explained to a reporter in 1979, "by acid and the words of Timothy Leary and Jerry Rubin."[43] From Jacques Michel's "Fume Ta Marijuana" ("Smoke Your Marijuana") to the offerings of Daniel Lavoie's first group, "Dieu de l'Amour vous aime" ("The God of Love Loves You") to Louise Forrestier and Robert Charlebois's extraordinary "Lindberg" (music by Charlebois, lyrics by Claude Peloquin), the prestige of youth counter-cultures drew Québécois artists into a new understanding of the relationship between popular music and social life.[44] They also made alliances with French or U.S. culture as a means of undermining the hegemony of English-speaking Canada. Unlike Anglophone Canadian singers like Stompin' Tom Connors seeking to establish a unified Canadian national identity capable of resisting identification with the U.S.A., Québécois artists expressed open identification with U.S. culture in a variety of ways, like Robert Charlebois's use of U.S. English slang along with Québécois joual or Diane Dufresne's nostalgic song about her memories of growing up in Quebec with a crush on Elvis Presley.

The golden years of Québécois music coincided with the growth of the nationalist Parti Québécois and its accession to power in provincial elections. For many Quebeckers, a decade of cultural revival and political mobilization led logically to secession from Canada and the establishment of Quebec as an independent nation. But the disastrous defeat of a Parti Québécois-sponsored initiative in a provincial referendum doomed these hopes for at least a decade, and devastated the political and social base that had given rise to nationalist Québécois music.

Political failure contributed to a dramatic shift in Québécois culture; during the 1980s sales of records by Québécois artists dropped significantly, local record companies and studios ceased operations, and individual artists turned to other genres. The identification with politics that had proved so lucrative for Quebec musicians in the 1970s became a liability in the 1980s, and a bitter sense of betrayal on all sides permeated the cultural politics of the province. Louise Forrestier stopped performing music in public, while Daniel Lavoie, Diane Tell, and other artists began to spend an increasing proportion of their time in France.[45] Robert Charlebois commented on the death of the dream of Quebec independence in a 1982 interview, noting,

I still see some people who have not come out of the delirium of those days, and it is not pleasant to see; most often, these people feel betrayed by those who have left their world. But surely they would trade their anguish for some confidence. After a while, revolution for the sake of revolution no longer makes sense.[46]

By the late 1980s, Quebec culture seemed more imperiled than ever. Poet Nicole Broussard told an audience:

Bilingual Canada is a fiction, a fake. We are six million French speakers living in a sea of English. English is the international language. There's TV, British and American music. We Québécois have the lowest birth rate in the world. We need daily political vigilance in the matter of language. If Quebec doesn't achieve independence, we'll be like the Americans. It has to happen in the next ten years. If not, it's all over.[47]

Yet, the institutions created through political struggle continued to play an impor tant part in Quebec's cultural life. In 1989, the Ministry of Cultural Affairs poured $234 million into artistic and cultural production in the province, spending twice as much on those endeavors as the much larger English-speaking province of Ontario. The provincial budget increased 22 percent between 1985 and 1989, but spending on cultural activities increased by 44 percent.[48] Like the centers for the study and preservation of indigenous music won through political struggle in Australia, these state expenditures in Quebec carved away space for local cultural production within the international market.

After years of decline, sales of music by Quebec artists increased significantly toward the end of the 1980s. Québécois musicians counted for nearly 40 percent of the artists whose recordings sold more than 50,000 copies in Canada in 1989 (ten out of twenty-six). The popularity of Gerry Boulet, Marjo, Michel Rivard, and Johanne Blouin sparked a revival in the province's commercial music industry that pushed revenues to an all-time high.[49] Richard Seguin, who had performed folk music in the 1970s with his twin sister Marie-Claire, re-established his career as a rock songwriter and singer in the late 1980s by restoring political themes to Quebec music. But the new politics of popular music in the province tended to address feminism, environmentalism, and pacifism rather than more narrowly nationalist issues. "We are all influenced by what's happening in society. Even our personal lives are affected, however much we may try and shelter ourselves," Seguin argued. Equating recognition as a musician as equiva-lent to standing on a speakers' platform, he complained that because politicians treat people like "kids in a nursery school," his role was to encourage rebellion. "And the stage is the perfect place for it," he continued, "because the audience expects it to be used as a platform and they understand all the rituals."[50]

In an indirect and unexpected way, federal politics played an important role in the revival of Québécois culture and politics. The policies of the Progressive-Conservative Party under the leadership of Brian Mulroney eroded Canadian sovereignty significantly through a series of agreements with the U.S.A., especially through the North American Free Trade Agreement. In the name of privatization, Mulroney's government weakened national communication and transportation networks and made Canadian markets more accessible to U.S. products. By reducing differences between Canada and the U.S.A., these policies gave more power to Quebec within the federation while calling attention anew to the ways in which Francophone culture made the province different from the rest of the nation. In the 1993 elections, a coalition from Quebec emerged as the second largest force in the Canadian Parliament. It is not clear whether this prefigures either separation from Canada or more autonomy within the federal system for Quebec, and it is not at all clear what Quebec independence might mean for the rights of indigenous peoples or women or immigrants in the province. But it is clear that popular music in Quebec has played an important role in creating and maintaining a sense of common identity for millions of French speakers within the province and across Canada.

African nationalists, reformers, and revolutionaries, Australian indigenous and Native American activists, and Québécois separatists have all used popular music as part of their strategies for securing, shaping, or stunting the power of the state. They have deployed music as an important weapon in battles to create a cultural basis for new nations, to transform alliances and identities within already existing states, and to unmask the power imbalances that give regions, languages, and ethnic groups very different relations to the state they supposedly all share.

The plurality of practices that connect popular music to politics around the world often revolve around the peculiarities of place and history. Attacks on the state by anti-apartheid crusaders or Indian activists can enhance inter-cultural sensitivity and understanding, but when the official policy of the state has been anti-racist, attacks on the state can be regressive. For example, "The Skinhead Marching Song" by the Hungarian band Mos-oi attacks the legacy of totalitarian state power in that country by resorting to despicable forms of racism against immigrants, "gypsies," and Jews.[51] The mere fact of opposition to the state does not guarantee progressive, democratic, or

egalitarian politics; the mere fusion of popular culture and politics does not automatically mean better culture or better politics. But in the contemporary world it is hard to
see how culture can ever serve emancipatory ends if it does not confront the power of
the state at some point, and it is equally difficult to imagine any progressive political
practice that does not have a cultural dimension to it.

When cultural studies scholarship started, critics often questioned whether it made
sense to call cultural practices and preferences political. They wondered whether the
music people play or the products they purchase have any real impact on public
struggles for political and economic power. These critics missed all-important connections between everyday life and politics; they failed to see the significance of how
popular culture creates its own micro-politics of organization, location, identity, and
affiliation. But in the era of de-industrialization, de-Stalinization, and post-coloniality,
we might better wonder whether *politics* can ever be political, whether political
discourse will ever again amount to anything other than a cultural performance
designed to divert attention from who actually has power and what they have done
with it.

Over the past twenty years in advanced industrialized nations especially, serious
political debate has been superseded by a succession of moral panics and moralizing
sermons. Instead of solutions to our most serious problems, candidates for office give
us idealized projections of personality. The state has virtually ceased to support its
citizens, but instead supplies us with spectacular exercises of military power for the
voyeuristic diversion of television audiences. Putatively socialist countries have suc-
cumbed to fraudulent "free market" hucksters who give full mobility and freedom only
to capital while confining citizens to ever contracting circles of suffering and silence.
"Third World" nationalists have seized state power by fair means and foul only to find
that the International Monetary Fund and transnational capital exercise even more
control over their countries than ever before.

The collapse of many kinds of political practice leaves commodities at the center of
social life. The atrophy of the nation state and the concomitant rise of private enclaves
of power and privilege answerable to no one leave little room for collective, coordin-
ated, public struggles for power and resources. The trade unions, electoral coalitions,
and community mobilizations that used to restrain the ambitions of capital and win
concessions for aggrieved groups were based on premises about the stability of capital
and the strength of the nation state that no longer apply. But as workplace- and
community-based social movements command less power and participation, new ones
emerge to take their place. Increasingly, these "new social movements" (see chapter 2)

revolve around cultural and social identity, coalition politics, non-ideological pragmatic concerns, and communities ranging in size from small neighborhood groups to
broad global alliances of feminists, ecologists, or anti-racists.

The new social movements face many problems, and it is difficult to see how they can
ever succeed by themselves unless they also attach themselves to more traditional forms
of struggle for control at the point of production and for political power through the
exercise of state power. But their existence emerges logically from new social relations
mandated by the supremacy of transnational capital. As the rapid flow of capital
undermines formerly stable identities and brings into being new networks and circuits
of communication, cultural questions take on crucial political importance.

African nationalists, reformers, and revolutionaries, activists from indigenous communities in Australia and the United States, and Francophone nationalists from
Quebec have faced different forms of state power in their struggles for self-determination. But for each group, popular music has provided a means of tapping collective
memories of the past and shared aspirations for the future. Popular music has helped
aggrieved groups to make their local struggles visible all around the world and it has
tapped the conduits of commodity exchange within commercial culture to build
coalitions capable of circumventing the political and cultural constraints of any one
nation state.

By playing on the contradictions between nation states and the capitalist economies
they sustain and support, popular musicians have sometimes successfully used commercial culture as a vehicle for political agitation and education. Their music reflects
the imperatives of the commercial and industrial matrices from which they emerge; in
challenging the nation state from time to time, they accept the centrality of commodity
exchange to contemporary culture and politics. Yet by operating through commodities, they also acquire authority and influence far beyond the borders of their own
face-to-face communities.

The critics of cultural studies may well be right to question what kind of political
practice can emerge from within commercial culture. Yet they would do well to
remember C.L.R. James's warning to his adult education class in Trinidad in 1960:

> In the end it is practical life and its needs which will decide both the problems of social and
> political existence and the correctness of a theory. But mankind today has reached a stage
> where action is conditioned by thought and thought by action to a degree unprecedented
> in previous ages. That indeed is the problem of the twentieth century. Whatever helps to

clarify this is valuable. And whoever, for whatever reason, puts barriers in the way of knowledge is thereby automatically convicted of reaction and enmity to human progress.[52]

NOTES

1. C.L.R. James, *Modern Politics* (Detroit, MI: Bewick Editions, 1973), 155.

2. Abner Cohen, *Masquerade Politics* (Berkeley: University of California Press, 1993), 120.

3. Philip Sweeney, *The Virgin Directory of World Music* (New York: Henry Holt, 1991), 50; Donald Clarke, ed., *The Penguin Encyclopedia of Popular Music* (London: Penguin Books, 1990), 638–9; Grand Kalle et l'African Jazz, *Merveilles du Passé*, Sonodisc CD 36503.

4. Don Snowden, "Zimbabwe Singer's Dream Helps Make the Revolution," *Los Angeles Times*, October 21, 1989, F6.

5. Julie Frederikse, *None But Ourselves: Masses vs. Media in the Making of Zimbabwe* (Exeter, New Hampshire: Heinemann, 1992).

6. Don Snowden, "Zimbabwe Singer's Dream Helps Make the Revolution," F6; Erik Goldman, "Thomas Mapfumo," *Option* (March/April) 1990, 43.

7. Rob Tannenbaum, "Fela Anikulapao Kuti," *Musician* no.79 (May) 1985, 30.

8. Don Snowden, "He's Philosopher, Rebel, and Passionate Musician," *Los Angeles Times*, November 12, 1986, calendar section, 6; Jon Pareles, "Fela Anikulapo Kuti, Nigeria's Political Activist," *New York Times*, November 7, 1986, C23.

9. Rob Tannenbaum, "Fela Anikulapo Kuti," 30.

10. Tom Cheyney, "Televisionary," *Option*.

11. Philip Sweeney, *The Virgin Directory of World Music*, 68; Donald Clarke, ed., *The Penguin Encyclopedia of Popular Music*, 68.

12. Philip Sweeney, *The Virgin Directory of Popular Music*, 69.

13. Chris Lawe Davies, "Aboriginal Rock Music: Space and Place," in Tony Bennett, Simon Frith, Lawrence Grossberg, John Shepherd, and Graeme Turner, *Rock and Popular Music: Politics, Policies, Institutions* (London and New York: Routledge, 1993), 249; Chester Schultz, "Aboriginal Music," in Marcus Breen, ed., *Our Place Our Music: Aboriginal Music* (Canberra: Aboriginal Studies Press, 1989), 3, 4.

14. Quoted by Chester Schultz in Marcus Breen, ed., *Our Place Our Music*, 27.

15. Coloured Stone, "This Land," and "I'm Going Back to Alice Springs," on *Island of Greed*, RCA, SPCK1088; Kev Carmody, "Thou Shalt Not Steal," on *Pillars of Society*, Larrikan Records, CDLRF 23; Archie Roach, "Took the Children Away," on *Charcoal Lane*, Aurora D30386; Kuckles, "Bran Nue Dae," on *Songs from Bran Nue Dae*, BND-001; Yothu Yindi, "Treaty," and "My Kind of Life," on *Tribal*

Voice, Mushroom Records TVD93358; Marcus Breen, "Desert Dreams, Media, and Interventions in Reality: Australian Aboriginal Music," in Reebee Garofalo, *Rockin' the Boat* (Boston MA: South End, 1992), 150.

16. D. Leila Rankine, "Aboriginal Music," in Marcus Breen, ed., *Our Place Our Music*, 3–4.

17. Marcus Breen, "Desert Dreams, Media, and Interventions in Reality", 161. According to one account, Kuckles took their name from a local shellfish (cockle) "with lascivious significance." Chris Lawe Davies "Black Rock and Broome," *Perfect Beat* vol.1 no.2 (1993), 54.

18. Chris Lawe Davies, "Aboriginal Rock Music," 252, 259; John Castles, "Tjungaringanyi: Aboriginal Rock," in Philip Hayward, ed., *From Pop to Punk to Postmodernism: Popular Music and Australian Culture from the 1960s to the 1990s* (North Sydney, Australia: Allen & Unwin, 1992), 27.

19. Rose Ryan, "Aboriginal Music," in Marcus Breen, ed., *Our Place Our Music*, 121.

20. John Dix, *Stranded in Paradise: New Zealand Rock'n'roll, 1955–1988* (New Zealand: Paradise Publications, 1988), 333. Dix relates that on the day that Marley died the Hawke's Bay freezing works had to close because of the large numbers of Maoris who stayed home from work to grieve over Marley's death.

21. Marcus Breen, "Desert Dreams, Media, and Interventions in Reality," 167.

22. Chester Schultz, "Aboriginal Music," 120.

23. Stephen Wild, "Songs of Experience," *The Musical Times* vol.133 no.1793 (July) 1992, 338.

24. John Castles, "Tjungaringanyi," 28.

25. Quoted in Tony Mitchell's reply to Lisa Nicol in *Perfect Beat* vol.1 no.2 (1993), 31.

26. Chester Schultz, "Aboriginal Music," 127. Maher was raised by a white family in Adelaide.

27. Lisa Nicol, "Culture, Custom, and Collaboration," 27.

28. For an argument that Yothu Yindi's pop success has come at the expense of their politics see Philip Hayward, "Safe, Exotic, and Somewhere Else," *Perfect Beat* vol.1 no.2 (1993), 33–42.

29. Chris Lawe Davies, "Black Rock and Broome," *Perfect Beat* vol.1, no.2 (1993), 56.

30. Karl Neuenfeldt, "The Djideridu and the Overdub," *Perfect Beat* vol.1, no.2 (1993), 75.

31. Karl Neuenfeldt, *Journal of Australian Studies* no.38 (September) 1993, 6.

32. Chester Schultz, "Aboriginal Music," 109–110.

33. John Castles, "Tjungaringanyi," 31.

34. Associated Press, "Death Sentence Ordered in Florida Slaying," *New York Times*, January 24, 1990, A18.

35. Marcus Breen, "Desert Dreams, Media, and Interventions in Reality," 150.

36. Rob Johnson, "Looking Out: An Interview with Kev Carmody," *Perfect Beat* vol.1 no.2 (1993), 44.

37. Lisa Nicol, "Culture, Custom, and Collaboration," 30.

38. Karl Neuenfeldt, "Yothu Yindi and Ganma: The Cultural Transposition of Aboriginal Agenda Through Metaphor and Music," *Journal of Australian Studies* no.38 (September) 1993, 1.

39. Chris Lawe Davies, "Aboriginal Rock Music," 255, 251; Philip Sweeney, *The Virgin Directory of World Music*, 176.

40. The song "Ebony Warrior" also references the group's dark-skinned back-up singer Michael Davis, who calls himself Michael D, the "ebony warrior."

41. Robby Bee and the Boyz from the Rez, *Reservation of Education*, lyrics, Warrior 604.

42. Nathalie Petrowski, "A New Direction for a Quebec Star," *Canadian Composer* (September) 1979, 26; "La Révolution Française," *Disco-Mag* vol.1 no.2 (1969), 41; P.V., "Les Québécois Perdent la Révolution Française," *La Presse*, January 29, 1970, 14; Richard Tardif, "Les Sinners: Ils Sont Revenus," *Pop Eye* (December) 1970, 14.

43. Nathalie Petrowski, "Interview," *Canadian Composer* (March) 1979, 18.

44. John Griffin, "Welcome Back, Robert Charlebois," *The Gazette*, October 8, 1983, H-1.

45. Andrée Laurier, "Passion Brings Songwriter Show-Stopping Success," *Canadian Composer* (May) 1986, 10; Gene Hayden, "Marketing Music in France Challenges Quebec Artists," *Canadian Composer* (November) 1987, 16.

46. Marc Desjardins, "No Fallen Hero, This Quebec Superstar Succeeds in France," *Canadian Composer* (April) 1982, 10.

47. Susan Ruta, "French Twists," *Village Voice/Voice Literary Supplement* (November) 1989, 34.

48. Stephen Godfrey, "Rich Cultural Life in Quebec Synonymous with Survival," *The Globe and Mail*, November 4, 1989, A6.

49. Stephen Godfrey, "Rich Cultural Life in Quebec Synonymous with Survival," A6.

50. Andrée Laurier, "Back to the Future," *Canadian Composer* (February–March, 1987), 8.

51. Laszlo Kurti, "How Can I Be a Human Being? Culture, Youth, and Musical Opposition in Hungary," in Sabrina Petra Ramet, ed., *Rocking the State: Rock Music and Politics in Eastern Europe and Russia* (Boulder, San Francisco, Oxford: Westview Press, 1994), 85.

52. C.L.R. James, *Modern Politics*, iii. I know that my postmodern friends may wince at this reference to "progress," since so much harm has been done to people in its name. But the teleology that James draws on here presumes that history should be seen as a struggle for democracy, self-determination, and decent lives for all people. Whatever problems we have created by assuming that progress is inevitable, whatever crimes we have committed in the name of history deserve to be exposed and critiqued and rejected. But to me, the goals James pursues are still absolutely the right ones.

8

"It's All Wrong, but It's All Right": Creative Misunderstanding in Inter-cultural Communication

SOUL VIBRATIONS

On a Sunday afternoon in 1951, eight-year-old Veronica Bennett (later Ronnie Spector of the vocal group the Ronettes) entertained her family in a flat in New York's Spanish Harlem by singing her favorite song. One of Bennett's uncles put an electrician's light inside a Maxwell House coffee can to make a "spotlight," while her father moved the coffee table to the middle of the room to make a "stage." As Bennett recalls:

> That light seemed to focus all the warmth in the room on me as I belted out Hank Williams's "Jambalaya" in my eight-year-old voice. "Jambalie, coldfish pie, diddly gumbo," I sang, with no idea what the words meant or if I even had them right. But when I looked around the room and saw all my aunts and uncles smiling and tapping their feet to keep time, I knew I must have been doing something right. In the middle of the song I stopped singing and improvised a little yodel. I was trying to imitate what all the cowboy singers used to do. And that was the beginning of the "whoa oh-oh-oh-ohohs" that would become my trademark as a singer.[1]

Bennett mangled Hank Williams's lyrics in her rendition, changing crawfish pie into "cold fish pie," and substituting "diddly gumbo" for file' gumbo. Her admission that she didn't know and didn't care what the words meant seems to provide strong support for critics concerned about the distracted and incomplete reception of inter-cultural messages in popular culture. Certainly few people would imagine the maximally competent audience for Hank Williams's country and western song to be Ronnie Bennett's inter-racial family in Spanish Harlem. But further investigation reveals some interesting dimensions to Bennett's choices in singing "Jambalaya."

Ronnie Bennett grew up as the daughter of an African-American/Native American mother and a Euro-American father. Her mother's sister Nedra married a Puerto Rican, making Ronnie's cousin Nedra a mixture of African-American, Native American, and Puerto Rican ancestry. This extended family lived in a neighborhood that "had Chinese laundries, Spanish restaurants, and black grocery stores." At school, Black children teased Veronica about her light skin, calling her "skinny yellow horse" and yelling "Hey, half-breed, get your ass back to the reservation."[2] She later recalled:

> the blacks never really accepted me as one of them. The white kids knew I wasn't white. And the Spanish kids didn't talk to me because I didn't speak Spanish. I had a little identity crisis when I hit puberty. I remember I used to sit in front of the mirror, trying to decide just what I was. Let's see now, I'd think. I've got white eyes, but these are black lips. My ears — are they white ears or black ears?[3]

Bennett appropriated "Jambalaya" from Hank Williams, who was no stranger to the kinds of cultural questions that confronted Veronica Bennett. Williams grew up in a white-working class family, but received his first vocal training and guitar lessons from Black street singers Big Day (Connie McKee) and Tee Tot (Rufus Payne). Williams habitually described himself as "part Indian," and his band, the Drifting Cowboys, included a Native American and a Mexican American. He wrote "Jambalaya" by taking the melody from the Cajun song "Grand Texas" and adding to it English lyrics that he thought sounded Cajun.[4]

So when the African-American, Native American, and Euro-American Ronnie Bennett sang "Jambalaya" for her Puerto Rican, African-American, Native American, and Euro-American family, she was imitating a version of a Cajun song written and recorded by an Anglo-American singer who thought of himself as a Native American trained by African Americans, and who played in a band with a Mexican American and a Native American! The "whoa-oh-oh-oh-ohs" that Bennett took from 'cowboy singers' and which later became her trademark vocal "signature" as the lead singer of the Ronettes, came from Euro-American efforts to imitate the African-American musical sensibility expressed through changes in pitch and use of "impure" tones.[5]

Ronnie Spector may not have known the correct words to "Jambalaya," but her attraction to it reflected more than a simple misunderstanding. It functioned efficiently to evoke the kind of mixed subject position in music that Bennett had experienced her whole life. From one perspective, her rendition of the song might seem ignorant or incompetent, but from another viewpoint it can also be interpreted as an uninterrogated and perhaps unexpected form of intelligence and competence – finding a song that turned cultural contradictions into a creative expression of cultural hybridity.

Popular culture routinely provides opportunities for escaping the parochialisms and prejudices of our personal worlds, for expanding our experience and understanding by seeing the world through the eyes of others. But it can also trap us in its own mystifications and misrepresentations, building our investment and engagement in fictions that misrepresent the lives of others and hide the conditions of their own production – the contexts of power, hate, hurt, and fear in which we live. Popular culture often reduces the lived experiences of gender, ethnicity, class, and race that contain and constrain people to exotic stereotypes that serve to build dramatic tension and texture, but which elide history.

In its most utopian moments, popular culture offers a promise of reconciliation to groups divided by differences in power, opportunity, and experience. Commercial culture puts people from diverse backgrounds in contact with one another, creating contrasts that can call attention to existing social divisions as well as to the potential for eventual unity and community. But inter-cultural communication in popular culture can also create new sources of misunderstanding, misreading, and misappropriation that exacerbate rather than remedy social divisions.

Inter-cultural communication, like all communication, involves some measure of miscommunication. We can never really know how the world looks or sounds through the eyes and ears of others; we use metaphors to convey our experiences because of the impossibility of communicating our experiences to someone else directly. As scholars from many disciplines have argued in recent years, the inevitability of representation always involves the necessity for metaphors that make direct, unmediated, and perfect communication impossible. But while we can never know the exact dimensions, resonances, or consequences of any act of communication, we nonetheless have to make choices about cultural messages by analyzing their impact on our understanding of the world and our ability to act in it.

Critics of commercial culture often condemn the properties of mass media that encourage consumers to expropriate cultural creations for inappropriate purposes. Long ago, Walter Benjamin noted how the mechanisms of mass production ripped cultural practices from the sites and circumstances that gave them meaning, marketing them as mere novelties for uncomprehending consumers. Certainly these propensities account for the seamy history of exploitation and appropriation of folk cultures around the world by the culture industry, for the ways in which forms of expression connected to concrete social issues in particular places have circulated around the globe stripped of their local meanings.

Yet, on the other hand, many of these commodities have drawn the investment and engagement of consumers because their moral and political messages have gained even more power when applied to a new situation. The role played by reggae music from Jamaica in articulating the aspirations of the African diaspora, or the appeal of Central American "magic realist" literature for European and American postmodern readers stem in part from the moral and political power of Caribbean and Central American strategies of signification and grammars of opposition to explain new realities for audiences encountering an increasingly cosmopolitan world. Even when listeners and readers have been ignorant of the exact original and local meanings of reggae or magic realism, they have often displayed advanced understanding about how they could use resonances of an "unfamiliar" culture to "defamiliarize" their own culture and then "refamiliarize" themselves and others with it on the basis of the new knowledge and critical perspectives made possible by cultural contrast.

The complexities of inter-cultural communication in popular culture compel us to look carefully at what might at first appear to be misunderstandings and mistakes.

People who appear to be "mistaken" about another culture sometimes really know things that can not be represented easily because their knowledge is illegitimate by existing standards and paradigms. Especially on issues of identity involving nation, race, gender, sexuality, and class, "mistaken" ideas often contain important insights. Without minimizing the very real dangers of cross-cultural appropriations and mis-understandings, we must nonetheless be open to the kinds of knowing hidden within some "incorrect" perceptions.

Similarly creative "misunderstandings" about popular culture pervade an important scene in Cheech Marin's film *Born in East L.A.* An I.N.S. officer questions Marin's character, Rudy, to see if he is a U.S. citizen or an undocumented alien. Rudy protests that he was "born in East L.A.," so the officer tests his familiarity with U.S. culture, asking him the name of the President of the United States. Flustered by the question, Rudy replies, "That's easy, that dude that used to be on 'Death Valley Days,' – John Wayne." Rudy's failure to identify Ronald Reagan marks him as "incompetent" in his civic knowledge. But of course, his conflation of Ronald Reagan with John Wayne reveals a larger truth: that Reagan's masculinist and paternalist politics and image "played" John Wayne for the American public, some of whom voted for the "Gipper" because they really wanted the "Duke."

In another scene in *Born in East L.A.*, Rudy attempts to teach some Mexican conjunto musicians "the most famous rock'n'roll song ever." He starts to play "Twist and Shout," but the other musicians hear the chord progressions and start singing "La Bamba." Rudy gets exasperated by their "incorrect" response, but the similarity between the two songs teaches the audience (if not the characters in the film) that Chicano identity is already sedimented within what might seem like a uniformly Anglo U.S. popular culture. In a film devoted to exploring the heterogeneous and composite nature of Chicano identity, it is appropriate that Rudy identifies "Twist and Shout," a song writ-ten for a Black singing group by Anglo songwriters who admired and attempted to copy Puerto Rican dance music, as his own, while missing its similarity to Mexican music. After the band shares "Twist and Shout" and "La Bamba," Rudy introduces them to other music that reveals the composite and dialogic nature of Chicano culture – a version of Jimi Hendrix's 'Purple Haze' where they bill themselves in an inter-lingual pun as "Rudy and His New Huevos Rancheros," and "Roll Out the Barrel," a Czech song that Rudy sings in German (which he learned in the military) but whose polka form brings to the surface the similarities (and interactions) between German/Czech and Mexicano music in the U.S.A.[6]

Chinese-American film-maker Wayne Wang employs similar strategies of creative misunderstanding in his film *Chan Is Missing*. While searching for Chan, cab driver Joe tries to draw on his cultural roots by "thinking Chinese," while Joe's nephew and partner Steve is more "American" in his approach. But neither approach succeeds in understanding Chan, who is not only Chinese, but also likes to dance to mariachi music at the Manila Town Senior Center. Chan is Chinese, Chinese-American, and inter-cultural; no one narrative, however perfectly understood, can contain or explain him.

Japanese-American poet Lawson Fusao Inada presents another creative misunderstanding in his prose poem "Fresno," where he reflects upon the Asian-American, Armenian-American, and Mexican-American neighborhood in which he was raised. Inada talks about African-American music as the glue that held these diverse groups together. For young people in Fresno, he remembers that Black music was the "lingua franca" that "enfranchised" and "conferred citizenship" on those who proved knowledgeable about it.[7]

On the surface, Inada's identification seems disastrously incorrect; how could identification with America's most disenfranchised group confer cultural citizenship on immigrants and their children? But taken less literally, his poem illumines a greater truth about what Albert Murray calls the "inescapably mulatto" nature of American culture. The Black music that Inada and his classmates regarded as quintessentially "American" was and continues to be one of the nation's great achievements, even if the credentialing institutions of society fail to recognize it as such.

Another kind of music offers an important insight in Oscar Zeta Acosta's *Autobiography of a Brown Buffalo*. The author wonders why the song "A Whiter Shade of Pale" holds such portent for him as he becomes more deeply involved in Chicano activism during the late 1960s. He hears it again and again on the radio, and it seems to speak directly to him. He writes, "The song moves me deeply. It reminds me of Luther's 'A Mighty Fortress Is Our God.'"[8]

Acosta never explains the importance of "A Whiter Shade of Pale," but in his confusion, he leaves some clues. Of course, one possible connection comes from the song's psychedelic imagery and the massive quantities of hallucinogenic drugs that Acosta's book suggests that he was taking. But "A Whiter Shade of Pale" also combines European forms – the melody is from Johann Sebastian Bach's "Air" from his Orchestral Suite No.3 in D Major – with African-American styles (the soul ballad tradition exemplified in the singing of Sam Cooke) in a way that resonates with Acosta's presentation of Chicano identity as a mysterious and always surprising entity forged from dialogue among Euro-American, Afro-American, Spanish, Indian, and Chicano sensibilities. Acosta's references to "A Mighty Fortress Is Our God" also contain musical accuracy since many of the devices employed to build a sense of majesty in "A Whiter Shade of Pale" appear frequently in Lutheran hymns. Acosta is not simply "confused" or "incompetent" about "A Whiter Shade of Pale," but rather his confusion brings to the surface things that he knows but cannot articulate except through his identification with the song.

Ethiopian-American film scholar Teshome Gabriel offers an example of yet another kind of creative misunderstanding in a story about an African friend of his who grew up believing that Pete Seeger was Black. Gabriel's friend knew that the folk singer participated in the Civil Rights Movement, that he sang freedom songs, and that he included Paul Robeson among his personal friends. When the African's view of Seeger's ethnicity got him involved in an argument after he came to the U.S.A., his adversary showed him a picture of Seeger that clearly showed him to be white. But the African remained adamant. "I know that Pete Seeger is Black," he replied. "Why should I change my mind just because I see his face?" In this instance, Blackness becomes a political position, something determined more by culture than by color. Although the African is factually wrong about the meaning of Seeger's identity within the context of U.S. culture, his "misunderstanding" also contains at least a strategic grain of truth.[9]

One can well understand how these kinds of "misunderstandings" allow people of color to see "families of resemblance" that reframe their separate experiences as similar, although not identical. But what about the danger of misunderstandings incorporated into Euro-American appropriation of the cultures of aggrieved populations? For example, Jefferson Starship's Marty Balin told an interviewer in 1983: "I grew up with the beat era; when I was twelve years old, I'd go down to the clubs and watch John Coltrane and Miles Davis. I didn't know what I was doing, but I could feel something happening."[10]

Balin's recognition that he didn't know what he was doing seems to confirm the views of critics who stress the limits of reception and the barriers to inter-cultural communication. Part of what Balin didn't know at the age of twelve was the way that his experiences as a listener had been influenced by the history of Euro-American appropriation, colonization, orientalism, and primitivism. But given the segregated nature of U.S. society, the censoring apparatuses of the culture industry and the state, and the systematic mis-education carried on by institutions of instruction, something else may have been happening in Balin's response to jazz at the same time. His sense that "something was happening" may also have been a recognition of the inadequacy of his existing language to know exactly how and why Coltrane and Davis affected him, how their music broke through the walls erected to keep them unknown to him, and how subversive their thinking might be to the culture in which Balin was raised. At the very least, it provided him with the inspiration to do more looking and listening, to see music as a potential site for the kinds of exciting and profound changes in human relations that Balin helped advance in his capacity as a member of one of the leading bands of the 1960s counter-culture.

Just as artists and audiences have been influenced positively by "creative mistakes," so too have artistic products themselves been enhanced by imperfect cultural exchanges. Artists from aggrieved communities have often profited from less than perfect knowledge about the exclusionary rules devised from within other cultures. Their "ignorance" of the intentions of others to exclude them has often served as an impetus to creativity; not knowing they were supposed to fail enabled them to succeed. Los Angeles Chicano artist Harry Gamboa, Jr. remembers learning about art museums only after he had been painting for years. His inspirations and models came mainly from comic books, neighborhood graffiti, advertising, and prints used on calendars. When he discovered that museums exhibited "art," he took his drawings to the curator of the most prestigious local museum, assuming that they would be exhibited if the curator liked them. They were rejected on the spot. Later, Gamboa went through more conventional channels, but got the same result. "We tried to get our work inside the museum, just like all the other Chicano artists in town," he recalls in reference to the origins of the guerilla art group "Los Four." Gamboa and his friends found the art museum uninterested in their work, "so one night, we went over there and spray painted our names on the outside of the building. We felt that if we couldn't get inside, we would just sign the museum, and it would be our piece."[11]

Gamboa and Los Four titled their tagging of the museum "Pie in De-Face," and their action generated enthusiastic support among community artists and audiences because it articulated accumulated resentments about exclusion from the establishment definition of "culture." This action succeeded, at least in part, because from the start Gamboa "failed" to learn the lesson his society was trying to teach him, that "art" didn't include him. By remaining "ignorant," he positioned himself perfectly to challenge rather than accept that judgment.

Technical "misunderstandings" can also often be productive for artists. In the 1920s, Bix Beiderbecke could make changes on the trumpet and cornet that no one else could master because he taught himself the instruments and learned all the "wrong" fingerings. The way he fingered the instrument would have been a detriment to skillful playing for most music written within the Western symphonic tradition, but within jazz they enabled Beiderbecke to perform maneuvers that came easily to him but that seemed highly skilled to most other artists and to audiences.

In another genre, blues guitarist Albert King developed a distinctive sound by playing a right-handed instrument with his left hand. Instead of inverting the strings the way most left-handed guitar players did, King left the strings the way they were but picked up on them instead of down. This "mistaken" technique brought an unusual but compelling texture to King's playing. His fellow blues guitarist, Lefty Dizz, had a similar experience. Unable to afford his own instrument, he had to borrow guitars from his right-handed uncles and learn how to play them left-handed. He explained,

> I couldn't reverse the strings, they weren't my instruments, you understand . . . If you're right-handed, you've got your dots for your positions. You see where you are: G, A, B, E. But if you flip that sucker over, there's nothing to go by, so you have to know, and you really have to concentrate on that. The way I did that, I would go in a room and close the door and play in the dark. Play in the dark and learn the fret board, you know.[12]

In the same vein, Black jazz musicians in turn-of-the-century New Orleans often confounded classically-trained musicians who tried to play with them because they played in so many "hard keys." They had no self-conscious intention of playing "difficult" music, but like Beiderbecke, they were self-taught, and the black keys on the piano felt easier to play because they were physically farther apart on the keyboard. Consequently, they developed a style of playing in keys like F sharp, making extensive use of what other musicians had been taught to ignore or treat as forbiddingly difficult. But these keys were only "hard" to those whose training started them in the key of C and others more commonly employed in the Western classical tradition.[13]

Charlie Parker's "mistakes" proved equally instructive. When he entered his first "cutting contest" (a bandstand battle where musicians tried to outplay each other), Parker didn't know about playing in key and was laughed off the stage. He took his saxophone with him to the Lake of the Ozarks where he spent an entire summer teaching himself to play in every key – an education that better-schooled musicians might see as wasteful for someone in a dance band where three or four keys were usually all that was required. But the ability he developed gave Parker exceptional resources as a musician that he explored more fully in his years as a leader in bebop composing and playing. In a similar fashion, Henry Roeland "Roy" Byrd, known professionally as Professor Longhair, used to confound night club owners by insisting on an upright piano rather than a grand piano. Most musicians considered the grand to be the superior instrument, but Longhair liked to kick the baseboard of the piano to help create the polyrhythms that made his playing so exceptional. His choice of instruments certainly added to the delight of his audiences, if not to that of club owners and their insurance companies when they discovered the damage that his kicks did to these instruments.

At times, musicians have to play in ways that are "mistaken" by one code in order to remain faithful to another. The indigenous Australian band Coloured Stone has had difficulty attracting a mainstream audience because their varying rhythms and uneven phrasing seem like "mistakes" to white audiences. But by refusing to suppress the indigenous elements in their music, Coloured Stone succeeds in securing the loyalty of Blacks – and even of a few white listeners who have learned to appreciate the group's "mistakes" as successes by another standard.[14]

Some musicians have used the shortcomings imposed on popular music by its industrial and commercial matrices to create new kinds of improvisational art. George Clinton spent so much time as a songwriter and studio musician concentrating on catchy "hooks," that he built an entire genre around them. "I learned how to write with clichés, puns, and hooks," he told a reporter. "So when I got to Parliament-Funkadelic, I just went stupid with it. Instead of one or two hooks, we'd have ten hooks in the same song. And puns that were so stupid that you could take 'em three or four different ways."[15]

In programming hip hop samples, sound engineers like the Bomb Squad's Hank Shocklee actually try to make "mistakes," to duplicate the "errors" that routine musical performance entails. As popular-culture consumers and listeners they have learned to take pleasure in the inconsistencies and irregularities that give recorded music its distinctive character. In order to give his songs the right feel, Shocklee knows that "you've got to recreate all kinds of stuff." He claims:

> You've got to simulate that laziness – when the drummer hits the snare and gets a repeating note because he didn't lift the stick up. Also, a drummer's stick doesn't hit the skin in the same place all the time, but that's what happens with a machine. That right there adds the funk: we've got to take these machines and recreate mistakes on purpose.[16]

Shocklee even programs a tape hiss into his recordings, claiming that "hiss acts as glue – it fills in cracks and crevices so you get this constant woooooofff."[17]

Many critics might think that Shocklee's choices have little to do with music, that in fact they stem from his inability to learn music the "correct" way. A newspaper reporter accompanying Milwaukee Symphony Chorus conductor Margaret Hawkins to a rap concert starring Dr. Dre, asked if what Dr. Dre played could actually be called music –

evidently expecting Hawkins to share her dismissal of rap. But the conductor astutely pointed out that the question revealed more about the limits of the reporter's understanding of culture than it did about the limits of Dr. Dre's performance.

Hawkins explained:

> You're thinking it's not music because you don't hear a melody. But melody is only one element of music. The rhythms are very complex. These people who say there is no music in rap are wrong. It's just that the main text is spoken like a poem. But in some ways it's more interesting than poetry. Rap relies on the rhythm for the words – and the rhythms change all the time. And the layers of sound – the bass and the harmonic progression . . . I was not bored for one second.[18]

Similarly, jazz musician Greg Osby feels that playing with rappers challenged him to hear music in a new way by forcing him to dispense with the rules that previously governed his playing. "You can't come into it with a lofty intellectual attitude thinking 'I'm a musician – I can deal with it,' because there's no key or center," Osby explains. "It's a sea of sound. You have to listen to the vibe, to almost unlearn what you've learned. It's some of the hardest music I've ever had to deal with, because it's so dense."[19]

At times, popular-cultural products make political interventions by "mistake." In totalitarian states like Hungary, Czechoslovakia, and the German Democratic Republic during the 1970s and 1980s, rock music groups with rather modest aesthetic and political ambitions often encountered serious repression because overly-zealous and defensive state authorities interpreted merely vague lyrics and group names as cleverly and intentionally satirical of socialist society. In the West Indies, prominent political figures and intellectuals attacked Kassav's 1984 hit song "Zouk-la se sel medikaman nou ni" ("Zouk is the Only Medicine We Have" – a song written with no conscious political intent), because they interpreted it as an attack on the backwardness of Guadeloupe and Martinique. At the same time, defenders of the song proclaimed that it properly invoked indigenous Creole *convivialité* as an alternative to neo-colonial culture.[20] In both Eastern Europe and the West Indies, enduring political tensions caused widespread "misreadings" of cultural products as covert statements about politics, but that very misrepresentation set in motion processes whereby the cultural products then gained an indisputable political meaning.

Whether in politics or in performance, the meaning of "mistakes" may have less to do with their transgressions of particular codes than with what they reveal about a broader field of action in which they are not "mistaken." I am not dismissing the serious consequences of cultural appropriation and exploitation. Neither am I claiming that all or any people ever have perfect competence in decoding the materials they encounter through popular culture. I am not saying that it is better not to know than to know. We still need cultural studies scholarship and political critiques grounded in history and ideologically attuned to understanding the limits of any one artist's or audience's subjectivity. But I do want to argue that people may know a lot even if they don't know the history of the literature they like or the names of the notes they play – that their imperfections as consumers or creators of inter-cultural communication do not necessarily render them oblivious to the effects and consequences of unequal power.

People make mistakes in any field of activity, including the practice of popular culture. But they are generally more curious, more resourceful, and more creative than their roles as consumers and citizens acknowledge or allow. Consequently, they often fashion fused subjectivities that incorporate diverse messages. They make mistakes often and they frequently distort what they see and hear. Sometimes they do violence to others by stealing stories and appropriating ideas, by indulging in forms of ignorance that have calamitous consequences. But they also display a remarkable ability to find or invent the cultural symbols that they need.

It is important to document the harm done by uncomprehending appropriation of cultural creations, to face squarely the consequences of mistakes in reception, representation, and reproduction of cultural images, sounds, and ideas. But the biggest mistake of all would be to underestimate how creative people are and how much they find out about the world that the people in power never intended for them to know in the first place.

NOTES

1. Ronnie Spector (with Vince Waldron), *Be My Baby: How I Survived Mascara, Miniskirts, and Madness or My Life as a Fabulous Ronette* (New York: Harper Perennial, 1990), 5.

2. Ronnie Spector (with Vince Waldron), *Be My Baby*, 1–2.

3. Ronnie Spector (with Vince Waldron), *Be My Baby*, 10.

4. Richard Leppert and George Lipsitz, "Everybody's Lonesome for Somebody: Age, Gender, and the Body in the Music of Hank Williams," *Popular Music* vol.9 no.3 (October), 1990.

5. Spector describes her vocal maneuver as a "yodel," but while it gestures toward the yodeling tradition, it doesn't involve the full form as expressed in the music of yodelers like Elton Britt or Eddie Arnold. Instead, it involves the changes in pitch, impure tones, and instrumentalized-sounding vocals that cowboy singers appropriated from African-American music.

6. See Rosa Linda Fregoso, "Born in East L.A." *Cultural Studies* vol.4 no.3 (October) 1990.

7. Lawson Fusao Inada, "Fresno," American Studies Association meetings, Costa Mesa, California, November 8, 1992. Author's notes.

8. Oscar Zeta Acosta, *The Autobiography of a Brown Buffalo* (New York: Vintage, 1989), 35.

9. Teshome Gabriel, "Every Individual Is a Crowd," presentation at the University of California, San Diego, April 12, 1991.

10. Marty Balin, "Starship Interview," *Trouser Press* (March) 1983.

11. "Interview with Harry Gamboa, Jr.," in *Murals: Sparc's Southern California Chicano Mural Documentation Project*, University of California, Santa Barbara Library, Special Collections, 1.

12. Steven Sharp, "Lefty Dizz," *Living Blues* no.112 (December) 1993, 40.

13. Burton Peretti, *The Creation of Jazz* (Urbana: University of Illinois Press, 1992), 102, 104. Irving Berlin also never learned to read music and preferred to use these hard keys while composing at the piano.

14. Marcus Breen, ed., *Our Place, Our Music: Aboriginal Music* (Canberra: Aboriginal Studies Press, Australian Popular Music in Perspective, volume 2, 1989), 65.

15. David Fricke, "George Clinton," *Rolling Stone*, September 20, 1990, 76.

16. Tom Moon, "Public Enemy's Bomb Squad," *Musician* no.156 (October) 1991, 72.

17. Tom Moon, "Public Enemy's Bomb Squad," 76.

18. Lois Blinkhorn, "Maestro Finds True Art at a Rap Show," *The Milwaukee Journal*, October 10, 1993, G6.

19. Larry Birnbaum, "Jazz for the Hip Hop Nation," *Down Beat* (February) 1993, 36.

20. Jocelyne Guilbault, *Zouk: World Music in the West Indies* (Chicago and London: University of Chicago Press, 1993), 23–4.

9

Albert King, Where Y'at?

BILLY PEEK

Many people writing today about the rapid movement of ideas, images, products, and people across the globe speak from their own experiences as migrants and expatriates caught between conflicting cultures. An extraordinary body of intellectual work in recent years by Asians, Africans, and Latin Americans living in Europe, North America, and Australia has called attention to new and complicated cultural questions arising from the emerging circuits, networks, and flows of transnational capital. At the same time, critical and artistic work by "women of color" in the U.S.A. has provided important epistemological and political grounding for heterogeneity, hybridity, and multiplicity as crucial ways of learning about and living in an interconnected world.[1]

This scholarship speaking from and for aggrieved communities has worked a curious inversion in intellectual life. People in countries that have traditionally been metropolitan centers of political, economic, and cultural power seem more unsure and more insecure than ever before about their identities and interests, while previously "marginalized" countries and regions like the Caribbean, the Indian subcontinent, and the Philippines have emerged as important sites for generating bold and confident theories about the world that is developing before us.

My approach to these issues begins from very different kinds of experiences and inclinations. Instead of facing the exhilaration and alienation of crossing boundaries and borders, I have spent a good part of my life trying to stay put. My cultural interests, political commitments, and intellectual concerns have focussed almost exclusively on the U.S.A., on its long history of inequality and exploitation as well as on its unrealized potential for democracy and social justice. Even more parochially, my most meaningful attachments have been to one place in the U.S.A., to the city of St. Louis, and to the people that I have known there. Part of my motivation for writing this book comes from my recognition of the inadequacy of that perspective, of the price we pay for remaining purely national in our thinking at a time when capital operates on a global scale.

St. Louis sits in the middle of the country, at a crossroads where Mississippi River traffic going north and south meets the railroad and highway commerce moving east and west. I moved there from my home in Paterson, New Jersey when I started college in 1964, and I spent the next twenty years trying to stay. It is not easy for me to explain how this decaying industrial city with its dire poverty and vehement racial antagonisms came to mean so much to me. Part of the answer lies in the social ferment of the times that I associate with my years in that city, in the civil rights, anti-war, and labor insurgencies that I encountered there that taught me so much about culture, politics, and power. Part of my affection for St. Louis also comes from the city itself – from its brick and terracotta buildings, its appealing and inviting public spaces, and its history – the ways that its diverse cultures have grown together into a complicated but compelling hybrid. But when I think of the many things that situate my sympathies in St. Louis, I always come back to music, especially to the blues and jazz.

Black music came to St. Louis from the American South, from the Caribbean, from Africa. Transplanted families and lone drifters brought blues and jazz music to the city as they rode in the railroad cars of the Illinois Central line, the cabins of the steamboats that followed the Mississippi from New Orleans to St. Paul, and inter-city buses that brought them from the plantation to the ghetto. In St. Louis, Victoria Spivey, Lonnie Johnson, and Peetie Wheatstraw sang the blues. Local culture enabled Scott Joplin, Louis Chauvin, and Tom Turpin to develop and refine ragtime. It was in St. Louis that Josephine Baker first learned to dance and sing and Bix Beiderbecke split his free time between afternoon symphony concerts and after-hours jazz joints. Jimmy Blanton transformed the string bass into a solo instrument in St. Louis, and Chuck Berry wrote his first songs there. Tina Turner and Fontella Bass developed their artistry as soul singers in Northside lounges and East St. Louis night clubs, and jazz musicians including Clark Terry, Miles Davis, John Hicks, Oliver Lake, Julius Hemphill, Hamiet Bluiett, and Lester Bowie developed their unique skills in the city's drum and bugle corps, youth orchestras, and blues bands.

Most, if not all, of these artists eventually left St. Louis to secure recognition and reward elsewhere. But they left a legacy behind. You could hear it all the time in the boogie-woogie rhythms and chord progressions of local rock bands, in the songs selected for airplay on local radio stations, in the emphasis on imagination and risk among jazz musicians. I encountered it most directly in the music of Billy Peek and Albert King, two blues guitarists and singers who operated out of St. Louis during the years I lived there.

Billy Peek grew up in a white working-class family in the Tower Grove District of South St. Louis. His parents had moved to the city from the Ozark foothills during World War II to work in war industries, and they stayed in St. Louis in the post-war period, working in the packing houses and warehouses near the Missouri Pacific railroad tracks in their neighborhood which they called "the Grove." Peek grew up listening to the country and western music favored by his parents, but one day at a corner candy store, a Greek-American youth – "the coolest guy in the neighborhood" – introduced him to Chuck Berry's music by playing "Maybelline" on the juke box. Peek liked what he heard immediately, and decided on the spot that he would learn to play and sing in that style. He began listening to Black disc jockeys who introduced him to an entirely new universe of sound, and he learned from them that he could hear Chuck Berry and other great musicians including Ike Turner, Little Milton, and Albert King by going to night clubs in North St. Louis as well as on the "East Side" of the river in Illinois where the bars stayed open all night.

Because he was under the legal age for entering establishments that sold liquor, Peek had to sneak into these clubs to hear his heroes. Sometimes he got ejected, but most of the time his determination earned him a first-hand look at the musicians he wanted to see. He noticed how the bands would start late and how their sets would unwind slowly. By four in the morning, though, they'd be letting loose with incredible sounds. Peek would practice what he heard over and over again, driving his parents to distraction with his efforts to make their home sound like an East St. Louis night club at four in the morning. Soon he began to play in blues bands – sitting in during sets with Ike Turner at the Club Imperial, playing roadhouses near military bases and in country towns, and eventually backing up Chuck Berry as a member of his band. Peek went on to tour with British rock star Rod Stewart for almost five years, before returning to St. Louis in the early 1980s to play the blues again in his home town.

Whenever Billy Peek played the blues, I tried to be there. He played at small clubs in suburban shopping centers for loyal and adoring fans who had followed his career for years. It is hard to explain exactly what he did with his tremendous repertoire of St. Louis-based blues songs, but no matter how hot or cold the weather was, no matter how tired and sick you felt, no matter how afraid and alone you might have been, listening to Billy play the blues made everything seem better. You knew it was going to be a good night just as soon as Billy started his sets by playing St. Louis classics like Ike Turner's "Prancing" or Albert King's "I'll Play the Blues for You."

The bars in St. Louis close at 1:30 a.m., about the time that the music starts to heat up on the East Side in Illinois. When I lived there, a local blues radio station featured live broadcasts from an East Side club. Many times I'd listen to them while driving home from hearing Billy Peek. Every so often, the disc jockey would yell, "Albert King! Where y'at? Albert King, get on down here! Come on Albert, come on over and play the blues!" King lived in nearby Lovejoy, Illinois, and invariably he'd respond to that call by driving over to the club and playing a few sets. I never really knew why they used the radio to summon Albert King, why they couldn't use the telephone, for instance. But I did notice that these appeals always worked, that once the disc jockey called out "Albert King, where y'at?" we were going to hear some terrific blues.

For me, the phrase "Albert King, where y'at?" became more than an invitation to hear him play on the East Side on any given night. When I had problems at work, when romances didn't work out, when I had no money, I'd ask "Albert King, where y'at?" and play some blues until I felt better. The blues were not just a collection of musical figures and devices, they were instructions for living in the world and assurances that somebody else had felt the way you did. But Albert King offered more than solace for disappointments. In his style of performance, his knowing persona, and the community he called into being through performance, he built bridges between people and showed them how life could be worth living. I discovered that many problems could be solved by asking, "Albert King, where y'at?" Maybe the grim facts and hard realities didn't change, but my attitude about them, about myself, and about other people, often did.

Albert King, Billy Peek, and the musical tradition they carried on, helped supply me with a secure sense of place in St. Louis. But in the early 1980s, that security slipped away. De-industrialization, capital flight, and economic restructuring devastated the industrial infrastructure of the city; the city's manufacturing establishments lost 44,000 jobs between 1979 and 1982 alone. I worked at a state university and the fiscal crisis that accompanied de-industrialization took my job too. I left St. Louis to take jobs in Houston, Minneapolis, and now San Diego.

When I read Marshall Berman's discussions of modernity as a process where people constantly see their "little worlds emptied out," I knew what he meant. Many times I have mourned the loss of the social world I knew in St. Louis, but every time I go back to visit I see more evidence that things there will never be the same again, that the industrial jobs that provided decent wages, inter-generational upward mobility, and a coherent cultural life are gone forever, that a chaotic new economy and culture based on low wages, declining opportunities, and desperate competition for declining resources will be in place for the foreseeable future. Sometimes, I have to play Albert King's music to remember that there was once another way.

Yet, the displacement instigated by de-industrialization in St. Louis makes me look at the past a little differently. The foundational realities I think of as firmly rooted in the St. Louis past, were themselves ephemeral developments, part of a dynamic inter-national process of migration, change, and transformation even then. St. Louis started out as a node in a network, as a port suited for trade with New Orleans, as a rail center linking the midwest with the south and west, as the gateway to the west, and a stopping-off point on the continental march toward trade with China. Little wonder then, that the railroads, rivers, and highways that brought different kinds of music to St. Louis also brought together in one place groups of Chinese workers from the west, Mexican workers from the southwest, black workers from the south, and white workers from the east. In the nineteenth century, expatriate liberals played out the unresolved problems of German politics in St. Louis's *turnvereins* and debating societies. During the early part of the twentieth century, Ricardo Flores Magon and his brothers organized opposition to the Diaz dictatorship in Mexico from offices on North Channing in St. Louis where they published their revolutionary journal, *Regeneracion*. St. Louis has always been a place that people passed through. To borrow a phrase originally meant to describe the state of Texas, it is not so much a place, but a commotion.

I think this history has much to teach us about the future that we sometimes feel we are not ready to face. The foundational stability and cultural solidity that appear to be eroding in the age of de-industrialization never really existed for most people. Industrialization, urbanization, and state-building wreaked havoc a hundred years ago and promoted anxieties about displacement and change that resemble much of what we feel today in the wake of de-industrialization, economic restructuring, and the neo-conservative attacks on the welfare state. This is not to say that we are not in crisis or that our sense of loss is not real, but rather than crisis and loss have been the norm rather than the exception for most people for most of the last two centuries.

Neo-conservative political leaders around the globe support policies and programs that create chaos. They destroy communities and disrupt lives in order to allow for unfettered capital accumulation everywhere. They give us fragmented lives, but demand uniform cultural behavior – prescribing one kind of education, one kind of family, one kind of patriotism, one kind of sexuality, and one kind of religion as the 'cure' to the disorder created by transnational capitalism. With romantic nostalgia for a past that never existed, they blame immigrants and oppositional movements for the sense of loss and displacement that so many of us feel. Yet when we examine the true nature of the world that we have lost, we learn that it has always been characterized by transformation and change.

Instead of looking to the past for compensatory stories about cultural uniformity, we need to build the future by learning lessons from individuals and groups whose histories have prepared them to make productive use of contradictions, to embrace the dynamism of difference and diversity. The blues and jazz music which seemed to me to define tradition in St. Louis offer important examples along these lines. The guitar originated in Spain, but took on its definitive modern characteristics in the hands of African Americans. The three-line twelve-bar blues originated in West African poetry but its chord progressions and flatted fifths, sevenths, and thirds came from the collision between European harmonies and the African five-tone scale. Blues lyrics often express displacement, but privilege movement over standing still and they rarely express any nostalgia for place. The principal practices that define jazz music originated in specific sites, but by privileging relentless innovation over static tradition they offered cultural, moral, and intellectual guidance to people all over the world.

Compare, for example, the curmudgeonly complaints about American culture by the historian C. Vann Woodward with the insights offered by jazz great Duke Ellington. In an ill-informed rant against "the cult of ethnicity," Woodward whines that "an outburst of minority assertiveness" in recent years has imperiled "the American tradition of a shared commitment to common ideals and its reputation for assimilation, for making a 'nation of nations.' "[2] Of course, minorities have always been assertive in America, but only recently has that assertiveness begun to penetrate elite institutions where even C. Vann Woodward has to notice. Woodward's presumptions about the past in this formulation differ sharply from the actual historical record, and they pose the problem with far less accuracy or subtlety than Duke Ellington did when he used to demonstrate the condition of Black people in America by playing a dissonant chord on the piano. "That's the Negro's life," he'd explain. "Hear that chord. That's us. Dissonance is our way of life in America. We are something apart, yet an integral part."[3]

The sense of being "apart, yet an integral part" located jazz and blues musicians both inside and outside of dominant U.S. culture. Although clearly emanating from African-American experiences, insights, and ideologies, jazz and blues did not remain Black music exclusively, but instead became a form of pan-ethnic expression that drew upon Black leadership for its core values and beliefs. John Storm Roberts notes that many musicians described as "creoles" in the early days of New Orleans jazz had Mexican ancestry and Spanish surnames. Ragtime virtuoso Louis Chauvin came from a mixed family of African Americans and Mexican Americans, while of course many white musicians have contributed to the evolution and development of the form.

The all-female International Sweethearts of Rhythm in the 1930s featured Chinese-American saxophonist Willie Mae Wong, Mexican-American clarinet player Alma Cortez, Native American saxophonist Nina de LaCruz, and Hawaiian trumpet player Nova Lee McGee.[4] Similarly, a wide range of blues and jazz musicians have had some Native American ancestry, among them T-Bone Walker, Lowell Fulson, Princess White, Joe Lee Williams, Hammie Nixon, Charlie Musselwhite, Helen Humes, Birleanna Blanks, Clarence Miller, Lillian Brown, Beverly Jean Hill, Wilbert Ellis, Tommy MacCracken, and John Trueheart. In recent years, Chinese-American musician Fred Ho (formerly Houn) has organized the Asian-American Art Ensemble to mix jazz with Asian-American cultural forms. Influenced by African Americans he encountered growing up in Amherst, Massachusetts including Max Roach, Archie Shepp, and Sonia

Sanchez, Ho became one of the first non-Blacks to join the Nation of Islam, although he balked at taking the name Fred 3X, arguing that his given name was Chinese and therefore not a slave name.[5]

Black cultural forms brought these people together for artistic expressions that had important political ramifications, if for no other reason than that they inverted the prestige hierarchies of white supremacy. The multi-cultural origins of jazz and blues performers demonstrate the importance of Black culture in combating the segregation that shapes so many areas of American life, but jazz and blues music also offer alternatives to dominant ideologies about connections between culture and social relations. When jazz drummer Max Roach told a reporter that "a jazz band operates more democratically than a society," he had more than the racial make-up of its members in mind.[6] Jazz and blues musicians offer an alternative to the atomized individualism of capitalist culture, they create collectively, privileging dialogue over monologue. They play music that tries to change life, to make an audience move, rather than just realizing abstract technical goals. As jazz pianist John Hicks remarks,

> People are always amazed, especially on piano, by technical displays. But working with guys like Little Milton, playing long slow shuffles and stuff, has always given me a certain feeling about keeping the blues in mind. A lot of people say, "You've had classical training, haven't you?" I mean, okay, I did that, it's cool. But I don't think that is as important as the feeling you get from some good old down-home swing.[7]

The practices that connect musical performance to social life in the jazz and blues traditions continue to inform many of the cultural forms we confront today as fundamentally new and postmodern. Hip hop engineer Hank Shocklee creates musical samples for Public Enemy and other rap groups by treating all noise as music. "We believe that music is nothing but organized noise," he explains. "You can take anything – street sounds, us talking, whatever you want – and make it music by organizing it. That's still our philosophy, to show people that this thing you call music is a lot broader than you think it is."[8] Although he sees himself working within blues and jazz traditions, Shocklee expresses disdain for jazz artists who "only mimic what they've heard in the past. And jazz was never like that. It was always an exploration music."[9]

Although clearly a product of the ways in which African, Caribbean, and European music and culture have interacted within the national context of the United States, jazz and blues forms that blend musical devices from all over the world have gone back out into that world with important implications for contemporary musicians all over the globe. Manu Dibango from Cameroon proudly affirms his allegiance to jazz and blues.

He describes music as "false singing" (even on the drums), and claims that the rhythm and blues saxophonist King Curtis perfected this art because of Curtis's grounding in jazz. In addition, he credits John Coltrane for making clear the connections between America and Africa, noting that "hautboy" (African oboe) players from North Cameroon sound very much like Coltrane even though they have never heard his music directly. "When you play music in this time," Dibango asserts, "it's better if you know jazz first, because jazz is a basic music for this century all over the world."[10]

In appreciating the importance of African-American jazz and blues to music all over the world, we cannot ignore the history of U.S. imperialism or the monopolistic domination by U.S. firms over global networks of commerce and communication. Coercion as well as creativity underwrites the worldwide dissemination of this music. But commercial calculations alone do not explain adequately the utility and adaptability of African-American forms to so many different contexts of musical production, distribution, and reception. The history of displacement, dislocation, and dispossession that gave rise to jazz and blues goes a long way toward explaining their enduring relevance to national and international cultural questions. They provide a crucial subtext for popular music all around the world precisely because they never belonged completely to cities like St. Louis, but instead told the stories of people who were passing through. Their skill at creating culture that could reflect and shape the experiences of migration, transformation, and change still has much to teach us.

At the end of Vincente Minelli's 1944 film *Meet Me in St. Louis*, Judy Garland exclaims that everything we need is right here in St. Louis. If that was ever true in the past, it will never be the case again. The world is too complex and too interconnected to allow for that kind of local chauvinism. But parts of our past can help prepare us for the future. Understanding how blues and jazz helped us "learn our place" enables us to see how people in other communities have used funk and punk, reggae and rai, bhangra and bugalu. We have something to teach and much to learn from the families of resemblance that unite people from diverse communities in similar struggles to determine their own destiny. In their own ways and their own languages, their music also asks "Albert King, where y'at?"

Yet space and place still matter; the global processes that shape us have very different inflections in different places. Cognitive mapping in the future will require both local and global knowledge, demanding that we blend rootedness in specific cultures and traditions with competence at mobility and mixing. This is a dangerous crossroads, one where it is almost impossible not to make mistakes. Our locations in specific historical and geographic contexts will mislead us many times, will make us misinterpret and misrepresent the plurality of cultural practices that we encounter. But if we learn to listen, we may find that experts come from unexpected places, that seemingly power-less people have more ways of understanding the world than their oppressors, and that the same global networks of commerce and communication that constrain us offer opportunities for cross-cultural resistance. When people turn to music in the modern world they deploy many different kinds of relationships and social practices. Some of them seem prepared to engage with the world that is emerging all around us. To paraphrase Ralph Ellison's narrator in *Invisible Man*, who knows? Maybe they speak for you.

NOTES

1. I thank Lisa Lowe for calling my attention to the epistemological and political importance of work by women of color. See also Gloria Anzaldua, ed., *Making Face, Making Soul: Haciendo Caras* (San Francisco CA: Aunt Lute, 1990) and Cherrie Moraga and Gloria Anzaldua, eds, *This Bridge Called My Back* (San Francisco CA: Persephone Press, 1981).

2. C. Vann Woodward, "Illiberal Education," *New York Review of Books* (May) 1991.

3. Barry Ulanov, *Duke Ellington* (New York: Harper, 1946), 276.

4. Hazel Carby, "In Body and Spirit: Representing Black Women Musicians," *Black Music Research Journal* vol.11 no.2 (Fall) 1991, 190.

5. Marpessa Dawn Outlaw, "A Chinaman's Chance in Jazz," *Village Voice*, October 23, 1990, 87.

6. Mitch Berman and Susanne Wah Lee, "Sticking Power," *Los Angeles Times*, September 15, 1991, 23.

7. Karen Bennett, "The Pleasure of His Accompany," *Musician* (June) 1991, 26.

8. Robert L. Doerschuk, "Hank Shocklee," *Keyboard* (September) 1990, 83.

9. Robert L. Doerschuk, "Hank Shocklee," 96.

10. Bob Palmer, "Big Manu Dibango: African Sounds, French Champagne," *Rolling Stone*, November 22, 1973, 18.

Index